FILIPPO BRUNELLESCHI
The Early Works and the Medieval Tradition

FLORENCE, SANTA MARIA DEL FIORE, DOME

FILIPPO BRUNELLESCHI

The Early Works and the Medieval Tradition

HEINRICH KLOTZ

RIZZOLI
NEW YORK

First published in German as a post-doctoral thesis on the
recommendation of the Arts Faculty of the University of Göttingen by
Gebr. Mann Verlag, GmbH, Berlin, with assistance from the Deutsche
Forschungsgemeinschaft. Translated from the German by Hugh Keith.

For Gertrud

First published in the United States of America in 1990 by
RIZZOLI INTERNATIONAL PUBLICATIONS INC.
300, Park Avenue South, New York, NY 10010

Published in Great Britain in 1990 by
ACADEMY EDITIONS
an imprint of the Academy Group Ltd, 7 Holland Street, London W8 4NA

ISBN 0-8478-1211-1
LC 89-64019

Printed and Bound in Hong Kong

CONTENTS

FOREWORD

FLORENCE, OSPEDALE DEGLI INNOCENTI, CENTRAL COURTYARD

In writing a monograph about Brunelleschi's work, one is exposed to the temptation of not just confining oneself to the limited works of the artist himself but of going further, and taking as one's framework the threshold between the Gothic and the Renaissance, the end of the Middle Ages and the beginning of the Modern Age, the line drawn between a past which has been 'overcome' and a new 'present', between the architecture of the fourteenth century and the first works of this new master of the Modern Age. But our view across this threshold would appear to be distorted by the very concept of different epochs. Such a line of demarcation becomes more of a barrier. And even interpretations based purely on the works themselves, which claim to be independent of preformulated definitions, have often merely discovered those aspects of Brunelleschi's work which confirm the existence of this demarcation line.

This may explain the remarkable indifference which exists towards the architecture of the late Trecento. Interest focuses on the high points of the epochs: Tuscan Gothic of around 1300 on the one hand, and Early Renaissance around 1420/30 on the other. The second volume of the comprehensive history of Trecento architecture *(Werden und Wesen der Trecentoarchitektur in Toskana)* by Walter Paatz has yet to appear; and Adolfo Venturi, in his basic multi-volume art history of Italy completely ignores the architecture of the Trecento. Sketchy introductions in Petro Toesca's *Il Trecento* and John White's *Art and Architecture in Italy: 1250-1400*, provide us with at least a start. But we do not really know what architecture in the second half of the fourteenth century actually looked like; the language with which to discuss it hardly exists and we have few insights into how things developed and how they related to one another. It is not enough

7

simply to describe what is there, for this does not help us to understand what is meant by 'overcoming' the Gothic. Was it simply a question of the new formal language of Classicism? We know even less about the traditions on which Brunelleschi drew. Was it only a question of referring to the buildings of the Florentine Renovatio (Proto-Renaissance)? What were the factors that directly determined Brunelleschi's works? Or were there none? Was his break with the past so radical that it completely severed historical continuity? These are all questions which relate to our understanding of history and which we must apply to Brunelleschi's work.

The idea of the present book was born of an interest in Gothic architecture in Tuscany. In order to do justice to the subject it would be necessary to gain a broad overview by starting with the first Gothic building in the region, the Cistercian Abbey of S. Galgano. From the multitude of forms one could then select here and there certain characteristics which Brunelleschi was able to use. But within the limitations of a monograph on Brunelleschi's early work, Gothic architecture has been considered only from the narrow point of view of its relevance to one question: to what extent can forms be found in Trecento architecture which pointed forward to new ideas and, specifically, may have inspired Brunelleschi himself?

Amongst the abundance of literature on this period H L Heydenreich's *Spätwerke Brunelleschis (Brunelleschi's Late Works)* deserves special mention, not just because it offers a basis for a critical approach to Brunelleschi's style in general, but also because his description forms both a complement to and a prerequisite for an understanding of Brunelleschi's late works, which form the subject of this book. The basic reading for any approach to Brunelleschi is, as always, the great work by Cornel von Fabriczy, which more recent monographs by Sanpaolesi (1962) and Luporini (1964) cannot replace.

A period of two years spent in Italy, made possible by grants from the Deutsche Forschungsgemeinschaft and the Institute of Art History in Florence, gave me the opportunity to get to know the buildings concerned rather better than would have been the case had I been confined to sporadic visits. It became clear that there was an urgent need for new photographic documentation of Trecento architecture in particular. The usual postcard views which are reproduced in their hundreds threaten to become the only valid 'view' of a building. There are virtually no detailed photographs. With Marvin Trachtenberg (New York University), I was able to produce a new series of photographs. Photography has become an important aid to the architectural historian. Unlike paintings, three-dimensional works of art provide much scope for photographic reproduction; an architectural photograph is always a product of an individual's 'eye'. I therefore regarded it as important that the photographs should bring out specific aspects of the buildings; in other words that they should be an interpretation in themselves. Photography cannot be an objective record of 'facts' but is rather a subjective art and is therefore no substitute for direct observation.

Finally, I must mention the Institute of Art History in Florence. It is a place of study which combines under one roof an unusual degree of openness with unique library facilities. I would like to express my thanks to the former Director of the Institute, Professor Ulrich Middeldorf, for his kind help with this work. I am similarly grateful to Professor Heinz Rudolph Rosemann for many helpful suggestions.

The manuscript was presented as a post-doctoral thesis to the Faculty of Arts of Göttingen University in 1968.

* * *

PART I

BRUNELLESCHI'S STYLE

FLORENCE, OSPEDALE DEGLI INNOCENTI

I THE COLUMN

FLORENCE, OSPEDALE DEGLI INNOCENTI, LOGGIA

1. Round and Octagonal Shaft

The column is an architectural metaphor of the human form: the base is the foot, the shaft the trunk, the capital the head. Its proportions, too, reflect those of the human body. Since Vitruvius, columns have been classified in anthropomorphic categories.[1] All classical[2] architecture can thus lay claim to being 'human', even though it often aimed at being merely monumental. In the nineteenth, and especially the twentieth century, an increasing need for the monumental destroyed the humanity of the column. It was reduced from being a metaphor of the human form to merely a formal expression of the function of support. Because of this, its proportions became merely incidental, indeed a deception. Being only decorative, they merged with the empty ornamentation of the rest of the facade. Thus ended an age at the beginning of which we find Brunelleschi.

One of Brunelleschi's major contributions was his rediscovery of the column as a metaphor of the human form and as the essential element in the proportionality of architecture. Even in his first creations the column can be found in all its canonic simplicity: an Attic base on which there stands a full, rounded shaft tapering towards the top and to which the entasis gives a graceful upward movement, perceived by the eye as an ascending growth from the foot to the head, i.e. the capital.

Brunelleschi set the column against the traditional composite pier, which was bound by no particular proportions, could stretch to any height and link in any way with other parts. It was an element which had lost the spatial independence reminiscent of the human body and had become merely one unit in a system of linked parts.

It may seem obvious that a column is round; but before Brunelleschi entered the scene, for more than a century in Florence there had been nothing but the octagonal pillar. Whenever simple colonnades were built – in courtyards, cloisters, large public rooms or

11

loggias and churches – the only type of support apart from the composite pier was an octagonal shaft, whose hard, parallel edges gave the pillar a crystal-like rigidity. The lively movement created by entasis had become impossible. The sharp edges suited the need to be able to stretch the pillar as high as required or to make it squat and powerful. Even though a sense for moderate proportions usually prevailed, there was still something random about them. The anthropomorphically defined proportions of the column which had been passed down by Vitruvius and were to be taken up again by Brunelleschi had been forgotten.

Only Alberti, in his *De re aedificatoria,* felt he had to stress the round shaft: 'The columns must be smooth and perfectly round.'[3]

There has been speculation as to whether the octagonal pillars on the walls of the Baptistry provided a model for the architecture of fourteenth-century Florence,[4] but since the excavations in Santa Maria del Fiore we have had an even more eloquent example: the octagonal shaft uncovered there,[5] which comes from the eleventh-century cathedral building, can also be taken to be the model used for the octagonal supports of the Chiostro dei Morti in Santa Maria Novella (c1280), which are probably the earliest from the Gothic period. Thus Santa Reparata, the first Florentine cathedral, was the original example for this tradition – a tradition to which the cathedral lent its particular authority.

With Brunelleschi's portico for the Ospedale degli Innocenti this tradition was suddenly broken. Even today, an observer used to the Gothic tradition finds this row of rounded columns on Attic bases with Corinthian-like capitals a breath of fresh air, a rebirth, almost a visual embodiment of the Renaissance. By contrast consider the loggia of the Ospedale di S. Matteo (1385-1410).[6] The consistent combination of sharp-edged pillars and crisp arches produces its own kind of perfection. The smooth tension of the walls of the loggia is echoed in the smooth octagonal faces of the pillars. Individual forms and the ensemble have a hard, unyielding, almost glassy effect. Unity of style is preserved, although such stiffness has made even the leaves of the capitals lifeless. They form rows like stamped tongues of tin. The naturalistic nomenclature for this Tuscan type of leaf, 'folia d'aqua', hardly mirrors their actual effect.

Brunelleschi restored an organic movement to the capital and gave the shaft a rounded form. Onto the sharply cut arcade of arches he put an archivolt relief so that the eye is led on, step by step, and does not come up against any sharp edge.

2. The Ground-Level Base

A line of steps lifts the colonnade of the Ospedale degli Innocenti off the ground. As you approach it you have to step upwards, leaving the square behind and beneath you and entering the higher spheres of architectural greatness. The building was not just a home for the orphans and foundlings of the city but also the most important official building of the Arte della Seta, whose coat of arms can be seen in the form of a tondo at either side of the exterior facade.[7] Together with the famous Children in Swaddling Clothes by Andrea della Robbia, these coats of arms are the only decoration on the portico – two contrasting symbols next to each other.

Once you have climbed the steps you find yourself on the same level as the columns, your feet next to the plinth and the base. Such a seemingly natural identity of position between Man and column was, however, just as unusual for the Florence of those days as were rounded columns. The octagonal supports of the Ospedale di S. Matteo rise from a raised base, as do the pillars of the cloisters in S. Maria Novella and S. Croce. This type of raised base was preferred in the fourteenth century. The pillars on the facade of S. Maria Novella, for example, stand on a series of complex blocks composed of various elements which have virtually obliterated the original simplicity of a pillar base. The plinths of the pillars in the Chiostro Verde of S. Maria Novella are half the height of the pillars themselves. These are not exceptions, but rather examples of a fashion which predominated in late fourteenth-century Florence.

With Brunelleschi's porticoed colonnade, the relationship of architecture to Man changed, because the columns stand on the same plane as the observer himself. The plinth is no higher than a shoe, without even the tiny stepped effect of the plinths in the interior of the Baptistry. It is as simple as those in S. Miniato al Monte. With his columns Brunelleschi won back the ground, the actual basis on which both columns and Man stand. The result is that, for all its majesty, the colonnade of the Ospedale retains a very intimate relationship with Man, not dominating him in the way that happened under

FLORENCE, SANTA CROCE, NAVE

FLORENCE, SANTA MARIA NOVELLA, COLUMN IN THE
CHIOSTRO DEI MORTI

FLORENCE, SANTA MARIA NOVELLA, PLINTH OF FACADE

FLORENCE, SANTA MARIA DEL FIORE, COLUMN FROM
SANTA REPARATA

FLORENCE, SANTA MARIA NOVELLA, CHIOSTRO VERDE

FLORENCE, OSPEDALE DEGLI INNOCENTI, COLUMN CAPITALS OF LOGGIA

Alberti.[8] When Michelozzo placed the columns of the cloister of San Marco on raised plinths he was once again sacrificing the intimacy and accessibility of the column for the sake of achieving a monumental effect. Developments continued in this direction, via Alberti, to Michelangelo and Palladio and right down to the Baroque. (In Maderna's facade for St. Peter's the columns may stand on ground level, but their bases are so enormous that they are themselves more than the height of a man.)

There is perhaps a special significance in the fact that the building which ushered in the Renaissance period in architecture made the entire construction rise from the level on which the observer stands. The heights to which the Gothic had aspired were reduced to the simplest conclusion and thus overcome; but even in later Renaissance architecture, there is hardly any colonnade rising from such a human level as that of the Ospedale or the Pazzi Chapel.

3. Repetition and Rule

For Brunelleschi it was sufficient to have achieved the most natural and obvious realisation of a column: to put it on the ground. He not only did this with the arcades of his basilicas, where it could be expected from the example of SS. Apostoli, but made it into an innovative principle to which he consistently adhered: in the facades of porticos, in cloisters, in the Barbadori Chapel and in the central light of the cathedral cupola. Only the wall pillars of the tribune-tempietti stand on a raised base, because here the bases had to be lifted above the already existing balustrade of the roof to prevent them from being completely masked.[9]

Someone like Michelozzo was much more flexible, changing his decoration at will, putting columns on ground level or on pedestals, choosing round or octagonal shafts.[10] Brunelleschi was concerned to remain consistent and to retain a certain austerity of decorative form. As a result all his buildings retain a very uniform character. It was characteristic of his art to apply certain principles consistently and repeat certain basic forms regularly. Even Alberti, whose theoretical writings have established him as the great normative influence of the fifteenth century, allowed himself greater freedom in practice than did Brunelleschi, and it was not just the fact that his foreman was constantly changing which caused this variety. Alberti, himself, determined the 'varietas'[11]

of his work by the variation of certain basic forms. From the pilaster motif alone he derived a host of different effects. The constant varying of his materials (Brunelleschi always used the same material) was another way in which he belied the normative image given by his theoretical writings. In Florence, for example, he reintroduced marble incrustation, not just on the facade of S. Maria Novella, where the Gothic building required this, but also for the Holy Grave of S. Pancrazio, where he had greater freedom.[12] But it was Brunelleschi who, through his work, set the standards. He was the revolutionary who created a new canon of forms which replaced the arbitrary regime that had held hitherto. He replaced the decorative imagination of the thirteenth century with an extremely restricted range of virtually constant basic forms. What he sought was the essential rather than the free play of forms; and he had to ensure that the new language he created was sufficiently consistent to be mandatory. Despite its variety, his work, like everything revolutionary, has certain dogmatic features. But even if Brunelleschi retained his vocabulary as far as possible unchanged, once it had been established, he seldom repeated himself.

The following generation, above all Michelozzo, was to make free use of the new forms and mix them happily with traditional Gothic elements. Brunelleschi's strict rules, his revolutionary crusade against the recent past, gave way to compromise. This is why Michelozzo is so important for the history of art, for he was the first to have at his disposal the vocabulary of both pure classical forms and Gothic ones. He let both speak without letting either reach the point of contradicting the other.[13]

4. The Corinthian Capital

Brunelleschi did not leave behind any theoretical magnum opus,[14] but any lack of theoretical works is compensated for by the canonic tendencies which his buildings reveal. Perhaps the most telling example of this is the capital. Brunelleschi preferred the Corinthian capital, which he used throughout his works in the form found on the Ospedale: its main features are two rows of leaves, one above the other, and the helical volutes.[15] These are unusually large on the columns and capitals of the Ospedale, but on all later buildings assume the usual proportions – a tendency already perceptible on the pilaster capitals of the Ospedale. In recent times three exhaustive studies have traced the changes undergone by Brunelleschi's Corinthian capitals in great detail and have highlighted stylistic differences such as, the way in which the leaf-work, originally much more natural, became increasingly stiff.[16] But such analyses merely serve to illustrate what should have been their conclusion – that there is an extraordinary consistency of the basic form.[17] The type of capital found on the Ospedale recurs on columns and pilasters. For example in his two basilicas, S. Lorenzo and S. Spirito, only the Corinthian capital can be found – on freestanding columns, wall-pillars and wall-pilasters.

The changes of style which can be perceived over a period of time (largely to the detriment of Brunelleschi's successors), are of a minor nature; they are indications of slight nuances which may be of interest to the art historian, but which do not put the typology in question. Brunelleschi's strictness of approach may be seen immediately by making the comparison with one work of Michelozzo – his tabernacle in S. Miniate al Monte. Here he juxtaposed four completely different types of capital, creating a decorative richness in strong contrast to Brunelleschi's austerity. Alberti did the same, thinking up different forms for the capitals of each building he created, even though both he and Michelozzo did display a preference for certain figures.[18]

5. The Throated Ionic Capital

Beside the Corinthian capital, the other type with which Brunelleschi was familiar was the Ionic. He added a broad throat to it and used it in specific places in his buildings.[19] Although he used a number of variations he always retained the basic form. The lantern balustrade of the Old Sacristy, which the inscription dates from 1429, is carried by a row of powerful columns whose Ionic capitals are formed by an unusually hard, wiry volute which sits on the egg and tongue moulding. The model for this was one of the small capitals on the window columns of the Baptistry. However Brunelleschi has shortened them even more, drawing the volute up to the egg and tongue moulding but setting the neck deeper so that a narrow throat is formed.

On the capitals of the Barbadori Chapel[20] the throat is elongated and delineated from the shaft by a second torus. This variant is generally richer and more decorative. The model for it was the Ionic capital of the

emporium in the interior of the Baptistry.[21] The volute is more tightly entwined and loses its angularity, becoming more rounded. The volute sides, held in place by a ring or a loop of cabling, return on Brunelleschi's capital. He has changed certain details: apart from the elongated throat the volutes, unlike their model, are given a further coil reminiscent of the great spiral volutes of his Corinthian capital. He has now left out the leaf and dart moulding as well as the interpolated plate which separates the volutes from the cornice. But despite these changes the original model is still recognisable. The variations on the theme range from the balustrade capital of the Old Sacristy and the capital of the half-columns in the Barbadori Chapel. Extreme simplicity and rich decoration contrast with each other.

A variation of the Barbadori capital can be found in the throated capitals of the Palazzo di Parte Guelfa.[22] The roof of the loggia is supported on consoles whose volutes are less tightly coiled and whose upper torus has become a band of cabling. (The capitals of the columns in the Loggia are like the wall consoles).

Even the Ionic capitals of the second courtyard in the Ospedale degli Innocenti are derived from the Barbadori type. The design is the same, but it can be seen that they were created at a later date.[23] One only needs to consider how stiffly the leaves of the volutes lie one above the other and how woodenly the volutes sit below the abacus. The great quality of the Barbadori capitals, whose volutes, like those in the Baptistry, are drawn together in the middle and curve elegantly outwards, is obvious. The capital of the Ospedale courtyard merges directly into the stunted cornice plate, whereas the abacus cornice of the Barbadori Chapel gently sits on the volutes with hollowed out spaces in between. Finally one can compare the volutes themselves in both cases: with Brunelleschi we find fine precision and detail; with Francesco della Luna, his chief builder, bluntness and imprecision! Such a comparison of details in itself should be enough to remove any doubts about Brunelleschi's responsibility for the Barbadori Chapel. The very similarity of the capitals allows such difference in signatures to differentiate the Master from his pupil.

In Masaccio's Tabernacle in S. Maria Novella and Donatello's doors for the Old Sacristy the capital from the Barbadori Chapel returns almost unchanged.

FLORENCE, SAN MINIATO AL MONTE, ALTAR TABERNACLE

FLORENCE, SANTA FELICITÀ, BARBADORI CHAPEL, CAPITALS OF COLUMNS

FLORENCE, OSPEDALE DEGLI INNOCENTI, COLUMN CAPITAL IN CHIOSTRE DELLE DONNE

FLORENCE, BAPTISTRY, WINDOW COLUMN

FLORENCE, SANTA MARIA NOVELLA, DETAIL FROM FRESCO OF THE TRINITY, MASACCIO

FLORENCE, BAPTISTRY, CAPITAL IN GALLERY

FLORENCE, PALAZZO DI PARTE GUELFA, DETAIL IN LOGGIA

FLORENCE, OLD SACRISTY, PORTAL

FLORENCE, OLD SACRISTY, COLUMN FROM LANTERN BALLUSTRADE

FLORENCE, SANTA MARIA NOVELLA, LOWER GALLERY IN DRUM

FLORENCE, PAZZI CHAPEL, BALUSTRADE

FLORENCE, SANTA FELICITÀ, BARBADORI CHAPEL, ALTAR

FLORENCE, PAZZI CHAPEL, PORTAL

Masaccio made the volutes smaller and drew the upper torus right round the throat; but here too one finds the sharply curving sides drawn tightly together with simple, unveined leafwork.

The restored capitals of the intercolumnar balustrade in the Pazzi Chapel are difficult to judge in detail. They are late successors which appeared only after Brunelleschi's death.[24] It is easier to pass judgement on the similarly restored capitals of the altar in the Barbadori Chapel. These are miniature editions of the capitals of the great half-columns in the same chapel, the only difference being that the volutes' spirals are shorter. Instead of the upper torus of the throat the cabling motif reappears which is familiar from the loggia of the Palazzo di Parte Guelfa.

The Ionic throated capital of the Barbadori Chapel is particularly worthy of note in this context. With its full volutes it provides a parallel to the Corinthian capitals of the Loggia degli Innocenti. Brunelleschi has here provided a paradigmatic example which was to be repeated often, first in Donatello's Tabernacle in Or San Michele and Massacio's Tabernacle of the Trinity, then in the architecture, both real and painted, of the Quattrocento, such as the pictures of Fra Angelico (e.g. the fresco of the Annunciation in San Marco) and the buildings of Michelozzo (e.g. the library and cloister of San Marco).

Probably because Brunelleschi's Corinthian capital achieved such an importance, his throated Ionic capital was largely ignored. He used it in less important places, for example, on small columns subordinate to the pilasters or on balustrades.[25] The formal purpose of the Ionic balustrade capital is contained in the frontality of the sequence of volutes. The multiple rows of miniature columns create an ensemble which follows the line of the balustrade.

In the entrance to the Pazzi Chapel the balustrade also fulfils the same purpose. It runs from the shaft of one column to the next in the first intercolumnar space of the left-hand colonnade. Clearly the original intention was to close the other spaces with such a balustrade as well, for the bottom ledges which would have linked the bases had already been constructed. The fact that they were part of the original plan can be seen from the corresponding ledges linking the bases of the rear wall pilasters.

6. 'Major' and 'Minor' Orders of Columns

Thus in an unusual manner a double 'order of columns' had come into being, the Ionic order of balustrades and the Corinthian major order. This may seem to be the chance result of combining two basic forms rather than a conscious juxtaposition of a subordinate 'Ionica' and a superordinate 'Corinthia'. The choice of Ionic capitals for the balustrades, as much a leitmotif in Brunelleschi's work as the Corinthian capital, could be explained 'functionally' in terms of the desire to create a sequence of volutes which emphasise the line of the balustrade. At the same time one must ask whether, in addition to this, Brunelleschi was thinking in hierarchical terms.

For it is striking that Brunelleschi gave the low balustrade a 'low' order, made the little columns into mere uprights in a fence and consistently 'assigned' to them the Ionic capital. The form of the balustrade became immutable, remaining constant for the internal galleries of the cathedral dome,[26] the anteroom of the Pazzi Chapel and the lantern of the Old Sacristy. It later returns in the facade of the Palazzo Pitti and on Michelozzo's flight of steps in the cortile of the Palazzo Canigiani. One could conclude that the Ionic column was not an 'order column' but merely a 'balustrade column'. But, as has been shown, it was also used elsewhere: precisely such 'balustrade columns' support the altar table in the Barbadori Chapel; single columns stand at the four corners of the stone slab; and it is also found, rather bigger and noticeably slimmer, as a half-column in the arcade of the Chapel, where it is now clearly subordinate to the Corinthian order of pilasters.

Without going into the precise significance, it can at least be stated that Brunelleschi made frequent use of the Ionic capital as a 'minor' order for less important positions. The Corinthian capital contrasts with this as a symbol of a monument's 'major' order. This systematic restriction to just two types of capital of visibly differing 'status' can only be explained as an expression of a sense of 'order' which clearly has little to do with the system of orders of columns applied by the Cinquecento.

To be clearly aware of the differences between the orders of columns would have required at least an acquaintance with Vitruvius. Brunelleschi could have found out what Ionic and Corinthian columns should look like from Vitruvius' *Ten Books on Architecture*. Now it is supposed to have been Alberti who was the first to consult Vitruvius in depth. But it is striking that it was not Alberti but Brunelleschi who almost exactly matched the classical forms of Corinthian and Ionic columns. The Florentine Renovatio could have offered him a wide range of capitals as models but, with the exception of the Ionic capital, he largely ignored them. Even the composite capital of SS. Apostoli which Michelozzo adopted, is only comparable with Brunelleschi's Corinthian capital in certain respects. Instead of a variety of forms he only allowed two types of capital to be valid. These are not only very close to the two orders of columns, the Ionic and Corinthian, but were also repeated by him in all his buildings. This strict concentration of two basic forms, broken only after his death by Michelozzo's lantern on the cathedral dome and the inner courtyard of the Ospedale, which was also completed by someone else's hand, must give food for thought.

In Brunelleschi's works the possibility of superposition only seldom occurred; his elevations are nearly always determined by only one order. When a major order dominates a minor one, as with the crossing pilasters of S. Lorenzo and S. Spirito, the Corinthian form was already determined by the arcade sequence of the nave, whose colonnade demanded full priority. Brunelleschi chose the Corinthian capital, identical on all sides, for the main motif of the whole building, i.e. the colonnade. The great colonnade of rounded columns was always for him a sort of 'general order' and the Corinthian capital, as the major form of all, was naturally part of it.

Three of the most important and earliest works of the Renaissance provide examples of a genuine direct combination of two orders: the painted tabernacle of the Trinity by Masaccio in S. Maria Novella, the tabernacle of St. Luke by Donatello in Or San Michele and the Barbadori Chapel in S. Felicità. Masaccio's tabernacle received its form with the cooperation of Brunelleschi, the Luke tabernacle was created by Brunelleschi's friend Donatello (with the help of Michelozzo), and the Barbadori Chapel is one of Brunelleschi's own first creations.[27] All three works are striking for the strict differentiation which they make between a lower Ionic order of columns which carry the arch and a higher Corinthian order of pilasters which carry the architrave. Again we find the capitals so typical of Brunelleschi, being set in a direct relationship to each other and clearly differentiated as separate orders.[28] Their reappearance in three different environments (fresco, sculptured tabernacle, chapel) points to a regularity which suggests a desire to establish clear categories. It would be highly significant if such a desire surfaced with the very birth of a new classical architecture and if subsequently a greater flexibility were regained.

The strict repetition of Talenti's model of a leaf-scroll capital for the nave piers of Florence Cathedral already indicates a certain systematisation which rejected any excessive variation of capital forms. 'Varietà', as understood at a later date by Michelozzo and Alberti, can be seen as a reaction against Brunelleschi's strictly regulated approach. The need for variety gives rise to a medieval richness of forms which was only finally overcome by the High Renaissance. The presentation of so many different forms of capital within one order of columns, such as created by Michelozzo in his tabernacle in S. Miniato al Monte would have been unthinkable in a building by Brunelleschi or Bramante.

7. Columns and Pilasters

The actual subject of this discussion has hitherto been the column, as though it were the main constituent in Brunelleschi's architecture. Goethe spoke of the 'three original concepts' of architecture: 'the base, the column (wall etc) and the roof'.[29] In the light of Brunelleschi's work, the relationship should perhaps be reversed and the column put in parenthesis with the wall as the main item, for it was not the row of columns but rather the wall which was for Brunelleschi the 'original concept'. The column is of course significant, and styles and intentions can be described, but in Brunelleschi's system of elevation it has a subordinate position as a constituent element in the wall. The Old Sacristy, the Pazzi Chapel and S. Maria degli Angeli consist purely of walls, with columns playing no role whatsoever in their elevations. What they contain instead are pilasters. In all his early works Brunelleschi made a basic distinction between free-standing colonnades which replace walls and series of pilasters which are linked to the wall. He only used half-columns in S. Spirito and the tempietti of the cathedral tribuna. Initially however, he made a strict differentiation between the physical qualities of wall and space: the flat pilaster is linked to the flat surface of the wall, whereas the round column stands in the

FLORENCE, SAN MINIATO AL MONTE, FACADE

FLORENCE, SAN LORENZO, CROSSING

FLORENCE, SANTO SPIRITO, ARCADE IN NAVE

FLORENCE, SAN MINIATO AL MONTE, CHOIR

three-dimensional space which surrounds it.

In the architecture of Roman antiquity there were two basic possibilities of using columns: in free-standing colonnades in temples or against walls. In all cases they bore a flat architrave. Columns as supports for the semi-circular arches of an arcade, as Brunelleschi liked to use them, were something which only came in at a later stage of antiquity[30] and were handed on to early Christian architecture. The colonnades in the naves of basilicas mainly had semi-circular arches.

While the classical Roman arcade was cut out of the fullness of the wall, which was supported by the heavy piers, and the half-columns were only decoration, the colonnade was independent of the wall although the arch itself was also cut out of the wall. The colonnade met it again at the end and was rounded off or supported by it. Brunelleschi retained this medieval combination of freestanding colonnade framed by a wall. This can be seen at the crossing of his basilicas where the pilasters, as an integral part of the wall, meet the end of the colonnade. The end column or pilaster leans against the crossing pier, which extends up to the architrave. Here the dependence of the column on the wall becomes clear. It is far from being a free peripheral column. The Roman wall system had thus been reversed: the half column supports the archivolt not the architrave, and the pier supports the architrave and not the archivolt. When, at a later date, Alberti demanded that the arcade should not be supported by columns but by piers,[31] he was calling for a return to the Roman system, which he realised on the facades of S. Francesco in Rimini and S. Maria Novella. It was probably under his influence that in the inner courtyard of the Palazzo Venezia in Rome, the piered arcade with half-columns was repeated and thus the basis for later developments was laid. The courtyard of the Palazzo Farnese and Bernini's facade for the Palazzo Barberini can be traced back to this model. In contrast to this, Brunelleschi took as the main support for his walls, not the piered arcade, but the framework of pilasters within which is the colonnade.

8. The Barbadori Chapel and the Medieval Tradition
The Barbadori Chapel is a typical example, where the pilasters rise up to the architrave and the half-columns are linked to the surrounding framework. The chapel takes the form of an open baldaquin crowned with a dome. Basically it has a Gothic framework whose counterpart is the round temple of antiquity also repeated by Brunelleschi in the lantern of the Old Sacristy, which is a tholus: a pure circular colonnade supporting the flat architrave. The frame of the Barbadori Chapel goes back to the traditions of the Gothic Trecento, while the tholus of the lantern goes back to the classical Renovatio of the twelfth century, for which the lantern of the Baptistry served as a model. Thus the two possibilities of continuing traditional forms in Brunelleschi's work are contrasted: a continuation of the Gothic, on the one hand, or a deliberate return to the medieval Renovatio, on the other.

If one compares the recently revealed fresco of a late Gothic baldaquin in S. Maria Maggiore in Florence with the structure of the Barbadori Chapel, it becomes clear what was meant by our reference to the Gothic framework. All four supports for the structure in the painting consist of a combination of a thin pilaster with a turned column. Above the capital the pilaster continues as a base for a pinnacle, and also supports the surround to the arch, whereas the column belongs to the actual archivolt. The tabernacle of St. John by Albizzo di Piero[32] in Or San Michele, built between 1415 and 1416 has a similar structure. But the crucial difference between these and the Barbadori Chapel is the fact that the column and the pilaster are of equal height and end in a common throated impost. The arcade field is correspondingly lacking in any upper border in the form of a ledge: the pointed arch rises up into the canopy. Brunelleschi converted this complicated Gothic verticality into a clear outline in which the pilasters are the major order and rise up to the horizontal entablature and the half-columns are a minor order and support the arches of the arcade.

The form of the Gothic baldaquin returns on a large scale in the Loggia del Bigallo (began 1352), albeit with a more complex system of supports. The arch is supported by piers which are linked to other corner piers; the inside columns, which merge straight into the archivolt are reminiscent of the pilaster/half-column motif, but retain a decorative nature. As in the previous examples, there is no attempt to differentiate between a major and a minor order. Above the common capital the corner pier begins again, rather like in the pinnacle-bases of the baldaquins. But, unlike the latter, the architect of the Loggia del Bigallo, which is, like the Barbadori Chapel, linked to the wall on two sides, has created a clear framework in the form of a horizontal ledge. Instead of a pointed arch which rises into the canopy, there is a semi-circular arch which virtually touches the horizontal ledge. Thus a clearly delineated arcade field is created. The Loggia is the Gothic precursor of the Barbadori Chapel. What they have in common is the basic framework. The wall forms a pilaster frame which holds the colonnade, a structure which was unknown in antiquity. Even the Romanesque had a completely different approach to similar buildings, as will be demonstrated elsewhere.[33] These complex Gothic creations whose decorative exterior contrasts so strongly with Brunelleschi's clear, simple forms, have to be reduced to their basic structure in order to see that they provide the traditional background against which Brunelleschi produced his entirely new, sober structures. When it is stated that the architecture of the early Renaissance owed as much to the medieval period as it did to classical antiquity, then this is a concrete example. It is not just the cathedral dome with its lofty ribbed shape which comes from the Trecento! But, on the other hand, the Barbadori was no longer a Gothic construction, as can be seen from the pendentive dome and the simple, clear lines of the pilaster/half-column framework.

Brunelleschi differentiated between major and minor orders. He broke down the capital frieze of the Loggia del Bigallo, giving the half-column an Ionic capital and the pilaster which stands next to it a Corinthian one. The individual elements have become independent entities. Even in the buildings of the Florentine Renovatio the relationship, as regards orders, between the framing wall which ends the colonnade and the half-column, was unclear. This was the critical point in a system which linked the colonnade with the wall; and the classical Roman half-column system had its revenge on the medieval one. Even the facade of San Miniato al Monte, with its classical effect, is no exception: the outer half-columns run up an undefined strip of wall which, as in the Gothic baldaquins, is cut by the impost-like cornice of the column. The naked sandstone of the wall contrasts with the marble column next to it. The possibility of combining a pilaster of a major order with the column was not considered. Thus the architrave hangs in a vacuum, so to speak. The decorator was concerned only with providing a framework for the arches of the arcade with a strip of wall. For him this solution, which we judge through Brunelleschi's eyes, was completely unproblematic. The fact that such a combination of naked wall and half-columns was acceptable is demonstrated by other facades of the 'Proto-Renaissance' such as S. Stefano in Florence, or the Collegiata in Empoli. On the other hand, Arnolfo di Cambio's corner piers on the exterior of the Baptistry must have seemed really problematic. The columns were replaced with heavy striped piers and the sides of the arches were held by faced props which run vertically down the piers.

The half-column arcades of the choir of S. Miniato end with a pilaster which is not part of the arcade but rather stands at an angle and carries the chancel arch. The arcade itself now ends in a vertical strip. This gives rise to an unusually ambiguous combination of half-column and pilaster which on the one hand has all the characteristics of a medieval arcade and on the other hand, with its apparently random linking of both elements, anticipates Brunelleschi's double order. If one imagines the continuation of the arches not into the curve of the choir, but rather straight ahead to the pilaster, then one has the arcade of S. Spirito or the Loggia degli Innocenti.[34] If one shortens it to one arcade, then one has the elevation of the Barbadori Chapel. These widely differing arcades with framing pilasters are all based ultimately on one basic system.

What is missing in the choir of S. Miniato, is the genuine relationship of pilaster and half-column which can be found in the gallery of the Baptistry. Here the order of columns has become a balustrade, so that they are not at the same level as the pilasters. But one finds here, clearly laid down, the differentiation between a major order of pilasters which carry the horizontal architrave and a minor order of half-columns. It is not chance that we find here, once again, the Ionic half-column capital from the Barbadori Chapel. But, following Vitruvius' orders, Brunelleschi replaces the pilaster capital with a Corinthian capital. This, too, is highly significant.

Two different traditions – the Gothic baldaquin and medieval Classicism – meet in Brunelleschi's work.

The arcade of the Ospedale differs from the Barbadori Chapel in that, instead of a combination of half-column

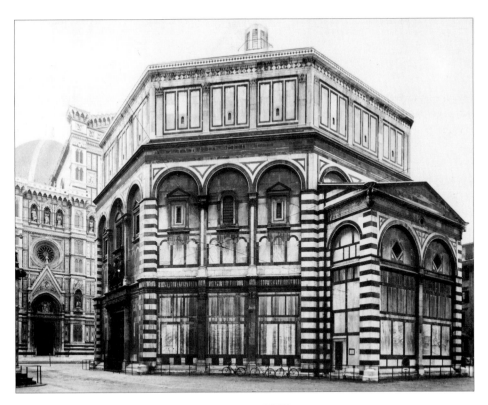

FLORENCE, BAPTISTRY

FLORENCE, BAPTISTRY

FLORENCE, OR SAN MICHELE, TABERNACLE OF ST. JOHN

PIENZA, PALAZZO COMUNALE, LOGGIA

FLORENCE, SANTO SPIRITO, BASE OF CROSSING PIERS

FLORENCE, SANTA MARIA NOVELLA, BASE

FLORENCE, CAPPELLA DEL BIGALLO, LOGGIA

FLORENCE, SANTA MARIA MAGGIORE, FRESCO ON PILLAR

FLORENCE, OR SAN MICHELE, ORCAGNA TABERNACLE, BASE

FLORENCE, OSPEDALE DEGLI INNOCENTI, COLUMN BASE IN COURTYARD

FLORENCE, BAPTISTRY, GALLERIES

and pilaster, one finds here a complete column which stands independent of the pilaster. This detail does not change the principle involved, but this combination brings out the problem of combining the framing wall (pilaster) and the free-standing colonnade even more clearly. Brunelleschi wished to retain the independence of the column at any price.[35] The tondi in the outer spandrels of the arcade were also not to be bisected but merely sliced, so that the emblem of the child in swaddling clothes did not have to be fragmented. Thus the archivolt is separated from the pilaster by a ledge which sits above the capital: a form which Brunelleschi found in the external arcades of the cathedral tribuna, where the arches are also separated from each other at each angle of the wall by horizontal ledges. Here, for the first time, we see Florence Cathedral being considered as an important traditional influence on Brunelleschi's work.

As late as 1460, the Palazzo Comunale in Pienza, founded by Pius II, retained the motif of the Ospedale portal, the free-standing arcade column next to the wall pier. The significance of this example lies in the fact that there is no pilaster. The framing pier consists merely of cut stone blocks which descend at the corners of the portal. These corner piers thus form the actual substance of the construction and are the supporting elements, with the columns taking a secondary role. Such a simple construction, whose structure is not hidden by any architectural decoration, makes clear the extent to which the architecture of the Quattrocento was determined by medieval assumptions. The corner pier corresponds to the framing sandstone strip on the facade of S. Miniato al Monte. In as much as, when defining a style, one is looking at more than just the classical decoration, one will recognise that the tectonic structure of the Palazzo Comunale in Pienza is closer to the Middle Ages than to the High Renaissance.

9. The Nave Arches of S. Lorenzo

Brunelleschi puts a half-column at either end of the nave arcade of S. Spirito, which is linked either to the inside of the facade wall or to the crossing pilaster, which this time is smooth and unfluted. The system from the Barbadori Chapel has returned, and is extended here to the multiple arcade of the basilica.

In his first church Brunelleschi chose a rather differ-ent way of ending the colonnade. In S. Lorenzo the outer columns were converted into a form of pilaster-like pier. This was the most obvious solution to the problem of ending a series of free-standing columns with a wall. Here the apparent independence of the colonnade is not rescued with the help of the outer half-columns, but rather the pier directly replaces the column, thus admit-ting that it is actually the pier and not the column which should support the arch. The wall sends out an anta to receive the arch.

By doing this Brunelleschi was taking up a medieval form which he had not found in SS. Apostoli, which provided so much of Manetti's inspiration. In that church the arch ends with half-columns in the wall. It was the cathedral of Pisa which offered a solution for S. Lorenzo. On the interior of the facade and at the crossing the arch curves down to simple antae.

Fabriczy pointed out certain general similarities between Pisa Cathedral and San Lorenzo.[36] In both cases a flatly-roofed central nave is combined with vaulted side-aisles and the crossing is crowned with a dome. In the context of our discussion it can also be noted that the high pilasters which support the crossing of S. Lorenzo recur in Pisa Cathedral as slim piers. The combination of an arcade anta with the crossing piers creates a cross-section in the form of a short-armed Greek cross.

It is significant that in his first basilica Brunelleschi adhered to the traditional medieval solutions to the question of arcade structure. The main characteristics are the antae piers and the extremely slim crossing piers, which here become fluted pilaster-piers. If, with his crossing pilasters, Brunelleschi was ignoring all 'Vitruvian' proportions which had been adhered to for the columns of the nave and the pilasters of the arcade antae and the side-chapel, then what he was doing was allowing the medieval relationships of these tectonic elements to come to the fore: with all the fragility of engaged columns, rather than canonic proportions, the crossing piers rise up to the chancel arch. The crossing, a characteristic element in a medieval basilica, has left its mark on S. Lorenzo. If Brunelleschi wanted to link the antae-pilasters with the crossing pilasters then, for the sake of retaining the correct proportions, their width had to match. It was the height which became a variable; in the same breath the unity of the canonic proportions had been broken. The crossing pilasters in S. Lorenzo have an effect similar to flat Gothic 'strip piers' like those in S. Trinità in Florence; so not only Pisa Cathedral but also this Florentine Trecento church was a precursor of S. Lorenzo.[37] The traditional Florentine choir is combined with the important motif of a row of nave chapels. The narrow strips of the crossing piers against which the subordinate arcade piers nestle are closely related to Brunelleschi's group of pilasters. This impression is reinforced by the systematic consistency of all elements. The relief depth of the thin strip piers equals that of Brunelleschi's crossing pilasters.

In S. Spirito Brunelleschi has given the pilasters heavier proportions. The crossing pilasters have become more independent of the nave arcade and no longer need to relate to the width of an anta. Instead of this, a half-column with which we are familiar from the Barbadori Chapel, which has retained its own proportions without forcing these on to the crossing piers, sits against the unfluted pilasters. Thus Brunelleschi has transferred to his second basilica the pier/half-column motif which he had developed, whereas with his first church he took over the medieval crossing piers with their cross-shaped section. This variation of approach should be seen in the context of the different wall design of the two basilicas; the crossing pilasters of S. Lorenzo equate to the pilasters in the side-aisles, whereas the crossing columns of S. Lorenzo relate to the half-columns of the side chapels.

10. The Base Ring

Both the crossing piers of S. Lorenzo, with their cross-shaped section resulting from the combination of four pilasters, and the piers of S. Spirito and S. Felicità (Barbadori Chapel), with their half-columns, are highly complex unclassical formations which are closely related to the medieval composite pier. The individual elements form a larger whole; their interdependence as equal parts of a greater whole becomes particularly clear if one looks at the base of these structures. The attic base, separated from the ground by a simple plinth and almost predestined to be an individual form, becomes a unifying ring which snakes round the half-columns and the pillar corners, holding them together. The basic geometric figures of square and circle, base and plinth, become a synthetic figure.[38] The base becomes a 'super-ordinate', or rather 'co-ordinating' form. In principle there is little difference between the base of the crossing piers of S. Spirito and the base of the arcade piers of the Barbadori Chapel. The only difference is that in the former, the corners of the plinth project completely, whereas in the latter they are rounded off in line with the bases of the half-columns. The bases in the Barbadori Chapel are notable for the close link they have with the traditional forms of the Trecento. The composite piers at the corners of the Orcagna tabernacle in Or San Michele consist of a pier-like angular core with attached half-columns. The Gothic structure is unmistakable. The model can be seen here, not just for the base but also for the rounded plinth which follows the same line. But it is not just the rounded corners of the plinth which differentiate the bases in the Barbadori Chapel from the classical attic base as found in Brunelleschi's portal for the Ospedale and the crossing piers in S. Spirito. There is also the broad throat which separates the thick torus mouldings from each other. One can still see here the influence of the Gothic proportions of the Orcagna tabernacle,[39] and this strengthens the assumption that Brunelleschi created the Barbadori Chapel before work began on the Ospedale.

Roman antiquity knew the type of base moulding which incorporates wall pilasters, such as one finds in the wall of the entrance hall of the Pazzi Chapel. In the 'Proto-Renaissance' the equivalent moulding was applied to configurations with half-columns, as in the choir of San Miniato al Monte. However, all classical ideas of form objected to the idea of joining up the bases of free-standing columns, as happened in the portal colonnade of the Pazzi Chapel. Here it fulfils its purpose as a base for the balustrade, but it clashes all the more with the individualistic principles of classical forms. The Gothic, which linked everything with everything else, made no exception in the case of the bases of columns. A search for similar structures leads us once again to the school of Orcagna, whose workshops were responsible for the high altar in the cathedral of Arezzo. At the back of the altar there is a colonnade on a moulded plinth which curves round the base of each column, enclosing them all in a sort of chain-effect. Whether Brunelleschi was consciously making reference to this or merely hit on a similar solution to a similar problem is not certain; what is certain is that in doing so he demonstrates his links with late Trecento Gothic.

FLORENCE, SANTA TRINITÀ, CROSSING PIERS

FLORENCE, BAPTISTRY, GALLERIES

II THE WALL

FLORENCE, SANTA MARIA DEL FIORE, SIDE WALL, NORTH

1. 'Membri e ossa'

The typical building material used in classical antiquity was marble. Brunelleschi however used no marble at all on his buildings. Exceptions are the central light and the ribs of the dome, and the corner tempietti of the choir of Florence Cathedral, whose marble incrustation was predetermined by the Trecento facings of the nave. But all Brunelleschi's other works, in other words all those which he initiated himself, are of sandstone. Or, to be more precise, Brunelleschi's language consists of plastered walls, and ochre and grey pietra-serena or pietra-forte structural elements.

This is, in itself, food for thought. Here is Brunelleschi, the 'Classicist', whom his first biographer, Manetti, and later Vasari credited with 'rediscovering' the ancient Roman architecture, ignoring an essential element in all classical architecture: i.e. marble.

The problem of Brunelleschi's Classicism has appeared in a different light since it was recognised[40] that

it is not so much the architecture of classical antiquity which provided his models as that of the Florentine Romanesque, in other words a classical style passed on via the Middle Ages. It was by returning to the Florentine tradition itself that he was able to break with the Gothic.

But this still does not explain the fact that Brunelleschi uses no marble, for the Florentine Romanesque tradition also used it to a considerable extent. Pilasters and architraves, which were realised in white and dark-green marble, reappear in Brunelleschi's buildings as pietra-serena elements. Nor did he imitate the walls with their marble slabs; his are covered instead in plaster.

Thus the man credited with 'overcoming the Gothic' himself followed the Florentine Gothic tradition.

Ever since the mendicant orders used naked stone to its full effect with the churches of S. Maria Novella and S. Croce the Romanesque tradition of marble incrustation had been broken. The facade of S. Maria Novella, as the important public face of the church, may have still been clothed in marble, but the sides of the building were not. In the interior the Dominicans used only plastered walls, in places decorated with frescoes, and yellow-brown pietra-serena piers.

The Franciscans followed this model with S. Croce. This, the largest building constructed by the mendicant orders, achieves much of its power through the monumental pietra-serena effect of the piers and arcades. All the structural elements, including the lesenes and consoles, stand out against the plastered walls. Although frescoes cover the pilasters and arcades in the choir, the contrast between stone pilasters and plastered, painted wall remains in the side chapels of the transept. Likewise the columns and arcades of the nave have, presumably, always been unplastered. The effect of the stone has been carefully calculated so that the lower smooth quarter of the columns contrasts sharply with the rough, upper section. There are only a few medieval family coats of arms painted on the octagonal sides, which shows how the columns were deliberately kept free of fresco decoration.

For the mendicant orders, buildings constructed of stone blocks and plaster provided an expression of the monastic ideal of poverty. Expensive marble was replaced by simple, uncut stone or shaped, undecorated blocks, which served to increase the general effect of monumentality.

The cathedral, which is richly decorated in marble on the outside, uses on the inside the material of the churches of the mendicant orders. With perfect clarity the structural elements deliberately stand out as a dark pietra-serena framework against the light plaster walls.

The great cathedrals of the north were built entirely of stone blocks.[41] At most the web of the vaulting was built of brick or tufa. In the Tuscan cathedrals, the unity of the structural elements and the walls was maintained; a significant example of this being the cathedral of Lucca (1372 ff) which was based loosely on the model of Florence Cathedral. In this, the second great construction of the Tuscan Trecento, the contrast between structural elements and walls was again relinquished in favour of the unity of stone walls.

Florence Cathedral was also originally intended to have a cut stone finish. Arnolfo di Cambio's internal facade leaves us in no doubt as to this. When, around the middle of the century, Talenti continued the work, there was a return to the local architecture of the mendicant orders. Columns and arcade arches were finished with stone blocks, while the walls were plastered. The dark, flat arches of the arcade are framed by a thin, sharp-edged ledge which lifts around the columns as though to cut down the spandrel of the pietra-serena arch. Although the sandstone structure should be part of the wall surface it is separated from this by the ledge imposed on the surface. This is a principle applied to the building in its entirety: the structural elements and the wall surfaces, the stone blocks and the plaster, are all clearly delineated from one another.[42]

The same ledges run across the marble of the exterior wall of the cathedral. Their purpose is not just to mark off zones with different materials but also to fulfil the general need for delineation. They take over the role of the stepped profile, but do not penetrate the substance of the wall, rather being added on to the surface of the marble slabs. The surface of the wall appears impenetrable, the ledges running like metal rings round the canopy tondo of a side door.

Talenti developed this form of delineating ledge in the upper storey of the Campanile.[43] The stone surface is untouched and the pointed arch of the window is separated solely by the bevelled ledge. Even at the beginning of the fifteenth century the external walls of the choir tribuna were formed in this way under Ghiberti. This purely external surface decoration was something which Brunelleschi broke with. He brings the structural elements out from the wall surface. The light plaster background provides a foil for the pilasters, architrave, tondo and window frames, which stand out, not just because of their darker shade, but also because they are physically proud of the wall. The pilasters project by the width of one or half a flute, and the architrave and arches of the archivolt similarly protrude as independent elements. Manetti called them the bones (ossa) of the building.

This was the decisive innovation introduced by Brunelleschi to the walls of his buildings. The flat surface is given a degree of movement and each structural element, each framework stands out from the surrounding wall. The stone elements are no longer, as in the nave of the cathedral, merely separated from a flat expanse of wall by an added ledge, but rather 'in-

FLORENCE, SANTA MARIA DEL FIORE, NAVE

FLORENCE, SANTA MARIA DEL FIORE, ELEVATION OF NAVE

FLORENCE, SANTA MARIA DEL FIORE, EXTERNAL WALL OF CHOIR TRIBUNE

corporate' in themselves a separate relief surface. Thus perhaps the most salient characteristic of all Trecento architecture, the way in which the taut, flat surface of the wall dominates, was overcome.[44] On the other hand the other possible link with Gothic, a staggered sequence of elements one behind the other, a sign of 'diaphanous' structure, does not occur. The elevation of Florence Cathedral has retained signs of its diaphanous origins despite the extension of the structural framework. The flanks of the piers protrude, leaving the engaged piers on a separate plane, while the wall forms a third layer at the back. Brunelleschi created the wall and its structural elements as two thin layers, one in front of the other, thus reducing the relief effect to two levels, the wall surface and the pilaster/architrave level, which stands proud by the thickness of a flute. All that stands out further are the consoles, the cornices and the capital volutes.[45]

What has become important is not that the structural elements should be matched with the surface of the wall, but rather that they should stand out from it. The 'two-dimensionality' of Brunelleschi's early elevations is not the flat surface of Trecento architecture, nor are his relief effects the same as the diaphanous structure of Gothic architecture.

2. The Florence Baptistry as a Model
If one inspects the walls of the gallery in the Florence Baptistry, with its thin pilasters, which sit in front of the wall surface and support the classical architrave, projecting imperceptibly, then the parallels to the Pazzi Chapel and the Old Sacristy become clear. In all three cases six rows of fluting run down two-thirds of the length of the pilasters, with the lower third left flat which was a traditional Roman form.

This structure of pilasters forms the basic motif for Brunelleschi's early elevations where there is not an actual colonnade forming the main structural element in an elevation. Does this mean that all Brunelleschi has done is to transfer the order of pilasters from the Baptistry at the same time using more modest materials: as befitted the cathedral, a combination of pietra-serena structural elements and a simple plastered wall?

It is not just the distinct depth of the wall relief and the slight protrusion of the pilasters from the wall which is important, but also the degree of movement within the relief.

In the Baptistry the marble slabs create an effect of rigidity. By way of contrast, the plaster wall of the Old Sacristy seems more permeable. Brunelleschi expressed a feeling of movement into and out of the wall by giving the flanks of the pilasters in the Old Sacristy one single row of fluting which suggests that the other five rows, in other words the entire depth of the pilaster, have been sunk into the wall.

In the Pazzi Chapel the pilasters stand proud of the wall by the width of only half a row of fluting, whereas in the Old Sacristy they project by the width of a whole row and the fluting runs down them. In the Baptistry the pilasters have no marking, and sit against the wall, which takes on an unyielding quality. The degree of relief is indeterminate and changes from area to area, being almost flush along the gallery and protruding next to the half-columns, though without revealing any fluting.

In the Pazzi Chapel and the Old Sacristy Brunelleschi allows the full body of the pilasters to protrude at the corners of the chancel arch. This motif, of a pilaster connected on one side to the wall, was something he also found in the Baptistry; not in the gallery but at ground level. The pilasters support in its entirety the architrave running in front of the niches, whereas Brunelleschi makes the archivolts of the chancel arch protrude from the pilaster. The structural elements match the thickness of the walls, apart from the shallow relief on them.

Logically speaking the pilasters should be almost completely embedded in the walls at the corners, and this is in fact the case in the choir. The walls, which run together at ninety degrees, only reveal the edge of the fluting; in other words, the edge of the pilaster emerges only to the depth of the relief layer. The capital, too, is enclosed by the walls; only the edge of the volute protrudes. At this point the logical consistency of the wall structure becomes clear. The 'ossa' are complete elements deeply embedded in the wall, like bones in the flesh of a body.

However, Brunelleschi deviates from this principle at the corners of the main area. The pilasters are broken up: in the Old Sacristy in the ratio of 3:3 rows of fluting; in the Pazzi Chapel, in accordance with the elongated plan, which emphasises the sides, in the ratio of 5:1. The optical effectiveness was more important than the rational consistency of the structure. In the Old Sacristy it was the supporting elements which had to come to the fore. They consist, in this case also, of the corner pilasters on which the heavy entablature rests. This fluting could never form a visual counter to the weight of the architrave. Moreover, next to the full pilasters of the chancel arch there was a need for pilasters of appropriate width in order to maintain the harmony of vertical elements. In addition, the arch above the cornice needed a support. The breadth of the pilasters had to match that of the arch.

On the other hand, in the corners of the smaller of the choirs where the moulding of the arches is also thinner, total consistency was possible. A form such as this cannot be found in the Baptistry, where, in the corners of the choir, there are rounded columns. These were, of course, added later, at the beginning of the thirteenth century, and no one knows how the master of the gallery might have solved this problem. Without answering this question, we return to the cathedral in Florence.

3. Florence Cathedral as a Model

Hitherto we have been concerned to differentiate certain elements in Florence Cathedral from Brunelleschi's architecture. Now, in returning to this building, we shall establish certain formal features which influenced Brunelleschi's style and were at least as important as the Baptistry for its development. Here, however, the relationship is less transparent than in the case of the classical buildings of the Florentine Renovatio.

So far we have only looked at the arcade wall of the nave and contrasted it with Brunelleschi's wall structures. Now we shall look at the area of the upper storey. The curve of the vaulting runs up the wall, from which it is separated by a pointed arch. In contrast to the arcades where the plaster area of the spandrel extends flush with the arch and is separated from it by an added ledge, a stepped relief effect is formed which brings out the arch as a plastic element. At all points where the vaulting meets the wall, i.e. also in the side aisles and in the chapels of the tribuna, the same relationship between wall and arch occurs.

The interior of the tribuna chapels is structured by the thin stone ridges of the engaged columns and ribs. It is not so much the detail which can be compared with the Old Sacristy, as the relationship of the structural elements to the wall. As in the Gothic chapel, we find structural elements only in the corners – pilasters here,

engaged columns there. Otherwise there are nothing but large, light areas of wall framed by the slender strips of the arches, but also linked by these to the vaulting. In the Gothic building the ribs of the web pick up the downward movement and guide it into the vertical. A fine console frieze provides a border between rib and web. Brunelleschi used the rich moulding of the classical cornice to form a link with the pendentive, a form which already existed in the cornice frame of the cathedral vaulting. Just as the moulding of Brunelleschi's semi-circular arches stands out from the rest of the surface of the wall, so, too, on the cathedral chapels, the arches are proud of the wall. It can be seen that the archivolts and Gothic arches take on similar tasks and have the same relationship with the wall and the vaulting.

In the tribuna chapel the arch is drawn down into the vertical. There are two ledges on the engaged pier, which, as in the nave, takes the form of a polygon rod which fills the corner between the sides of the pillars and seems to protrude from the wall as a narrow edge. The corner pier in one of Brunelleschi's choirs sits in the wall in a similar manner. The leaves of the capital press into the white plaster in a similar fashion; the difference being that in the one case they belong to a composite pier, whereas in the other they belong to a pilaster.

In the Pazzi Chapel there is a heavy, continuous architrave on top of the capital, whereas in the cathedral there is an architrave-like impost which is similarly embedded in the wall. The vertical framework of the Gothic building lacks the horizontal division between the arch and the wall below.

Brunelleschi put the classical elements based on the Baptistry into a context already created for the Gothic structural elements of the Tribuna chapel. He established classical decor as an intentional, revolutionary return to the archaic architecture of the Florentine Renovatio. He took over the link between the wall and the structural elements as though it had never been in question, as a product of the latest development of Florentine architecture. The actual language of the forms could become controversial, so that he quite deliberately set pilaster against composite engaged column, archivolt against pointed arcade and fascia against moulded arch. This was an important aspect, if not the entire essence of the innovation. His view of how

FLORENCE, SANTA MARIA DEL FIORE, TRIBUNE CHAPEL

FLORENCE, SANTA MARIA DEL FIORE, CORNER ENGAGED COLUMN IN TRIBUNE CHAPEL

FLORENCE, PAZZI CHAPEL, CORNER PILASTER IN CHOIR

FLORENCE. SAN LORENZO

FLORENCE. SAN LORENZO. SIDE AISLE

LUCCA. CATHEDRAL. ELEVATION OF NAVE

structural elements should be linked with the wal had to be much less deliberate, altogether more natural and closer to tradition.

On the other hand, the replacing of the classical marble elements with traditional pietra-serena and the resulting retention of the plastered walls as the contrasting substance must have occurred on a totally conscious level. Brunelleschi retained the specific effect of the elevation of Florence Cathedral and applied it to the new formal language he had painstakingly established. A link thereby emerged between the Early Renaissance which had been born with his work and the Late Gothic of the Trecento. But the Gothic of Florence Cathedral already contained elements pointing forward, out of the Gothic.

The important link between the cathedral and Brunelleschi's development is proved not just by the fact that the dome was put in his hands. He had already been involved as a consultant for the vaulting of the choir,[46] and therefore must have had a close familiarity with the problems of Gothic structures.

4. The Elevation of the Side-Aisle Wall in S. Lorenzo

It was not just the interrelationship of the wall and its structural elements, so characteristic of all Brunelleschi's buildings, which was inspired by Florence Cathedral. In addition to this the cathedral provided the model for certain basic aspects of Brunelleschi's internal elevations. Such a connection will, admittedly, not be found by comparing the nave elevations of his basilicas with that of the cathedral. What was a revolutionary innovation in these buildings was the way in which he abolished the Gothic composite pier system and the Gothic vaulting. The return to the colonnade and to an independent upper storey separated by a broad architrave and lit by large windows, above which was the coffered roof, created links with the Romanesque architecture of SS Apostoli or even early Christian buildings such as S. Paolo Fuori le Mura in Rome. The break with the recent past was total.

Even the wall of the side-aisle of S. Lorenzo[47] takes up the basic note of the new classical decor from the central nave, but at the same time reveals certain residual Trecento touches. The linking of a row of side-chapels into a vaulted aisle creates a wall in which the classical decor serves to lift what is basically a Gothic system

into an entirely different sphere. The wall pilasters serve as supports for the architrave and semi-circular archivolts which rise above this, while the arcade structure remains below and forms a series of frames for the arches of the chapel. Above this rises the semi-circular vaulting, so that a sort of aisle upper storey is formed.

This basic design matches the central nave of Florence Cathedral. A heavy gallery balustrade separated from the pointed arches below by a ledge divides the wall into two zones, clearly separating the upper storey from the arcades. This is an original device which differentiates Florence Cathedral from churches with a similar elevation such as S. Maria Novella or S. Petronio in Bologna. In these the arcade rises uninterrupted into the upper storey with its oculi. The horizontal division introduced in the cathedral, which draws attention to the direct superimposition of two sets of arches, marked a distinct change in this design tradition[48] which had roots going back to the early thirteenth century.

Brunelleschi took the basis of this design for the side-aisle walls of S. Lorenzo as a cue to give a classical flavour to the Gothic structural elements[49] by replacing the composite pier with pilasters and the balustrade with an architrave which thus separated the arcades from the arch of the vaulting just as did the gallery in S. Maria del Fiore.

The link between the Gothic elevation and Brunelleschi's design of the side aisle walls becomes even clearer if one compares it to one of the many architectural paintings produced in the Trecento. Tadeo Gaddi's painting in the Baroncelli Chapel in S. Croce represents Florence Cathedral in a simplified form, changing the gallery into a flat ledge and the pointed arches into rounded ones. This motif is still found in S. Maria degli Angeli.

Attention has already been drawn to the arches of the upper storey in the cathedral and to the particular relationship between the wall and the structural elements. As in the aisle of S. Lorenzo, the stone strips stand proud of the wall and a large oculus sits in the centre of the wall under the arch. The similarity in form of the two buildings is brought home to us once again. As in the upper storey of the cathedral, Brunelleschi surrounds the window with a ring of stone which protrudes from the surface of the wall.

5. Moulding and Frames

In the cathedral the angled moulding of the great round windows emerges directly from the wall, but the dark stone makes it an element in its own right, like a heavy ring which has been embedded in the wall, its front edge turned in round the edge of the wall to form a frame for the window.[50]

If we compare it to the upper-storey oculi in S. Maria Novella, the important change which has taken place becomes clear. In S. Maria Novella the round windows are let directly into the walls without any architectural framework whatsoever.

But the contrast between Gothic moulding and the window frames in Florence Cathedral should also be pointed out. The moulding is an integral part of the wall itself, merely delineating the interruption formed by the window, whereas oculi frames such as these have a form independent of the wall; they stand in their own right as something more than a mere frame for the window. We should, therefore, in the case of the cathedral windows, speak in terms of a 'sleeve' frame rather than a moulding. The same goes for Brunelleschi's windows and oculi. Their moulding is similarly framed by a sleeve-like frame which emerges from the wall.

Thus whenever windows or niches had to be framed, Brunelleschi used moulding which stood out from the plane of the wall. Here the late Gothic architecture of the Trecento provided models.

The windows of the cathedral nave are framed on the inside by a strip which sits against the wall: Talenti's traditional string course. The completely smooth-sided cut in the wall only has at the front edge such a strip as a projecting frame. The strip frame returns in the windows of the Palazzo di Parte Guelfa as an edge for the broad fascia which forms the projecting frame of the window. Thus Gothic and classical forms are united.

A second example is provided by the frames to the niches in the tempietti of the tribuna. Once again there is a sharp-edged strip, this time separated from the wall by a ledge. It links to a cornice which runs round the inside edge of the niche like a collar. The oculi of the upper storey of Florence Cathedral has a similar cross-section.

Brunelleschi favoured creating a frame which combined a sharp-edged strip superimposed on the wall with a cornice. The strip followed the direction of the opening in the wall, or, like in the oculus of the Old Sacristy, was set into wall itself, or emphasised the curve of the niches of the tempietti. Even the apse-like choir niches of the Old Sacristy are framed by such a cornice; in this case it is an unusually broad one which leads into the shallow niche, starting with a torus and curving gently inwards, leading the eye inwards from the wall to the niche before ending abruptly.

The side chapels of S. Lorenzo are framed in this way, rather like pictures. The cornice provides a frame for the entire space of each chapel. In contrast to the windows of the Palazzo di Parte Guelfa, where the ledge is superimposed on the wall, it is here embedded in the wall. An entire arcade becomes a frame, starting from a projecting foot, leading up to the curve of the arch and down again to the foot. Thus a peculiar combination occurs of pilasters and arcade arch without an impost. This device was to recur frequently in the early Florentine Renaissance, for example in Ghiberti's architecture on the second bronze door. Alberti, too, uses it in the chapel of Mantua Cathedral.

Such an arch reaches enormous proportions in the side naves of S. Spirito and takes on the dimensions of an 'order' comparable to the pillared arcades themselves. The massive arch has a frame whose cross-section has deep shadows in the crevices.[51] The Gothic profile seems to have come into its own again. The impression is created by Brunelleschi's use of a succession of concave and convex curves which he sets against each other,[52] thus brilliantly achieving an effect of both leading the eye into the niche and letting it rest on the arch itself. When the top plate of the column impost meets the front moulding, there are immediate associations with Gothic forms. The frame of the chapel breaks through the ledge of the impost and becomes a 'transcending' element.

This effect came from the intention to lend overall unity to the system which in S. Lorenzo still consisted of an accumulation of individual elements. This desire to unify diverse elements and to link the columns with the wall of the niches led to such a 'transcendental' form, slightly reminiscent of Gothic systems, which also used continuous and linking arches. The heavy tori of the niche frames take on the character of engaged columns.

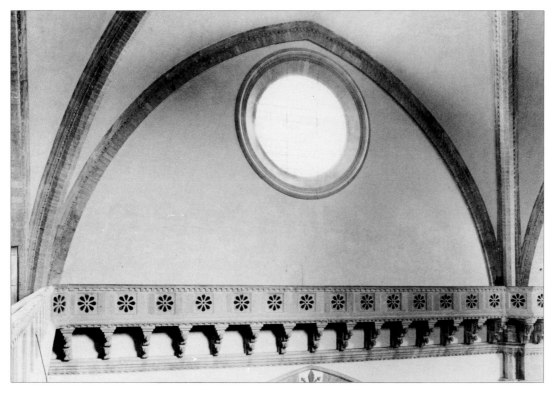

FLORENCE, SANTA MARIA DEL FIORE, CLERESTORY

FLORENCE, SANTA MARIA DEL FIORE, CLERESTORY OCULUS

FLORENCE, OLD SACRISTY, OCULUS

6. The Ribs of the Umbrella Dome

Since the building of S. Maria degli Angeli, Brunelleschi had emphasised not so much the flat qualities of wall surfaces as the massivity of the wall itself.[53] As the bulk of the wall increased, the structural elements became heavier too. The basic differentiation between wall and structural element, brought out by the difference of the materials used, remained the main characteristic of Brunelleschi's elevations. In the side chapels of S. Spirito, it is not so much the wall itself which expresses massivity, as the projecting edgings and the curves of the half-columns. It is the relationship of the structural elements to the wall which qualifies the qualities of the latter: it possesses both surface and bulk.

This multivalent property of the wall comes out particularly clearly in the pilasters of the Old Sacristy, which break up before the corner and then sink into the wall (choir) and only project an edge from the corner.

If the webs of Brunelleschi's umbrella domes seem paper thin compared with the niches in S. Spirito, then this effect is achieved by the slender ribs which, instead of sinking deep into the semi-circle, sit against the front edge of the webs.[54] The webs curve from rib to rib like wind-filled sails between masts. Such an interpretation is supported by Brunelleschi's own view of this form. In the vaulting of the smaller choir he dispensed with the umbrella web and created a smooth cap, a symbol of the skies: against the dark blue background one sees the constellations and, at the bottom edge, instead of a ledge, one finds a bulge of reefed sailcloth. The 'blind' has been drawn back leaving a clear view of the heavens. This illusionist effect deliberately changes the nature of the stone; the vaulting becomes a sail and the actual dome becomes the firmament. Another effect derives from the surface of the wall. The ribs of the main dome form a framework which radiates out to the edge of the dome. Between the spokes the individual segments swell like sections of an open umbrella. In Roman and early Christian antiquity similar vaults had no ribbed subdivisions. The individual sections were joined with thin ridges. Brunelleschi, however, wanted a clear setting for the light-coloured webs of the dome and used projecting ribs, unmistakably derived from Gothic models. A common form of Gothic ribbing was a band with slight supporting spurs, and Brunelleschi's ribbing is reminiscent of this. But the Gothic ribs were always a factor of the ridge-like joins of the webs, whereas here the ribs have an entirely different task: that of framing the light-coloured sections of the dome. Thus they do not run to a central ring but curve away before meeting the ring round the central light, and run back down the next rib. The wall section, or in this case the umbrella web, now has a particular function: the eye is led by the framework to the cut-out sail, not by the engaged columns and ribs, as was customary in Gothic buildings.

7. The Empty Surface

In our interpretation of Brunelleschi's elevation design we assumed that the wall against which the dark pietra-serena structural elements stand out was covered with a uniform, light-coloured plaster, as though it were a white 'canvas' on which the architectural sketch is drawn. Devoid of any fresco decoration, the pale surface forms a background against which the structural elements form a 'picture'. At the same time, dark stone frameworks create empty arch shapes on the wall, as though the surface itself were an aesthetic treasure worthy of being framed. Examples of this are the arch shapes in the Pazzi Chapel or the choir niches of the Old Sacristy.

Such a deliberate decision to contrast the wall surfaces with the structural elements seems to have offered only one possibility: to make the wall into an empty expanse constituting a background against which only the architecture can stand.

And yet such a purity was seen as being impossible, and Brunelleschi's buildings were given fresco decorations which destroy the interplay of wall and structural elements and reduce them to a mere vehicle for illusionist painting which dominates the architecture.

A generation which was discovering the colourfulness of medieval cathedrals and Greek temples, and was thus moving away from the sterile whiteness of the historical Classicism of around 1800 could only imagine Brunelleschi's buildings being decorated with frescos.

Heinrich von Geymüller's criticism of the Old Sacristy uses precisely the 'lack' of painting as its strongest argument. When he complains 'that in the total structure, which is conceived as a configuration of supporting, framing and linking elements, the strength of the elements does not seem in proportion to the function which they fulfil', he finds this impression strengthened 'by the barbaric whiteness of the plaster.

This whitewash makes structural elements, which perhaps should only have had the function of providing a frame, appear to have a supporting function without possessing the strength actually to carry this out. Instead of architecture, what we see is partly just a framework. Both weaknesses would have been largely or even completely removed by the painting which Brunelleschi certainly must have intended to be added. That this was his intention, or indeed that such paintings existed, can be seen both from individual traces and also from the need to make this element available to the master, lest the weaknesses listed above detract from his reputation in a manner entirely unworthy of him.'[55]

To back up this statement Geymüller points to the remains of colour which existed in his day and were, in the restoration work which followed, extended to form the colourful ensemble as we know it now: a blue dome in the choir with gold constellations, the golden coat of arms of the Medici with the red spheres, the coloured version of the Donatello relief and some gilding of the ornamentation. But on the walls no traces of colour were found. They remained white, as indeed they would have been from the start. The concentration of colour on the pictorial elements, the choir ceiling, the coats of arms and the reliefs would seem to be the result of a deliberate decision to leave the wall, even with its different sections, undecorated, so as to bring out the architeture all the more strongly. The individual touches of colour concentrate the eye on the pictorial message of individual elements, such as the coats of arms of the founders.

The thin gold band on the ring of the dome brings out particularly clearly this deliberate limitation to only selected colourful elements. The architecture itself has to remain unaffected. Another example of Brunelleschi's 'pure' architecture is the Pazzi Chapel, in which pictorial and colourful elements are confined to individual ornaments and the terracotta tondi, let into the thick walls playing an almost architectural role. Significantly, these take the form of reliefs occupying real space, rather than creating an illusion of space; thus remaining in the same dimension as the architectureitself.

The picture is isolated and framed like a window, oculus or coffer, and is thus fitted into the architecture. The Wall behind remains a bare expanse which has its own validity and serves as a foil for everything else, including the picture which sits against it, without changing it in any way.

Like the tondi above them, the great expanses of wall under the semi-circular arches between the pilasters are given powerful frames. This gives them the impression of being pictures, like the tondi. But the frames surround nothing but a bare expanse of wall, which thus becomes a centre of interest rather than just a foil for the rest, 'content' rather than background.

We can be certain that these expanses of wall were not intended to carry pictures if we compare them with the windows of the entrance wall. In the interests of the unity of the architecture, these are continued as blind arches on the other walls. The areas of wall within these arches remain bright, empty expanses to match the bright expanses of glass represented by the windows.

We cannot completely exclude the possibility that the walls were given coloured or even dark marbling, particularly in the choir, where Carl von Stegmann[56] claims to have discovered traces of dark colouring underneath the plaster. However it would seem more likely that the subsequent restoration of the chapel with a whitish finish, based on the colouring which was still in evidence, was correct. One thing is definite: it would be wrong to follow Geymüller and assume that the walls were painted and decorated like the chapel of the Cardinal of Portugal in San Miniato; neither can Michelozzo's Portinari Chapel in Milan be regarded as a model for the decoration of the Old Sacristy. By this time attitudes had changed from Brunelleschi's day.[57]

All Brunelleschis churches remained completely devoid of wall painting. How could one imagine painting the spandrels of the arcades and the long white plaster strips above? How could the light-coloured apse of a side chapel in S. Spirito, with its contrasting dark framework be decorated?

An isolated remark by Vasari can help us here. During the course of his painting of the Capella Martelli in S. Lorenzo he reports that Brunelleschi had intended only one large painting for each chapel.[58] One can still see what this looked like by looking at the choir chapels of S. Spirito, where the altars date from the Quattrocento and clearly indicate Brunelleschi's intentions. The white apse houses nothing more than an altar with a painted antependium and an oblong altar picture. Architectural decoration is limited to the colourful coat of arms of the endowers of the chapel which sits above the window against a light-coloured background.

Thus painted decoration is limited to a panel to which the two side pilasters and the entablature give an architectural framework completely independent of the architecture of the building which surrounds it. There is a certain awkwardness in the way the altar stands in its niche and the corners of the entablature fit uncomfortably against the wall. The strict separation of the painting from the building has an uncompromising character to it. Purified architecture has produced a purified picture, which now develops its own space. (It is no coincidence that now, under Brunelleschi's influence, exact perspective in painting was developing).

Brunelleschi banned wall painting from his churches. An architecture which itself now took on pictorial qualities was no longer a mere 'background' for painting. In vain Masaccio tried to find scope for his artistic activities in Brunelleschi's buildings. In Brunelleschi's work the two artistic genres became separated.

Hans Kauffmann observed the same process at work in sculpture: 'The first Renaissance buildings are contemporary with the last monumental statues. It had to be this way. For the new architectural style not only introduced a new approach to buildings but also, with its purism, dismantled the whole artistic system and broke down the "total work of art", the cathedral, into its constituent areas. The walls would now accept reliefs, but not statues. . . Thus the new style reduced and constrained the scope of sculpture.'[59]

A striking example of the new situation is the choir of S. Spirito where, even late in the Quattrocento, Brunelleschi's precepts were followed; here one finds a succession of altars, a veritable apotheosis of the emancipation of painting from architecture. The only exception to this rule is the marble altar by Sansovino in the left hand arm of the cross; here one witnesses just how drastically the artist of the High Renaissance deviates from Brunelleschi's purist approach: Sansovino's work follows the 'total work of art' approach and links up with the surrounding architecture, the shape of the marble altar echoing the curve of the apse. This was unknown to the masters of the Quattrocento. For them the genres were completely independent , as is echoed by the clash of the altar and the curved chapel wall.

From an initially revolutionary approach, Brunelleschi gradually developed towards a dogmatic consistency which sought to lay down new ideas as rules: it became an uninfringeable principle for him that the role of the wall was to serve as a background not for frescoes but only for the architectonic elements.

This was to change in the next generation, which was quick to return to the old interplay of the various genres. It is not Brunelleschi's works but rather the different approach of his successors which we find in buildings such as Michelozzo's Portinari Chapel in Milan, Rossellino's Chapel of the Cardinal of Portugal in S. Miniato, and Benozzo Gozzoli's private chapel of the Medici.

And indeed how could the great Florentine tradition of fresco painting have been supressed by the will of one man, even if that man was Brunelleschi! Nevertheless, at this early stage in the Renaissance, a basic theme had been established in a radical form which was to recur constantly at later stages and lead to a major problem for art: the separation, indeed the disintegration of artistic genres, which in itself led to many successful and also many unsuccessful attempts to revive the 'total' work of art, the 'Gesamtkunstwerk'. But for Michelozzo, who fitted naturally into the prevailing traditions, this problem did not exist. All he and his contemporaries had to do was to ignore Brunelleschi.

8. White

Sources tell us that during the construction of the cathedral dome Brunelleschi had iron hooks let into the vaulting so that, later on, scaffolding could be suspended and the dome covered in mosaic work.[60] This would have been a logical decoration for a ribless cloister vault, as already realised in the baptistry.[61] By contrast, the umbrella domes of the Old Sacristy and the Pazzi Chapel have remained without any mosaic work, the dark vaulting ribs framing a white surface.

With the process of purification of architecture, neutral, light-coloured or, where possible, white surfaces came into their own. It is a sign of Classicism, however, that these surfaces were not just left on their own but were enclosed in a framework, as, for example, in the case of the rounded arches of the Pazzi Chapel. Classicism meant the return of the empty, framed surface together with the marble white of the temples.

Ghiberti was already familiar with this sort of wall and, significantly, saw this as the whiteness left behind when barbarism had destroyed all ornamentation. 'During the times of the Emperor Constantine and Pope Sylvester it came about that Christianity became the dominant religion . . . and in order to eradicate all traces of idolatry it was decided to leave the temples white and undecorated. Severe punishment was meted out to anyone erecting a statue or any other form of artistic representation. Thus painting and sculpture and the teaching of these declined. And the demise of art meant that for 600 years the Houses of God remained white and undecorated.'[62] By contrast, when Alberti wrote his treatise on architecture he was 'completely convinced that the Heavens find greatest pleasure in purity and simplicity both in colour and in life', and he points to Cicero who, with Plato, believed that: 'his people should be exhorted by a law to reject all frivolous decoration in the temples and allow above all for pure whiteness'.[63]

Thus Brunelleschi's contemporaries were of diametrically opposed opinions. Ghiberti saw in the whiteness of the temples nothing but a sterility imposed by the barbaric asceticism of the early Christians. Alberti, on the other hand, saw the whiteness in terms of Cicero's moral justification of such deliberate limitation 'in which the Heavens find greatest pleasure'.

Implicitly he was acknowledging that Brunelleschi, probably the first to contradict Ghiberti, was right. But with his customary tact Alberti at once pays tribute to the need for decoration, in a statement which is often conveniently overlooked in attempts to make Alberti the pure classicist which he undoubtedly never was. ' . . . He shall earn praise who attempts to decorate the walls, ceiling and floor as artfully and splendidly as possible. . . For this reason for the interior a covering of fused or cut glass shall be particularly suitable.'[64]

Apart from the fact that Alberti here could point to Roman antiquity in making this demand, to surviving buildings such as the Pantheon, which was never just white but decorated with a variety of coloured stones, he is here also justifying the rich decoration of his own constructions, such as S. Francesco in Rimini.[65]

Thus Alberti agreed with Brunelleschi by citing the 'classical white' of Cicero, but at the same time left full scope for his own efforts and those of his contemporaries, and the desire for decoration displayed by Michelozzo, Rossellino and Alberti. But both Ghiberti and Alberti, in their theoretical statements, show that the white wall had become an object of debate now that Brunelleschi had given it a new meaning in his elevations. A newly discovered document relating to the building work on the Ospedale degli Innocenti makes it clear that Brunelleschi had planned white walls for this, one of his earliest works. The vaulting of the portal which was originally planned as cross-vaulting was intended to be painted white. Now of course such information would not allow one to draw general conclusions if it had not also been stated that a particular white was meant: 'di biancho San Giovanni' (San Giovanni white). The Florence Baptistry was a model for this, too.

' . . .Ciascuna di dette volti in croce e con sottoarchi, con gl'arcaletti centinati e con richasco. . . E di sopra bene amattonate e pulite; e di sotto bene intonichate con gli spigholi bene rilevati. . . E il detto amattonato e intonichato voglв si faccia a quello tempo e quando parrà a detti Operai e inbianchato di biancho San Giovanni.'[66] The two words 'San Giovanni' are in italics but are in the same hand as the rest of the text, which was probably written before 1424, when, instead of the cross-vaulting called for in this document, the suspended cupolas of the portal were constructed. The addition of 'San Giovanni' shows that the writer was aware of the thematic link with the form of the Baptistry and even regarded it as necessary to name the colour which was so crucial to the new Classicism of Brunelleschi. The document is the only one extant which specifically names the Baptistry as the model for the early Florentine Renaissance.[67] 'Di biancho San Giovanni' means that it was not the coloured cladding but only the marble white of the Baptistry which was recommended as the salient feature to emulate. Brunelleschi was able to push through this model vis à vis his client. He was able to point to a building which represented the entire city. The white of San Giovanni seems to have been the purifying force which justified the creation of empty spaces devoid of all ornamentation and painting. Brunelleschi achieved for architecture what Masaccio had for painting when he forwent the tiny ornamentation of Masolino and clothed his figures in single-coloured, generously cut robes which are undisturbed by patterns and thus accentuate the statuesque size of the individuals who wear them. Similarly Brunelleschi's hand makes even such a small building as the Old Sacristy into a peaceful space, opening out amidst uninterrupted expanses of framed wall.

FLORENCE, OSPEDALE DEGLI INNOCENTI, CONSOLE IN CHIOSTRO DEGLI UOMINI

PART II

BRUNELLESCHI'S EARLY WORKS

FLORENCE, OSPEDALE DEGLI INNOCENTI, CHIOSTRO DELLE DONNE DURING RESTORATION WORK

I BRUNELLESCHI AS A CONSTRUCTION ENGINEER

FLORENCE, PAZZI CHAPEL, DOME

Before the Arte della Lana gave Brunelleschi the task of creating the vaulting for the cathedral dome in Florence he had to prove against stiff opposition that he had the skill to create a cupola on a drum of a diameter almost equal to that of the Pantheon,[1] using free-standing scaffolding. Of primary relevance to the decision-making process was the question of the construction technique to be used.[2]

Brunelleschi's contemporaries lavished praise on his ability as an engineer. (It should be remembered that church-building represented the major technological achievement of the times, and the construction-sites of the great cathedrals were effectively the 'engineering institutes' of the Middle Ages.)

When Manetti in his biography of Brunelleschi tries to summarise his achievements, he frequently praises certain aesthetic qualities but at the same time emphasises Brunelleschi's skills as a builder. 'He studied the excellent and ingenious construction methods of the ancients and their musical proportions.'[3] 'Because his wonderful talent was recognised he was often asked for advice on building techniques.'[4] This appears to have occurred long before the building of the cathedral dome, for Brunelleschi's significance as a builder had been proved by his very first work, the house for his relative, Apollonio Lapi. The care Brunelleschi devoted to the actual building process is shown by the fact that he personally went to the brickworks and inspected the materials for the cathedral dome, sometimes brick by brick.[5]

A document published by Guiseppe Marchini in 1963 throws new light on Brunelleschi's involvement in the building of the cathedral, even before he took a more central role with his preparations for the construction of the dome.

As early as 1410 the builders had used Brunelleschi's knowledge as a builder and a stone-specialist and had paid him for a delivery of bricks.[6] In 1415 together with

53

Donatello, he took over an order for a statue which was to be erected on the crossbeam of the cathedral tribuna.[7] The same year he was in Pisa.[8]

Marchini's document dates from 1412: 'Prima dell' 11 di marzo erano venuti sul lavora 'e stettono di due' Nanni Niccoli e Filippo di ser Brunellesco 'capimaestri'. Il secondo altra volta 'venne a Prato a consigliarci per fatto della muraglia'; mentre Nicoló vocato Pela il 23 d'aprile 'venne a disegnare el modello e lo isguancio nella faccia della saggrestia . . .' 'Il 17 di luglio fu fatto onore' 'a due capimaestri che ci mandorono i sei per misurare la faccia dinanzi' dopodiche, il giorno seguente, viene inviato a Firenze al Pela maestro un modello per la facciata fatta Giovanni d'Ambrogio.'[9]

Nanni di Banco and Brunelleschi were thus called to Prato in 1412 in order to report on the building work on the facade of Prato Cathedral.[10] Giovanni d'Ambrogio, at the time 'Capomaestro' of Florence Cathedral supplied a model for the Prato facade.

There was a division of labour between the 'technicians', who were responsible for inspection of the construction work, and the actual 'architects and sculptors',[11] who supplied a model for the facade and had the task of realising the new portal. Brunelleschi represented the experts 'a consigliarci per fatto della muraglia'.

The document is very revealing if one compares it with other known information about Brunelleschi's activities at this time. We first hear of him as a construction expert in 1404 when, with Ghiberti and others, he inspects the errors made in the struts (sproni) of the cathedral tribuna in Florence.[12] In 1405, again with Ghiberti, he loses his job as *consiliarius*.[13] In 1410 Brunelleschi sells bricks to the builders of the cathedral, and in 1412 he reappears as an inspector of the Florentine builders in Prato, where he gives advice on the construction of the cathedral facade. Together with Nanni di Banco he is called *capomaestro*, which underlines his new importance.[14]

From extant documents we learn that Brunelleschi had specialised in construction matters relating to walls. Above all he concerned himself with stonework, gaining expertise which put him ahead of his rivals when it came to the competition for the task of building the cathedral dome. It was only then, in 1420, that he appeared as the great master-builder and, after displaying his skills in the plans for the dome, received in quick succession the jobs of the Ospedale, S. Lorenzo, the Old Sacristy, the Barbadori and Ridolfi Chapels and, indeed, the Palazzo di Parte Guelfa. These projects, which all commenced at roughly the same time, were to keep him occupied for the next ten years; and with the laying of the foundation-stone of the Pazzi Chapel in 1429 came the building which forms the transition to Brunelleschi's late works.

FLORENCE, OSPEDALE DEGLI INNOCENTI, ARCADE COLUMNS IN CHIOSTRO DEGLI UOMINI

II BRUNELLESCHI'S FIRST BUILDINGS

FLORENCE, PALAZZA VECCHIO, SIDE WALL OF SALA DEI CINQUECENTO

1. Sense of Style

Manetti names three buildings, whose precise identity has remained unclear, as being the first works of Brunelleschi, pre-dating the start of work on the Florentine dome: Apollonio Lapi's house, the tower of the Villa Petraia and the extension to the Palazzo Vecchio.[15] Manetti specifically mentions that the young Brunelleschi worked on the Palazzo Vecchio: 'Occorse ne' tempi della sua giovanezza, che s'ebbe a murare nel palazzo de' Priori l'Uficio e resedenza degli Uficiali del Monte e la stanza de' loro Ministri.'[16]

Manetti continues with some highly significant remarks on the characteristics of Brunelleschi's youthful style which, he says, differentiate his early works from later ones: 'And there [Palazzo Vecchio] one can see that he disliked the ornamentation customary for that period. . . and so he adopted another kind, though not that which he was to use later, for he did not yet know the works of the Romans.'[17]

Fabriczy underlined the significance of these words and concluded 'that the last named building, as well as the others, belonged to the pre-Roman period and, more importantly, that Brunelleschi's fine sense of form already led him to react against the decorative language of his time, even before he had delved more deeply into antiquity.'[18]

In other words, it was not the works of antiquity and their Florentine representatives from the eleventh and twelfth centuries which caused Brunelleschi to strike out in a new direction. Even before that, while he was still rooted in the traditions of the Trecento, he started to search for a new vocabulary which – 'si può vedere ancora' – was indeed different from the old one.

We are given here an interesting insight into the psychology of a process which we tend to label objectively as a 'stylistic turning point', as though such things occurred spontaneously. Manetti transfers the 'emergence of the Renaissance' to the individual, personalising the process and expressing it in terms of the individual's wishes and intentions.

There are few similar reports of such a stylistic discrimination extant. Brunelleschi's Flemish contemporaries, such as Jan van Eyck, must have been similarly aware. . . of the stylistic contrast that exists between Romanesque and Gothic forms and deliberately used it to express the antithesis between Judaism and Christianity.'[19]

However, it can be assumed that van Eyck did not just use Romanesque forms in order to make an iconographical differentiation between old and new, but rather that he was here undergoing a change in style similar to that of Brunelleschi when he turned to the Romanesque buildings of the Florentine Renovatio. The serene poise of semi-circular arches recurs even in situations where no reference to antiquity was required; namely on the inner sides of the Ghent Altar, where it is not just Adam and Eve's niches which have circular arches but also those of Mary and John the Baptist, and even those above the founders and their patron saints. Thus a style aimed at achieving a harmonious balance can overcome even a pointed Gothic arch.

A stylistic discrimination similar to that which Manetti ascribes to Brunelleschi, and which may be regarded as being at the very root of such a fundamental change in style can, significantly enough, be found two and a half centuries earlier at a time of similarly fundamental change. Abbot Suger of St. Denis was applying similar stylistic thought to his work, which was to mark the foundation of the Gothic, when he compared it with the old Carolingian church and contrasted his 'opus modernum' with the 'opus antiquum'. When the French Gothic later met the traditional styles of other countries, such a conscious underlining of specific stylistic characteristics recurred: 'Gervase of Canterbury deliberately sets out to analyse the contrast between the old structure and the new chevet begun by William of Sens in 1174 ('operis utriusque differentiam'), and not only brilliantly describes such differences as that between groin vaults and rib vaults. . .'[20]

The importance of such reports for art historians is not just that they mark the dividing lines between historical epochs, but that they also demonstrate that definitions of style are not just post-hoc rationalisations by researchers, but are actually something which the 'creators' of these styles and their contemporaries were conscious of, an awareness which formed an essential element of such stylistic watersheds.

Brunelleschi's works mark such a watershed: he himself was part of the Old before he created the New. The Ospedale marked such a sharp break with the past that since then we do not only see the 'Gothic' as distinct from the Renaissance, but also have difficulty in recognising Brunelleschi's early works as coming from his hand, so closely do we associate his style with that of the early Renaissance. It is only through written documents that we learn of his early works. The concomitant problems of identification, together with the radical difference in style, means that they are even further removed from the 'real' mature works. Only in more modern times have we been able to observe a similar process when, for example, an artist such as Picasso suddenly turns his back on the Impressionist style of his youth and founds Cubism thus splitting his artistic production into two periods so apparently independent that the very identity of the artist himself seems to be put in question.

2. The Extension of the Palazzo Vecchio

On the external wall on the north side of the Salone dei Cinquecento, whose rubble facade was only partly covered by the later facing, there are a number of blind arcade arches. The shape of the framework suggests that these date from earlier than the Salone itself, which was constructed towards the end of the fifteenth century by Cronaca. The possibility arises that the rubble wall, which is flush with the shaped stone wall beneath, already existed before Cronaca's extension.

The fact that the arches were themselves created earlier than the window aedicules can be seen from the square edge of the external pilaster, which covers one of the arches but leaves free part of the lower console ledge and the right-hand shoulder of the arch.

On the other hand, the evidence suggests that the wall was prepared for facing with shaped stones. The window arches are set further back than the front layer of Trecento stone blocks, which breaks off in an uneven fashion as though the facing was suddenly stopped. The arches have subsequently been let into the wall. They are flush with it, and were intended to be surrounded by smooth plasterwork.[21]

FLORENCE, PALAZZO BUSINI

FLORENCE, PALAZZO BUSINI, CAPITAL IN CORTILE

FLORENCE, PALAZZO BUSINI, CORTILE

Thus the following chronology emerges: an existing wall from the Trecento, prepared for facing, was, at the beginning of the fifteenth century – as stylistic analysis will demonstrate – pierced by arched windows with superimposed oculi. Instead of the stone facing originally intended it was now planned for the wall to be covered in smooth plaster. During a third building phase, the one in which the Salone dei Cinquecento received its final form, the arched windows were partially obscured by added pilasters.

The flattened arches, flush with the wall with no projections whatsoever and no jointing effects, were unusual for Cronaca's time. The consoles, which take the form of slightly downward-sloping ledges and provide a base for the window, but sit freely in the wall, have the traditional moulding of the fourteenth century. Even the window arch itself, which has a barely discernable point on the outer edge, displays Trecento characteristics. On the other hand, the inside of the arch is a full semi-circle and thus different from the flat segmental arch still usual in 1400. The window also receives a monumental character from the oculus which sits above the point. This was utterly unusual for the palazzi of the Trecento, and even in the Quattrocento only returns in the Palazzo di Parte Guelfa.[22]

All the stylistic characteristics discussed, the unusual vacillation between Trecento tradition and hitherto unknown vocabulary, which includes the combination of a full semi-circular arch with a slightly pointed outer edge, the jutting ledge of the window base and the oculus above the arch, give these windows an unusual character. Manetti's remark that in his youth Brunelleschi rejected the traditional ornamentation (conci) but did not yet know classical decoration could be given strong support by these windows. It is highly probable that the north wall of the Salone dei Cinquecento contains traces of one of Brunelleschi's early works.[23]

3. The Palazzo Busini

Manetti's statement that Brunelleschi built the house of his relative, Apollonio Lapi, is complemented by Vasari's remark that he also created the model for the Palazzo Busini 'with rooms for two families'.[24] Apart from Vasari, the Codex Gaddiano, Codex Petrei and Codex Strozziano all mention this building as one of Brunelleschi's.[25]

The fact that Vasari meant the Palazzo Busini in the Via de' Benci is corroborated by the Busini *catasto*, which mentions the Busini brothers, who both lived in a palazzo. Vasari's mention of 'rooms for two families' is therefore most helpful in identifying the building.

The date of the Palazzo Busini was uncertain. Only recently did Howard Saalman prove, from a study of the entries in the register, that the Busini brothers in 1427 mention it as being already in existence.[26] One can therefore say with some certainty that the building was started before 1427.[27] It is probably the first private palazzo of the Renaissance to be preserved with an arcaded inner courtyard in the shape of a regular square. Although the building was known to exist, little attention has been paid to it in the past.

The cortile which opens up behind the late Trecento facade should be of particular interest to historians of late Renaissance architecture. An evenly spaced colonnade of four columns per side surrounds the inner courtyard, from which it is separated by a slight step. The symmetry of three arches per side determines the harmony of the ensemble.[28]

Above the unframed arches, which are cut directly out of the wall, there is a dentilled string course, above which runs a second, rather more pronounced ledge under the windows. A broad strip of wall runs round between the arches and the windows and creates a unity, if one ignores the roof drains running down the corners of the square figure. Such strips of wall, bordered by ledges above the arcade, were used by the late Trecento, for example in the Loggia dei Lanzi, in order to create clear lines of division. There is also a distinctly late Gothic ring to the interplay of tongued capitals; the sharp, flat, unmoulded arcade and window arches; the thin, sharp ledges and the smooth, flat wall surfaces reminiscent of the Loggia di S. Matteo.

In contrast to these elements are the generous curved shafts of the columns on their attic bases, the heavy torus moulding of the capitals, the rounded arches and, above all, the slim arcades with their narrow spacing. The windows are, in Trecento style, undivided, but they echo the slim proportions of the pillared arcade and reflect its rounded arches. Such a matching of the proportions of the arcades and windows reveals a careful planning of the impact of the entire ensemble aimed at communicating clearly the relationships between the various elements. It is the symmetry which clearly marks this building out from the architecture of the Trecento, a symmetry which emerges both from the plan and the various elevations. A similar symmetry had been achieved in only a very few public palazzi in the Trecento, notable examples being the cortile of the Palazzo Pubblico in Siena (which is, however, given an asymmetrical note by the irregular entrance porch) and, less completely, the Palazzo Vecchio in Florence, where the southern colonnade runs at an angle and the eastern one disturbs the tripartite effect of the columns with a set of four. Compared with that, the cortile of the Palazzo Pubblico in Siena is a model of symmetry.

The courtyard of the Palazzo Busini which, with its fourfold 3:3 proportions of the arcade raises the 2:3 proportions of the Siena palazzo to a level of all-round symmetry, is the first example of such symmetry in a public palazzo.

The entrance of the palazzo is not in the axis of the house, but opens into the extension of the right-hand arcade into the courtyard. But another element which was to feature in future palazzi is found here: an entrance corridor with threefold ribbed vaulting, which leads one directly, indeed forces one without any possibility of deviation to left or right, either through a side stairway or to a seat, straight into the cortile. As you arrive, the narrow corridor leads you into the expanse of the arcaded courtyard, where you can pause. This deliberate contrast of atmospheres was to remain the leitmotif of private palazzi in Florence in the Quattrocento right down to the Palazzo Strozzi.

Within the courtyard itself the symmetry of the architecture is echoed in the scope offered for movement. In addition to the various small doors at ground level (which were given new frames in the Quattrocento) there are, in the centre of the two sides, almost on the axis of the centre arcades, the entrances to the staircases leading to the upper storey. Thus each side wing has its own entrance.[29] As you come into the courtyard you are led to the side, where you are faced with two entrances, one opposite the other, and must choose which of the two Busini brothers you wish to visit. Anyone familiar with the narrow staircases of earlier Trecento houses, which were often attached to the outside of the buildings, will appreciate the entirely new experience offered by the Busini staircases. To arrive and proceed into the house

becomes an event in itself.

Just how new this was is reflected in Manetti's words when he said of Brunelleschi's palazzi that they not only no longer had rough ('rozzi') walls as in the past, but that their interiors, too, offered much comfort and pleasure to the inhabitants: '. . . e vedesi, che v'è dentro assai del buono, del comodo e del piacevole.'[30] During later alterations the original division into rooms was lost. However the great front hall which united both families and the ante-room leading into it from the right with its colourful beamed ceiling, have survived. If you take the left-hand entrance you pass through a long corridor with similar cross-vaulting to the downstairs entrance, directly into the great hall, which stretches across virtually the entire front of the building. This was the public room of the Busini family.

The roof beams sit on Trecento voluted consoles. The painted decoration of the smaller side room, the typical cable moulding which Brunelleschi found on the underside of the architraves in the Baptistry, and the chain of simple squares set diagonally, are all early Renaissance motifs.

The row of windows in the main hall with their original hinged shutters are indistinguishable from the usual windows of Trecento houses, with deep seating niches and flat segmented arches over the outside. Similar forms can be observed in the great hall of the Palazzo Davanzati (circa 1370-80). Consideration of what is peculiar to the building, reveals that it is an interesting combination of traditional late Trecento forms and classical ones; it is easy to recognise this as typical of a transitional style.

We should ask ourselves whether a building like this really represents a moment of stylistic change, whether the new forms have emerged by a process of 'mutation' from the old ones, almost as though the very moment of change has taken concrete form, as though the classical columns of the cortile have not yet found their corresponding classical capitals. The almost shocking contrast of the rounded shaft on an attic base and the Trecento tongued capitals is the first thing to strike the eye when one enters the cortile. But the heavy torus moulding of the capitals, the clearly formed calathos in front of which the *folie d'aque* rise and the curved abacus show that even the capitals have the most important elements of a classical capital. The Trecento form thus

FLORENCE, PALAZZO BUSINI, UPPER CORRIDOR

FLORENCE, PALAZZO BUSINI, ENTRANCE CORRIDOR

FLORENCE, PALAZZO BUSINI, CONSOLE IN UPPER CORRIDOR

FLORENCE, PALAZZO BUSINI, CONSOLE IN COURTYARD ARCADE

SAN FRANCESCO AL BOSCO, PORTAL CAPITAL

FLORENCE, PALAZZO BUSINI, CEILING IN GREAT HALL

FLORENCE, PALAZZO BUSINI, GREAT HALL

FLORENCE, PALAZZO BUSINI, CEILING IN SIDE ROOM

FLORENCE, PALAZZO CARIGIANI, CONSOLE IN LOGGIA

FLORENCE, PALAZZO DAVANZATI, GREAT HALL

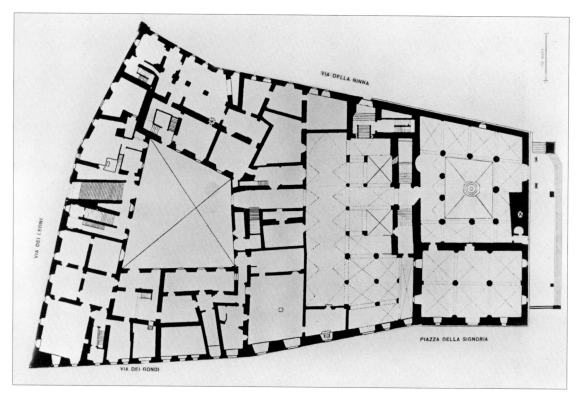

FLORENCE, PALAZZO VECCHIO, GROUND PLAN

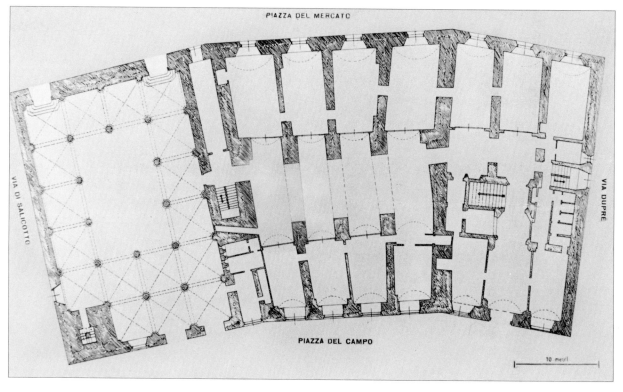

SIENA, PALAZZO PUBBLICO, GROUND PLAN

takes for granted classical early Renaissance forms. In the columns in the Ospedale entrance Brunelleschi reached back once again to the Trecento and used similarly typical motifs from the past, without being able to turn his back on the early Renaissance style.

Even the wall consoles of the courtyard cannot hide their early Renaissance inspiration. The elegantly curved point ending in a boss, is based on consoles by Michelozzo such as are found in the courtyard of the Palazzo Canigiani. The same goes for the vaulting consoles in the corridor, which end elegantly in a curved raindrop form.

An inspection of detail reveals what is true of the entire palazzo; namely that the transition from one style to another turns out to be a compromise. It is not as though we have here preserved in stone the very moment of birth, but rather that this building reveals a desire to take up the new forms of the Renaissance but at the same time to retain the traditional forms of the Trecento. It is mixture of forms, rather than the birth of new forms, which characterises a transitional style, though it is only too easy for a historian to think he has lighted upon the actual moment of emergence itself.

The portal of the Ospedale degli Innocenti had stylistic unity from the start. Even though, as will be shown, it too displays Trecento elements, one cannot separate out the new from the old as one can in the case of the shafts and the capitals in the Palazzo Busini. A conscious choice between one and the other, between a classical column and a Gothic capital resulted in an eclectic combination, made it possible to take over the new without relinquishing the old. What we have here is a deliberate choice which clearly differentiated between innovation and tradition. And such eclecticism becomes all the more attractive when it discriminates between a public building which can make full use of the new Classicism and the house of a private individual who did not wish to be so ambitious, but preferred to remain within the bounds of 'propriety'[31] and use, the eloquence of a capital to give a novel form of palazzo stylistic overtones appropriate to its origins. But such compromise would not be typical of Brunelleschi; it would be much more likely to come from Michelozzo. On the other hand one would not expect the latter to be capable of such a symmetrical, carefully planned palazzo in the early 1420s. But every architectural detail bears the stamp of Michelozzo. The thin ledges which separate the arcades from the windows are typical of him, and can be seen in the portico of the Biblioteca di San Marco. There one finds again the 'raindrop' console, though this time decorated with cable moulding.[32] It is the capitals, however, that speak loudest in favour of Michelozzo; they bear the unmistakable signs of his hand.

Finally the attribution of the Palazzo Busini to Michelozzo is supported by a comparison with the capitals of the entrance portal of S. Francesco al Bosco (c1427). Here the Gothic capital has been given an unexpectedly stocky form, with the leaf scrolls becoming little more than relief-work, but the generous echinus, which seems to hover around the neck of the column is the same as in the Palazzo Busini. Brunelleschi never put such rings round below his capitals, but gave them a more subtle link to the end of the shaft.

The possibility that this building could be one of Brunelleschi's early works, as Willich and, more recently, Sanpaolesi[33] attempted to prove, must be excluded. This would mean that it is Michelozzo who was responsible for the earliest extant Renaissance cortile. In this connection it is worth mentioning the symmetrical courtyard of the Palazzo Capponi in the Via de' Bardi, built in the early fifteenth century, which reveals a similar mixture of forms. What Manetti said of the Palazzo Lapi also goes for the Palazzo Busini; indeed, with its symmetry and its round-columned cortile, the latter can only have been inspired by the new language developed by Brunelleschi. The design of the unbuilt Palazzo Barbadori, which Manetti mentions in the same context as the building of the Barbadori Chapel[34] must have played a significant role in the development of the private palazzo in the Early Renaissance period. In ascribing the Palazzo Busini to Brunelleschi, Vasari is perhaps expressing his wish to find a convincing replacement for the unbuilt palazzi of Brunelleschi's early period.

* * *

FLORENCE, PALAZZO DI PARTE GUELFA, SIDE WALL IN VIA DELLA TERME

III THE PALAZZO DI PARTE GUELFA

FLORENCE, PALAZZO DI PARTE GUELFA, LEDGES

Brunelleschi's Palazzo di Parte Guelfa was constructed at roughly the same time as Michelozzo's Palazzo Busini, from 1421-22 onwards.[35] A comparison of the two buildings shows to what extent the two masters differed in their approach; although of course it is not easy to compare them directly, for the Palazzo di Parte Guelfa, as a public building, had an entirely different role from the private palazzo of the Busini. Civic modesty had caused even Cosimo de' Medici to reject Brunelleschi's grand design for a new palazzo. But the important and powerful Parte Guelfa in Florence was all the more able to call for a massive architectural approach to its headquarters.

Another difference lay in the basic task itself. What Brunelleschi was called upon to do was to add an extension to a palazzo already built in the late Trecento. A cortile like that in the Palazzo Busini, was not envisaged from the start. Manetti supplies us with the necessary details: 'And after the extension to that part of the Palazzo di Parte Guelfa on the Via di Porta Santa Maria had been started and the work planned and completed by the most highly-regarded masters usually employed for such works, up to approximately two cubits under the balustrade of the windows of the main floor, it was decided that Brunelleschi would complete the rest: the office *(udienza)*, the entrance hall connecting the old hall, and the new hall itself.'[36]

Brunelleschi often found himself in the situation of continuing work already begun by other architects. The drum of the cathedral dome, with its enormous proportions, demanded the very best from him, and because the existing architecture demanded such a unique completion, it is worthy of the dome itself. This was not the case with the Palazzo di Parte Guelfa. Brunelleschi reduced the existing early fifteenth-century building to playing the role of a mere base, refusing to continue any of the themes it had established, and constructing instead a completely unexpected continuation, reducing the ground floor below it to a characterless block which only 'prepares' for the upper floor in that it offers a stark contrast to it.

If we examine the side of the palazzo in the Via delle Terme and look for the connection with the earlier parts of the building, it is then that the uncompromising violence with which Brunelleschi set his massive extension against the traditional Trecento facade is brought home to us only too clearly.

The builders who preceded him had intended to extend the division into storeys from the old building to the new; they had continued the wall of flat, shaped stones and the arches of the ground floor, and had also intended to continue the line of the ledge: next to the window ledge there is a line of stone of equal width which continues the line of the ledge along the side of the palazzo, but was cut back, probably by Brunelleschi. This is where the critical line has to be sought: the building had – in Manetti's judgement – reached two *braccia* below the windows when Brunelleschi took over. The floor of the great hall runs somewhat below the line of the ledge and well below Brunelleschi's entablature, which does not mark the division between storeys, but is merely an external window ledge.

Brunelleschi appears to have raised the bottom storey by some inches before he added his heavy entablature and started on the upper elevation. The pilasters, which exceed all customary proportions, ruthlessly cut through the windows of the existing palazzo. A link between the traditional elevation and Brunelleschi's new facade was simply not conceivable. If ever one could speak of a revolutionary change in style then one can here, in the drastic, uncompromising break between the old facade and Brunelleschi's new one. The old *graffito* facade, with its three storeys separated by cornice ledges, is largely similar to that of the Palazzo Busini. Given the contempt with which Brunelleschi treats the traditional forms in the Palazzo di Parte Guelfa, it would seem unthinkable that he could have been responsible for the Palazzo Busini. Like a pointing finger, the New, in the form of the corner of Brunelleschi's classical entablature, points at the Old, in the form of the segmental arch of the window. Brunelleschi's employers must have identified with their architect to a very great degree for such a statement to have been permitted.

Just as Brunelleschi used the pilasters to delineate clearly the new from the old facade, so he used the broad, full entablature to provide a heavy horizontal border between the ground floor and the rest. He took as his model the Baptistry. The architrave and cornice were separated by a broad frieze; the jutting cornice, the drip-stone, the egg and tongue and dentil frieze were all to be found there. Certain characteristic, though almost imperceptible changes were made to the classical model: Brunelleschi changed the sloping geison cornice into a level one, gave the lower fascia of the architrave a torus and in compensation finished the upper cornice with a sharp edge, instead of repeating the toros of the Baptistry architrave.

This is the first time that a classical entablature appears on the exterior of a palazzo. Later it hardly ever reappears with a moulded architrave and a broad frieze on palazzi. On the facade, even to mark the divisions between storeys, the usual cornices of the Trecento soon returned (see Michelozzo's Palazzo Medici, and also the Palazzo Pitti, Strozzi, Antinori etc) and now could be combined with dentil friezes. In its pure classical form it was demonstrated immediately on the Palazzo di Parte Guelfa and was only repeated by Alberti on the Palazzo Rucellai.

The massive pilasters were also new; they frame the edges of the facade. Alberti later changed, Brunelleschi's pilaster motif into a regular series of small pillars on the Palazzo Rucellai and thereby created the foundation for the facades of Renaissance palazzi. The massivity of Brunelleschi's elevation had no effects in the Quattrocento. This huge order of pilasters, sitting on a storey constructed of stone blocks, which limited the elevation to two storeys only, disappeared as suddenly as Brunelleschi had introduced them. Manetti specifically praised Brunelleschi for not wrapping the pilasters round the corner but rather allowing the narrow corner of the main wall to come through. He could not possibly have matched the thin rounded edge of the lower storey with joined-up pilasters. Instead he creates a subtle link to the previous building. Michelozzo had already joined up the corner pilasters on the tower of San Marco and Baccio d'Agnolo did the same with the tower of Santo Spirito.

1. The Proportions

The main hall rises up with surprisingly monumental proportions which it would be difficult to find elsewhere

FLORENCE, PALAZZO DI PARTE GUELFA

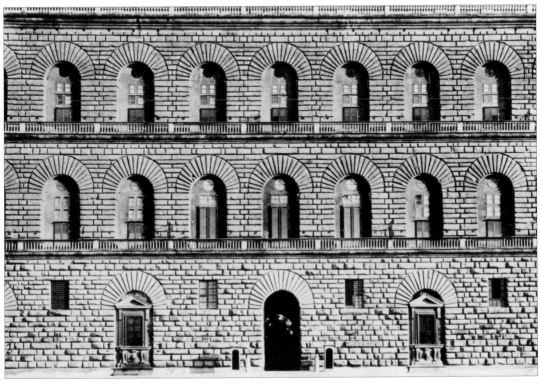

FLORENCE, PALAZZO PITTI

FILARETE, PALACE OF THE PRINCES IN 'SFORZINDA'

FLORENCE, SAN MARCO, TOWER

FLORENCE, SANTO STEFANO, FACADE WINDOW

FLORENCE, SANTO SPIRITO, TOWER

in Trecento architecture. Suddenly the palazzi from the past, themselves not ungenerously proportioned, appear almost mean in comparison. The regular reduction of the successive storeys, which was compulsory in Quattrocento Florentine palazzi, has been totally ignored as a design principle for this facade. Brunelleschi instead reverses the tradition and makes the upper part of the building rise higher than the lower storey,[37] so that it seems to sit majestically on a pedestal.

The great order of the Renaissance came in with the introduction of the new architectural language of that period, but remained without any direct successor. With it one finds for the first time the use of proportions on the *piano nobile* principle: on a baselike *rustica* order there sits the main storey with its order of pilasters, a design not confirmed until the High Renaissance with the two-storeyed palaces of Raphael, Bramanti, Sanmicheli et al. In Florence, on the other hand, the traditional three-storeyed *rustica* palazzo persisted.

2. The Windows

The Florentines, accustomed as they were in the Trecento to windows which were by no means small, must have been challenged by the Palazzo di Parte Guelfa to think in altogether new proportions. The windows of the Palazzo di Parte Guelfa are, as tradition demanded, large openings without any division. But this is all they have in common with the palazzi of the Trecento. One has to turn to church windows to find similar proportions. In S. Stefano, for example, not far from the Palazzo di Parte Guelfa, a window had been created in the late fourteenth century which had a fluid, rounded arch with a finely-moulded surround. The curve of the arch is uninterrupted by either an impost or the slight angles of a segmental arch. But it is the proportions of this broad, yet high window which point directly to Brunelleschi's palazzo windows.[38]

The finely-cut surround, whose moulded rods rest, in the Gothic style, on small plinths, has the character of a frame, as it does not cut deeply into the wall, but rather forms a broad flat surface. The rounded rods stand out and are themselves framed by finer ones. The entire frame is part of the wall itself, and is not superimposed on it, like Brunelleschi's, but gives an impression of flatness to the eye and, in its breadth, is reminiscent of the windows of the Palazzo di Parte Guelfa.

A comparison of this kind is particularly revealing because it demonstrates how near the Gothic style, within its own limitations, comes to Brunelleschi's own style. Here we see the beginnings of the decorative broadening of a surround and its transformation into a frame. What is missing is the final decisive step of bringing the surround out of the wall and creating a frame which lies in the same plane as the pilasters, proud of the wall itself. Now an oculus or a window could be an independent element, the frame being a separate entity.

In Brunelleschi's early work, namely the windows of the Palazzo Vecchio which still survive in part, one can see for the first time in secular Florentine architecture the motif of a row of windows with oculi above. But the individual forms remained within the tradition of the late Trecento: the flat window frame was already an independent element, but remained deeply embedded in the wall. The proportions, too, retained the restraint of the Trecento: the oculus is close to the tip of the arch, whereas in the later facade it rides triumphantly high above the window. If it is possible at all to compare the works of the young with those of the mature Brunelleschi, then this is a good example of, on the one hand, the slow development 'out of the spirit of the Trecento' and the break with the past, on the other.

The motif of a window with an oculus above it had been presaged on the sides of Florence Cathedral. An encrusted rose window is linked to the pointed arch, an utterly Gothic configuration which Brunelleschi already transmutes when he uses it on the Palazzo Vecchio. The idea is, once again, based on the Gothic, but its development leads into the High Renaissance. In palazzo architecture the motif recurs in Filarete's treatise as an idealised example in his theory of design. He sketched a palace for his idealised city of Sforzinda which has an oversized Palazzo di Parte Guelfa facade with continuous pilasters above a loggia with rounded arches.[39] In the architecture of the High Renaissance the grand order of pilasters with a mezzanine floor developed into a common design element which, of course, no longer has its roots in Brunelleschi's facade alone.

3. The Hall

It is uncertain to what extent Brunelleschi was directly involved in the building of the hall itself. It was Vasari who gave it its coffered ceiling.[40] Prior to that, in 1450, Maso di Bartolommeo had worked on capitals for the palazzo which are probably the eleven saddle volute capitals: 'the other five are based on an old model which Brunelleschi seems to have left behind'[41] wrote Manetti, who already complained of the work being unfinished. However he must have seen the building in an advanced state of development to have been able to make the judgement that the hall exceeded everything which the formal rooms of the Palazzo Vecchio could offer in those days.[42]

As on the outside, the internal walls are divided by unusually large pilasters, in this case fluted, and by sharply angled window frames. The oculi are, however, not visible, for Vasari's ceiling runs between these and the windows, thus creating a separate, low oculus storey. Although Vasari specifically states that he acted 'secondo l'ordine di Filippo',[43] it is to be doubted whether Brunelleschi would have accepted stone pilasters meeting a wooden ceiling without any architrave in between.

Geymüller assumes that a broad architrave was intended to sit on the pilasters, above which were to rise semi-circular archivolts around the oculi, thus creating the typical divisions of the wall into 'fields' which one finds in the side aisles of S. Lorenzo.

Salmi's reconstruction, based on Geymüller's suggestion, makes the design clear.[44] The outer archivolt arches are separated from the corners of the room by a short sectiozn of architrave. This contrasts with the Old Sacristy, whose arches are closely joined by a corner pilaster, the sets of arches standing clear of each other. Brunelleschi clearly wished to match the inside with the outside by not wrapping the pilasters round the corners. The Old Sacristy thus contrasts with the Palazzo di Parte Guelfa, but the particular device used in the latter reconstruction is corroborated by a detail of the Loggia degli Innocenti: the archivolts above the pillars which stand separately next to the great framing pilasters run into the pilasters with a similar short tongue of architrave. In the last analysis Geymüller's reconstruction must be the only possible one.

In order to demonstrate how totally different Brunelleschi's world of architecture was, we can compare the Palazzo di Parte Guelfa with an example of a Trecento hall; that of the Palazzo Busini. In the latter, the window niches float in the wall, the areas between them being unmarked. The wall is framed only by its natural limits where it meets the ceiling, the floor or a corner. Yet the influence of traditional forms persists in Brunelleschi's work; for example the window niche with its gently curving window arch surmounted by the broad segmental arch of the niche itself. Brunelleschi knew no such flat segmental arches; he reduced the geometry to horizontals, verticals and semi-circular arches. Thus, in his hands, the unusual combination of two superimposed segmental arches changes into a clearly delineated horizontal combined with a semi-circular arch of the outer window which fits into the rectangular shape of the niche. The dark stone brings it out from the rest of the wall.

The rectangular frame for the inner arches has Gothic echoes. There were no models for this in Classical antiquity. On the other hand the Gothic had not been capable of bringing such elements out of the wall and giving them a life of their own.

4. The Entrance Hall

Manetti records that Brunelleschi also built the *udienza* and the connecting corridor between the old hall and the new one in the Palazzo di Parte Guelfa. The latter is a long corridor with windows on one side only and a wooden ceiling with a brocade effect, which sits on a cornice. From here a door leads to the Loggia, whose lower columns have tongued capitals; above this a second row of columns has the throated capitals which we have already analysed and which belong to the group of Brunelleschi's Ionic capitals.[45] Apart from a door, whose frame is very much Brunelleschi's, what strikes the eye are the windows whose surrounds are strongly moulded. They are genuine Gothic openings cut straight out of the substance of the wall. The emphasis of a single line of torus moulding, held in place by concave mouldings, is reminiscent of the internal moulding of the great drum oculi in the dome, which had been produced as early as the 1940s under Giovanni d'Ambrogio. The window surround is a genuine transitional character, but the strong individual forms, with the torus moulding,[46] point forward to Brunelleschi's mouldings.

The ceiling cornice leaves an even stronger impression of being a transitional form. The row of limp leaves was not something which Brunelleschi used in his main works. Since Giovanni Pisano's facade for the cathedral

FLORENCE, PALAZZO DI PARTE GUELFA, HALL (SALMI'S RECONSTRUCTION)

FLORENCE, PALAZZO DI PARTE GUELFA, HALL

FLORENCE, PALAZZO DI PARTE GUELFA, CORRIDOR CEILING

FLORENCE, PALAZZO DI PARTE GUELFA, CORRIDOR WINDOW   FLORENCE, SANTA MARIA DEL FIORE, DRUM OCULUS

in Siena, this motif had become part of Tuscan Trecento Gothic. The square billet frieze and the egg and tongue moulding had also existed in the Trecento. Even the individual leaves, with the irregular tips of the side leaves, which curl slightly, had been commonplace since the 1370s in Tuscany. Similar motifs can be found, for example, on the capitals of the Palazzo Davanzati. It was Brunelleschi's first capitals in the Ospedale degli Innocenti which marked the replacing of the Trecento type of leafwork with a classical one based on the model of the Florentine Renovatio.

The moulding of the entire ledge adheres to the usual Trecento forms. The combination of two cornices was a motif which can already be found on the facade of the Palazzo Vecchio. Only the lower egg and tongue moulding was unusual; and the sharp edge below it is a detail from the vocabulary of the Florentine cathedral works in the late fourteenth century. Thus almost all elements in the ledge go back to the Trecento; it is only the twisted fabric motif immediately below the ceiling which is a specific detail from Brunelleschi's repertoire, and the identical motif was used to round off the ledge in the choir dome of the Old Sacristy. But it is not just these details which announce the dawning of a new age. The most powerful pointer is the positioning of this, largely Trecento, ledge. A ceiling had never before been supported by such a heavily ornamented, projecting stone ledge round the entire room, giving it a very definite border. The console has been replaced with an elaborate ledge such as is found under the ceiling of S. Lorenzo. The ornamentation does not allow this ledge to be dated as later than 1420. Its transitional nature is already clear from the elaborate leafwork. Michelozzo may have used the palm-leaf of the Trecento at a later date; but as soon as he created an acanthus capital, the leafwork on Brunelleschi's composite capital in the Ospedale served as a direct model. The side-leaves of the Trecento decoration, which curl over the main leaves left edges too indistinct and allowed the stone-carver concerned too much freedom. Michelozzo cannot have been the master here.[47] Although it is difficult to prove with any certainty, Manetti may have been right when he named Brunelleschi. It would seem obvious that Brunelleschi created a direct connection between the old and the new halls even before he created the latter on the base of the existing building. The spacious corridor is, in a double sense, a genuine bridge between the Trecento and the Renaissance.

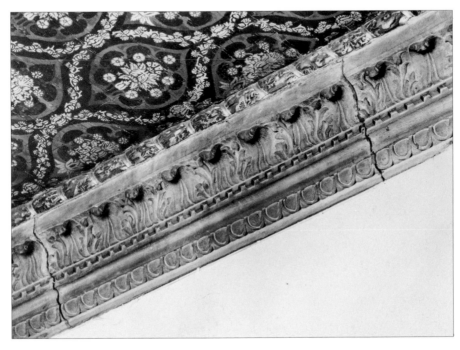

FLORENCE, PALAZZO DI PARTE GUELFA, CEILING CORNICE IN CORRIDOR

FLORENCE, VIEW OF SANTA MARIA DEL FIORE

IV THE DOME OF FLORENCE CATHEDRAL AND THE CONSTRUCTION OF DOMES IN MEDIEVAL TUSCANY

FLORENCE, SANTA MARIA DEL FIORE, TEMPIETTI

1. Gothic and Renaissance

None of Brunelleschi's works represents such a drastic break with tradition as the Palazzo di Parte Guelfa; and no other work of his has such close ties with previous traditions as the dome of Florence Cathedral.

The history of this construction – one of the greatest of all time – has already been written. Countless documents about the building process have been published and analysed.[48] There is hardly a single detail of the dome which has not been given consideration. Important studies have examined and illustrated the architectural structure of the double-skinned dome.

In addition to this the position of the dome in the history of Western architecture has been discussed; its origins have correctly been identified in the dome of the Florence Baptistry; its impact on later works can hardly be summed up in a few words. Michelangelo's dome for St Peter's is undoubtedly its most famous successor. The dome of the church of Madonna dell'umiltà in Pistoia,

started as early as the fifteenth century, is less well known. Brunelleschi's dome was the first in a whole series of post-medieval domes. With it the 'monumental' form of modern architecture was born. Even the domes of the state capitols in America have their roots in the Florence dome.[49] Thus Brunelleschi's edifice has to be seen as *the* 'modern' building which marked the end of the medieval period. Taking into account its effect on later architects, interpretation of the dome has had to emphasise the original aspects of the work. But when it was realised that the structure of the dome made it no longer possible to maintain the division between Renaissance and classical, and therefore the definition of the modern age was put into question by it, Brunelleschi's major work was hastily set aside from his other works as far as definitions of Gothic and Renaissance style were concerned. It was therefore the Ospedale degli Innocenti which was seen as marking the beginning of his 'modern' works, and the dome was seen as a medieval work and left for the previous chapter in the histories of art to deal with. 'Later critics were right when they saw in him the great innovator of Italian architecture. Only the dome, his greatest engineering feat, had nothing to do with his work as an artist.'[50]

'A double dome was already planned, and its size and outline had been laid down ten years before the Master's birth. This fact means that the famous construction which is normally used to mark the start of the new style has to be excluded from our considerations: neither the task nor its formal solution and the construction itself have anything to do with the Renaissance.'[51]

This point of view, predominantly taken by German scholars, was couched in such radical terms that even at an early stage voices were raised in opposition and put the counter argument in a similarly extreme manner.

Manetti's emphasis of the fact that Brunelleschi used Roman building techniques to achieve a free-standing dome was intended to underline the general characteristics of the work.[52] F D Prager's important statement, that with his stone model, Brunelleschi did not just wish to prove that vaulting could be produced without ground scaffolding, but also 'that a vault of the octagonal form required could stand without the help of buttresses and without visible, transverse chains'[53] does not justify the conclusion that the dome was completely devoid of Gothic elements: 'In this sense, the Florentine dome is not a Gothic structure, executed by Filippo as assumed by modern writers, but the main work of the originator of the developed Renaissance, as clearly implied by the older biographers'.[54]

The heavy Roman cupolas, set into massive masonry supports, have nothing in common with the lofty, gently curving dome in Florence. Nevertheless the Gothic elements in the dome should not prevent us from seeing it as a work of the early Renaissance. These constructional and aesthetic characteristics do not mean that it does not fit into his oeuvre, for right until the building of Santa Maria degli Angeli Brunelleschi's work was never exclusively 'classical', but rather always contained Gothic elements. If such stylistic categories are to be used at all then they must not be seen as mutually exclusive; this would have particularly serious consequences if the divisions of art history into eras were to be based on such judgements.

H V Geymüller has a helpful contribution to make to the problem of defining style: 'I now began to feel that the influence of such attitudes was making me see Brunelleschi's appearance as altogether too miraculous and sudden. I realised that the break with the past was by no means so abrupt and that the early Renaissance did not suddenly appear, like Minerva from the head of Jupiter, as a sharp contrast to the Gothic. It [the Renaissance] necessarily requires the collaboration of antique and Gothic elements. . . '[55] 'It is an artistic attitude which modifies a Gothic conception, removing part of the Gothic and replacing it with something from antiquity.'[56] Even though Geymüller's definition may attempt to weigh up the various components in a rather too mechanical and quantitative manner, it is nevertheless more appropriate than any attribution of the work to one style only. More recent attempts to define a specific 'Renaissance' style do not measure it purely according to the quantity of classical or Gothic motifs.[57]

Neither does one come any closer to the originality of Brunelleschi's work by taking refuge in a phenomenological approach which attempts to bring out the 'essence' of a work purely in its own terms. Apart from anything else it is a matter of didactics rather than methodological ideology that one wishes to draw comparisons with traditional forms in order to perceive both the original, creative elements and the influence of traditional ones in the work in question. Manetti's report that Brunelleschi sought new forms because the old ones no longer pleased him is proof of a conscious turning away from tradition. This statement can now be contrasted with documentary proof of Brunelleschi's close links with that tradition.

In 1434, when a decision had to be taken as to how to prevent the apparently imminent collapse of the nave of Florence Cathedral, Brunelleschi suggested building a ring of chapels round the triple-naved building, which would not only support the walls but would also increase the beauty of the church: 'Ac etiam actento quod corpus ecclesie prefate erit pulcrius et magis ornatum fieri et de novo edificari certas cappellas a quolibet latere navium dicte ecclesie, eo modo et forma prout stant cappelle ecclesie Sanctae Trinitatis de Florentia; que cappelle erunt catene totius ecclesie, et quod ecclesia erit pulcrior et orniator.'[58] This document offers us an authentic proof of a model for Brunelleschi which was not to be an antique or a quasi-antique building but rather a

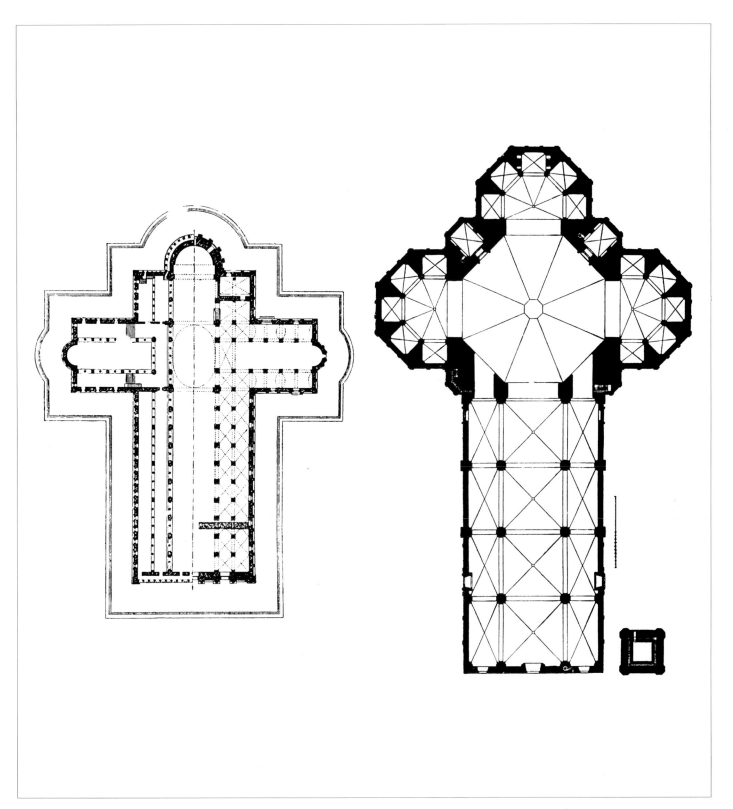

L TO R: PISA, CATHEDRAL, GROUND PLAN; FLORENCE, SANTA MARIA DEL FIORE, GROUND PLAN

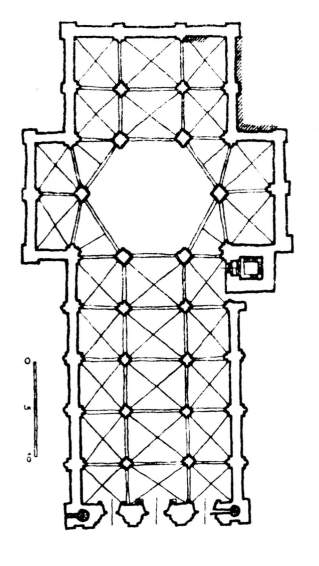

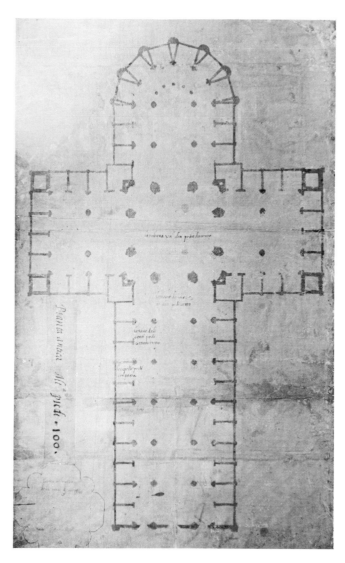

L TO R: SIENA. CATHEDRAL., GROUND PLAN: BOLOGNA. SAN PETRONIO, GROUND PLAN

Florentine church of the Trecento – Santa Trinità. Its ring of chapels ('catene totius ecclesiae') was to be the model for the ring planned at Florence Cathedral, 'quod ecclesia erit pulcrior et ornatior'.[59] It is doubtful whether such chapels would have actually had the same form had they been built round the cathedral. Brunelleschi would have come into conflict with the minute Gothic incrustations of the exterior: at least he must, as for the tempietti, have planned a similar marble incrustation. If it was not possible to prevent too radical a break by adapting what already existed, the unity of the entire building was at stake. Undoubtedly, Brunelleschi would not have been able to find the direct link as he did between his dome and Giovanni d'Ambrogio's drum.

2. The Building in its Immediate Environment

Looking at architecture in developmental terms tends to lead to an individual work being viewed as an example of a particular style, so that its immediate 'environment' is not its topographical situation but rather its position in the history of architectural styles. As a result it is treated in isolation from its physical environment and is related only to stylistically similar works.

The environment of the Florentine dome then becomes, for example, the dome of St. Peter's, Rome, rather than the city of Florence above which it rises. But the city is part of the architecture of this dome and not just a background 'sea of houses' above which the huge cupola towers. Rather, it forms a constant factor in the architectural form itself. The fact that the dome is clad in red tiles – a fact that seems so utterly natural that no-one has considered it worthy of further thought[60] – gives it a special character, a homely, municipal feel, which stands in contrast to the Baptistry or Michelangelo's bronze cupola in Rome. It is not just a question of a difference in materials; the whole intention is different. Similarly the topographical situations of the two domes are different: the one in Florence is in the centre of the city to which it belongs, whereas the one in Rome is outside the city, indeed today is politically separate, on sovereign territory. It forms a counterpoint to the city, having its own separate silhouette. As a symbol of papal greatness it remains aloof from the city, not only geographically but also architecturally. It could be objected that there is a time-lapse between the Florentine dome and the one in Rome which accounts for the difference in form.

However this is not enough to explain the differences. The entire St. Peter's complex is based on the surrounding space. It not only rises to a great height but also extends horizontally, occupying a large amount of space. It is ringed by four small satellite domes (two complete) which mark the corners of the central area. In contrast the four tribuna-tempietti of the Florentine cathedral lie next to the dome and the buildings of the city itself sit closely round the outer curve of the choir. It is significant that the erection of the houses which curve round the line of the choir, echoing its form, coincided with the building of the choir itself. Thus the houses and streets of the city became a framework for the dome. Brunelleschi's own creation builds, in architectural terms, on the basis of the Trecento, but also on the basis of the city's topography which was determined by municipal ideas. This dome is the high-point of the city which surrounds it, quite simply the highest and most beautiful of all the tiled roofs of the city. In contrast the dome of the Papal Cathedral in Rome is a tangible expression of his highest authority, a symbol of power for all to see, which rises in its own space. It is significant that the later domes built in Florence, including even the Baroque sepulchre of the Medici at San Lorenzo, retained the tiled roof.

3. Central Tower and Triple Apse

It had been an old motif from Romanesque architecture to mark the central crossing of a basilica with a tower. The point where the nave and the transepts met was the point to which the eye was drawn by the main sight-lines of the building. An example is the eight-sided central tower of Worms Cathedral. In the medieval churches of northern Europe such a central tower never developed into a broad dome.

The transepts and choir tended to form a movement out and away from this central crossing point. In contrast, when there are three apses, the semi-circular recesses seem to gather round the crossing. The first large-scale example of this type of church in Western Europe is Santa Maria in the Capitol in Cologne. A centralising tendency can be observed within the nave itself.

Both basic architectural types, the long basilica and the pure centralised building, could be combined though not always successfully. In particular the Knights Templar developed this type of church. The Church of the Holy Sepulchre in Jerusalem was the major model for this type.

The tribuna of the Florentine cathedral cannot be compared with any of these three basic types – and yet it contains the seeds of all three. It is a triple apse design, centralised and in a certain sense also a 'crossing tower', although extended on to the side aisles and therefore beyond the scope of such a tower.

A treble nave leads into the area under the great dome, which forms a link between a basilica and a centralised church. From the centre the 'transepts' and 'choir' run off, but they have become apses and close around the centre of the dome area in a polygon. The conches are themselves central areas under domes, for small domes sit round the large one. This ring of domes is closed by the tempietti which sit close to the drum. Half and three-quarter domes surround the central dome, forming rich variations on the main theme.

This basic plan, with the exception of the tempietti[61] must have been laid down since the 1367 model. The master in charge was Lapo Ghini.

4. The Dome over the Crossing

The Florentine dome becomes easier to understand if it is regarded not so much from the point of view of ecclesiastical architecture in general, but rather against the background of the tradition of Tuscan cathedral building. Only in Italy, and in particular in Tuscany, had the dome become the dominant centre of the basilica. The cathedral in Pisa, the first fortified city in Tuscany, had provided the basis for this development. At the same time the very model of a centralised building, the Florence Baptistry, was being built. Thus in Tuscany two models for the future were available for large-scale architectural projects. The Pisa basilica, with its lack of tower and its five aisles, has a central dome above the crossing which is located at the point where the crossing tower would normally be, but with its broad curving shape is only distantly related to the normal Romanesque motif of the central tower. It forms the highest point of the basilica and is thus the heart of the entire building.

The solution found to the question of how to place a dome over the crossing was unusual and indeed clearly derived from the new intention. The inner square of piers was not big enough, and so the dome was elongated and stretched beyond the bays to the triumphal arch and the nave. The transept arms were separated from the nave by a system of arches so that the dome received side-support. The dome forms a narrow oval shape which conforms laterally to the dimensions of the crossing, but along its other axis extends beyond the nave bay without, however, extending beyond the breadth of the three-aisled transepts. It is a clever solution and yet still an experiment!

Logically speaking the next step was undertaken in the cathedral at Siena, which displays an even stronger experimental character. The difficulty of combining a nave and a dome which now extends laterally as well as lengthwise was greater. One can still find in architectural details of the building the attempts which were made: originally it was intended that, as in Pisa, the side-aisles would continue into the crossing. But at the side the dome rests not on a treble arcade of arches but a double one. However the centre piers were moved into the transepts, thus creating a very irregular ground plan. The central piers, by being shifted outwards create a greater breadth for the dome and the centre of the dome expands, but at the same time this creates a conflict with the ground plan of the nave. The centre pier has lost its original place in the crossing axis but has not reached the line of the external wall of the side-aisle. It thus stands in the middle of space without being related to any line of sight and the overall ground plan is disturbed solely in order to allow for a lateral expansion of the dome. In such a case there is a sharp conflict between the form of a centralised building and that of a basilica. The dome rests on an irregular six-sided arcade system. The shifted centre pier moves the arcade outwards as well, bringing the arch out of the line of the arcading of the nave.

This is the critical point of the ground plan. In the Florentine cathedral it can also be seen, but here a new unity between the dome space and the nave has been achieved. After the oval dome of Pisa and the irregular six-sided one in Siena it was the octagon, with its regular sides, which offered the solution. The model came from the Florentine tradition. The Baptistry, whose arcades reappear on the incrusted external wall of the cathedral apses, was connected with the cathedral nave; the line of the side-aisle walls coincide with the outer lines of the octagon, the breadth of the central nave runs into the front, and the triumphal arch of the choir apse into the eastern side. The diagonal sides create the link and cover

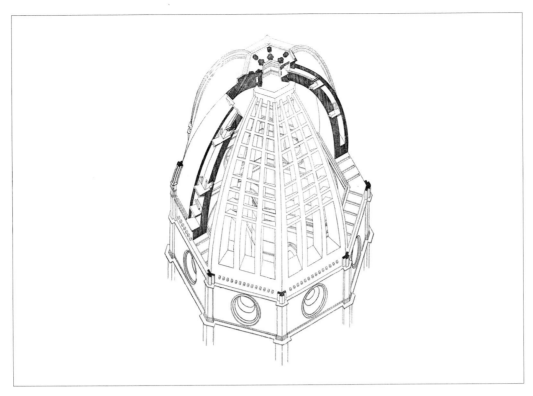

FLORENCE, SANTA MARIA DEL FIORE, CROSS-SECTION OF DOME (AFTER SANPAOLESI)

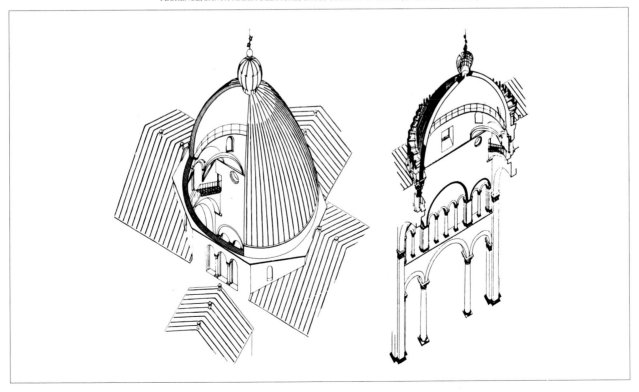

PISA, CATHEDRAL, CROSS-SECTIONS OF DOME AND CROSSING (AFTER SANPAOLESI)

MASSA MARITTIMA, CATHEDRAL, AREA BENEATH DOME

MASSA MARITTIMA, CATHEDRAL, DRUM OF DOME

MASSA MARITTIMA, CATHEDRAL

FLORENCE, OSPEDALE DEGLI INNOCENTI, CHIOSTRO DELLE DONNE

FLORENCE, OSPEDALE DEGLI ▶

NTI, CHIOSTRO DEGLI UOMINI

FLORENCE, SAN

ARIA DEL FIORE

FLORENCE, SAN LORENZO, OLD SACRISTY

FLORENCE, SAN LORENZO, DOME OF OLD SACRISTY

FLORENCE, SANTA FELICITÀ, BARBADORI CHAPEL

the breadth of each side-aisle. But the problem of linking the nave and the polygonal centre area is still visible in the manner in which the great piered arch, with its double function of ending the line of arches in the side aisle and being part of the diagonal arch of the octagon, leads the eye in two contradictory directions. One is reminded of the angled arch of the dome in Siena.

The three major medieval cathedrals in Tuscany have, over three centuries, varied the great theme of combining the basilica principle with that of the centralised building. This is the major feature which they have in common. Florence Cathedral represents the most successful solution of the problem. It again was an example for San Petronio in Bologna, which itself served as a model for the two cathedrals of the Renaissance – Pavia and Santa Maria in Loreto.[62]

5. The Gothic Structure of Pavia Cathedral
If one looks from the side aisle of Pavia Cathedral into the dome area, the eye is caught by the sharp edge of an angular pilaster the position of which is reminiscent of the displaced composite piers in Siena Cathedral. The Siena solution to the problem of linking the dome area and the nave obviously had an effect which lasted to the end of the fifteenth century.

In the plans for San Petronion in Bologna the massive piers of the Florence octagon have given way to individual supports marking the corners of the octagon. Instead of heavy walls it was planned to erect once more Gothic composite piers, which were changed into composite pilasters in the corner piers of Pavia Cathedral. This building, which was created largely under Bramante, still displays the Gothic vertical system of composite supporting elements. The classical forms of the pilaster and entablature were inappropriate for this structure: the supports rise up above the architrave of the first row of pilasters as further pilasters without capitals or order, which lift the great arches of the octagon high up under the drum. It was only the massive Roman pier used first in the High-Renaissance by Brunelleschi in Santa Maria degli Angeli and then by Bramante during the reconstruction of St Peter's, which broke with the tradition of the composite pier.

6. The Dome of Pisa Cathedral
Nowhere in medieval Italy were so many possibilities of building domes realised as in Tuscany. Looking back it is almost as though this was a large-scale experiment in which all possible variants were tried out and finally one kind, the Florentine model, was developed. It was probably in Pisa that the simplest solution was found: the central rectangle was linked by squinches to an elongated octagonal drum. The dome itself, consisting of a simple thin shell rising up relatively shallowly, sat on its edge. Later on the drum was strengthened with blind arches, creating a broad ambulatory platform on to which the jagged decoration of the canopies was added in the late Trecento. Above this the great dome rose up. Also in the Trecento it was given its roof of metal plates and its onion on which the golden apple with the cross stands. The great apses of the transept and choir counteract the outward movement created by the arms and make for a concentration on the centre, the dome. Prior to the Florentine tribuna only Pisa Cathedral had such an effect.

The flat drum, which only rises slightly above the triforium, intersects with the roof of the nave and choir which rises to the bottom of the curve of the dome. It is only on the sides towards the transepts that the side of the drum is free; the result is a very irregular effect as though the sloping roof of the nave and choir had not been taken into account.[62]

7. The Dome of the Cathedral in Massima Marittima
It was probably Giovanni Pisano who took the cathedral of his native city as the model for the dome of Massima Marittima. With the building in its present state it is not possible to reconstruct the actual cupola in its original form, but the remains of the drum up to the ledge of the arcade is clearly early Trecento. Like in Pisa it is set into the roof of the nave and cuts into the slope of the roof, standing free only at the sides. The wall carries the motif that was so interesting for the drum in Florence: a round window which opens out towards its periphery and, in this case, has Gothic mullions in the form of a rose. The interior of the building is also similar to Pisa Cathedral; however, instead of triple arched arcades there are only two arches which combine with the arch of the nave and the triumphal arch to form an almost square crossing above which the regular octagon of the drum sits on squinches. The rather ugly join between the drum and the roof is unavoidable because the projecting squinches

had to be covered by the roof. The curve of the dome itself dates from a later restoration. It is probable that as early as the fourteenth century a domical cupola had been planned which would have made possible a direct link to the octagonal sides of the drum, and avoided the problem faced in Pisa of rounding off the corners to achieve the transition between octagonal and oval cupola.

There is a very similar dome in San Donato in Siena. It was, however, extensively restored in the nineteenth century. There are traces of Trecento work in the drum and the Baroque piers of the crossing hide a Romanesque core; the broad arches of what is now a regular crossing reveal the Romanesque elements.

8. The Dome of Siena Cathedral

We have to rely on views of the city produced in the fourteenth and fifteenth centuries in order to see what the dome in Siena originally looked like. The present cupola with its heavy lantern dates from Bernini; the outer stone skin was renewed after a fire in the nineteenth century.

The first cupola, which was completed in 1264 was, like the one in Pisa, covered with copper plates and, as in Pisa, had an onion crowned with a 'mela'. For the first time in Tuscany it was planned to build a drum which stood free above the roof, surrounded by a large arcade above which was a second, smaller one. But as early as 1290, when the clerestorey of the nave was built,[63] and towards the end of the century, when the choir came into being, the drum was set deep into the nave, which now overlaps with the arcade. Inside the sequence of arches can still be seen on the outside of the nave arch and the triumphal arch.[64] In Siena the dome also sits on a drum with squinches which forms the transition from a six-sided figure to an irregular twelve-sided one, almost circular in effect. To increase the number of sides of the cupola base was a clever experiment. The strangely irregular layout can be seen from the ledge on which the cupola sits: the idea had been to make the width of the squinches roughly equal to one complete side of the drum, and to make the latter as far as possible the same as the lines of arches in the arcade – a daring improvisation! But the dome was given a second upper drum which can be seen from the outside as a small arcade, and from the inside emerges as pillars under an architrave. Four windows under curved arches on the sides of the dome create a second light zone above

the tripartite groups of windows in the drum.

The purpose of all this – in addition to expanding the dome space – was to emphasise the drum. This was not achieved by raising it high above the central nave, but rather by planning to dispense with the clerestory. Only the second arcade rose before the beginning of the cupola, slightly beyond the crest of the roof. That the drum was originally intended to be a free-standing piece of impressive architecture is corroborated by the richly incrusted arcade arches with their double pillars and their broad, heavy cornice. Thus, already in the first half of the thirteenth century we see an attempt being made to create a dome as a 'monumental' and decorative element which sits above the rest of the church. The addition of arcaded ambulatories was intended to give it external space which was clearly accessible to the observer.[65]

9. The Pendentive Cupola: The Arezzo Pieve and S. Paolo in Ripa d'Arno in Pisa

In addition to the simple cupola with squinches, there are two examples in Tuscany of pendentive cupolas: it was a type which had travelled from San Marco in Venice to S. Antonio in Padua. It had also become known in Pisa – perhaps independently of the Veneto – for Pisa had always been open to oriental and Byzantine influences. San Paolo had a hanging cupola erected over its crossing probably in the thirteenth century. The ends of the pendentives join together in a pointed arch and support the cupola itself, which sits on a round ledge. This was the only place in Tuscany where Brunelleschi was able to study a complete system of pendentives and cupola. In the Pieve of Arezzo all he could examine were the pendentives themselves. The stone cupola had been replaced by a wooden one with internal beams. Interestingly enough – probably to hold the wooden construction together – a drum, lower but freer than the one in Siena, with a decorative arcade, was set on the pendentive ring. The cupolas of San Marco also had a narrow drum-like ring, but this merely formed a wall against the shoulder of the cupola and as such was only visible from the outside. In Arezzo there was one of those peculiar mixed forms so typical for Tuscany. Thus there had been many experiments prior to Brunelleschi's cupola. But the stonework of the pendentives in the Pieve of Arezzo is of a perfection unmatched anywhere else.

SIENA, CATHEDRAL, DOME, EXTERIOR

SIENA, CATHEDRAL, DOME, INTERIOR VIEW

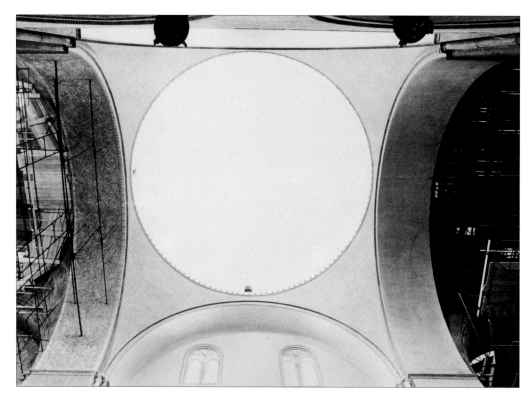

PADUA, SAN ANTONIO, DOME

AREZZO, PIEVE, DOME

10. The Florence Baptistry and the Cathedral Dome

None of these domes either in their outward form or in their internal construction can have served as a model for the one in Florence. Only the Baptistry dome, unique among the traditional cupolas of medieval Italy with their squinches and pendentives, served as a starting point for Brunelleschi.[66] Both buildings have in common the basic structure of a large octagon continuing into the steep lines of the cupola topped by a lantern. In addition to this Brunelleschi's double-shelled construction is found also in the Baptistry. Groups of four struts at right-angles support the sideways thrust of the cupola. They are linked by barrel vaulting which, together with the struts, stretch up one third of the height of the cupola. Above this the cupola stands free. A pyramidal roof hides the inner framework.

The important new element in medieval cupola construction was that the inner shell was given vertical supporting piers which provided a 32-piece framework around the cupola. Brunelleschi took this idea but converted the supporting struts into continuous ribs which run right up to the lantern, thus completely changing not just the morphological structure of the cupola but also its entire outward appearance. Brunelleschi may have used the Baptistry as a model for the original constructional notion, but with what at first seems to be a purely quantitative extension of the struts he creates a framework which is stylistically entirely different from the Baptistry's buttressing, based as it was on the Roman Pantheon.[67] The Baptistry cupola points stylistically in two directions: it derives from the Pantheon, but frees the latter's supports from the wall structure and makes them into a separate framework which prepares the way for the ribbed structure of the cathedral dome. In the latter, however, the supporting struts are not confined to the lower third of the cupola but rather follow its curve right to the top. By way of contrast to this, the Baptistry retains the Roman principle of restrained support which holds the cupola. Just as in the Pantheon the wall of the drum rises above the beginning of the cupola, here the upper pilaster level surrounds the inner strut system which replaces the heavy shoulder. Brunelleschi coverts this system of struts supporting the cupola on the outside into a self-supporting skeleton of ribs, thus creating a completely different structure. The difference is most clearly visible at the corners of the octagon: in the

Baptistry the struts extend like claws, holding the edge of the cupola section on either side but allowing the edge itself to run down between them, until it is caught by a squinch niche above the drum. The struts and the cupola are independent elements which are linked.

Brunelleschi replaces this complicated solution with one single heavy rib which itself forms the edge between the sections of cupola. In principle Brunelleschi's cupola is a Gothic construction, with its corner ribs emphasised by their thickness and by the white marble strips applied to them on the outside. The eight ribs of the cupola form, as it were, the primary skeleton, and everything else is of lesser quality and size: the two intermediate ribs of each side which hold the huge webs; the horizontal supports which prevent the webs from collapsing inwards, hold the lateral pressure and prevent the ribs from being pressed outwards. The unusual depth of the ribs, which link vertically into the web and, as such, are reminiscent of the struts of the Baptistry, made the division of the cupola into an inner and outer shell necessary. The two concentric shells converge with the ribs towards the lantern. The thin outer shell hides the network of ribs which stiffen the inner shell. The cupola of the Baptistry is 'held' from the outside by a system of struts which forms a shoulder which stops as the cupola stretches upwards and which is hidden by the shallow pyramidal roof. By contrast Brunelleschi's cupola is a ribbed construction which allows the shell to rise up with the ribs, creating externally a form which matches the curve of the inner shell; thus an 'extroverted' form is created, a dome which rises freely up from the drum and – as Alberti put it – casts a shadow over the land. The Gothic conception of ribbed vaulting had radically changed the Romanesque/Roman idea of shoulder supports.

11. The Elevated Outer Shell

In thirteenth-century Venice the tendency to elevate the cupola more sharply had already resulted in the steepening of the flat cupola of San Marco. It was an easy solution: using a framework of beams built up on the shoulder ring of the drum and the cupola itself, the outer surface was created, thus resulting in a primitive form of 'double-shell' dome! A similar solution can be found on the cupola in Siena, whose steep lines are depicted in contemporary pictures from the Trecento and Quattrocento.[68]

12. The Tabernacle of Or San Michele

The cupola of the Orcagna tabernacle rises in a similarly independent manner above the vaulting of the baldaquin. There is no link between the inner vaulting and the steep lines of the cupola, which has little function other than to catch the eye from the outside. Like a ribbed helmet[69] it rises above an eight-sided drum.[70] Although it could in no way set a firm example for the construction of the cathedral dome, it nevertheless has stylistic connections with the latter, sharing with it a tendency for the cupola to rise freely and steeply above an eight-sided drum. By adding crockets to the ribs of the webs their lines were emphasised just like the ribs of a Gothic helm roof, as shown in Giotto's design for the Campanile.[71]

The dome of Orcagna's tabernacle (1349-59) may well have received the form of a model created for the cathedral dome. Failing this it may have formally influenced the later model of 1367 which Brunelleschi worked from. The model of Florence Cathedral (c1350)[72] painted by Andrea da Firenze in the Cappella Spagni (1365) certainly shows a less steep line for the cupola, but includes the crockets on the ribs. No other formal element underlines so clearly the Gothic nature of these domes than the lines of crockets, which turn what was originally an inwardly directed architectural form into one with an external orientation whose webs join the upward lines of the whole construction.

13. The Drum

The idea of sitting a cupola with a steep profile of pointed arches on an independent drum goes back to Orcagna's times. Only with this drum, erected under Giovanni d'Amrogio, was it possible for the cupola to stand so free of the roof of the church. Now the perfect solution, sought after also by the master-builders of Siena Cathedral, had been found.[73] Andrea da Firenze had carried the clerestory of the nave straight into the drum so that the cupola – as in Siena – started at the height of the eaves and met the roof at its base.[74] Now, however, the roof extended up to the second, free drum ring, which freed the cupola from all links with the nave and lifted it high above the roof. Thus, in a very real sense, the cupola had been liberated from the basilica system. It received the profile of a monumental, free-standing element, with the tribune chapels below looking like a mere base for the

drum and its cupola. The heavy jutting ledge at the bottom of the drum separates the animated chapel area from the cupola. The need to raise the building like a monument on a pedestal had been recognised in the building of the hall in the Palazzo di Parte Guelfa; the 'stylobate' of the Ospedale portal serves the same purpose, as do the bases of the tribune tempietti. It remained a characteristic of Renaissance architecture that buildings were set on a pedestal, thus creating a monumentality which set them apart from the smaller world about them, just as, ideally, the were also free-standing, separate buildings (Palazzo Strozzi).

The same goal is served by the great areas of marble incrustation on the drum,[75] which, while taking up the basic elongated form of the Gothic marble surfaces, relinquish the restricted proportions of these and cover the entire wall in a few strokes. The generous round windows which open wide into the exterior similarly break with traditional proportions. Giovanni d'Ambrogio could – for the sake of consistency – have adhered to the diameter of the clerestory oculi. But here, too, the old proportions were massively exceeded: the oculi take up the entire breadth of the wall spaces. They positively command attention. The forms are the old ones, thus creating the link with the rest of the building below, but the proportions are new and force the eye to judge the dome by different standards.

14. The Model of the Cathedral

As early as the Trecento consideration had been given to the idea of two drum rings one above the other. The first would be linked to the nave, transferring its height to the cupola, and the second would supply the cupola with a massive, free-standing pedestal. Such a solution can be found in a picture by Ambrogio Lorenzetti (c. 1330) Interestingly the ouli (with tracery) continue the line of the clerestory and pierce the lower drum ring. The upper ring is blind and linked to the pointed roof of the upper nave. On this rests the usual semi-circular cuppola, which seems devoid of any ribs; it seems Lorenzetti assumed there would be an external, metal-plated wooden shell of the Venetian type.

The best impression of the pre-Brunelleschi cupola is given by the wooden model in the Florence Museo dell'Opera del Duomo, which is possibly based directly on the 1367 model. It is so similar in form to the actual

SANO DI PIETRO, VIEW OF SIENA, PALAZZO PUBBLICO, SIENA

AMBROGIO LORENZETTI, ALTAR FROM SANTA MARIA DEL CARMINE, PREDELLA (DETAIL), PINACOTECA, SIENA

ANDREA DA FIRENZE, VIEW OF SANTA MARIA DEL FIORE, FLORENCE, SANTA MARIA NOVELLA, CAPPELLA DEGLI SPAGNUOLI

ANDREA DA FIRENZE, DOME, DETAIL OF ABOVE

FLORENCE, MODEL OF DOME OF SANTA MARIA DEL FIORE,
MUSEO DELL'OPERA DEL DUOMO

BOLOGNA, MODEL OF DOME
OF SAN PETRONIO

FLORENCE, MODEL OF TRIBUNE OF SANTA MARIA DEL FIORE, MUSEO DELL'OPERA DEL DUOMO

BOLOGNA, MODEL OF SACRISTY OF SAN PETRONIO

FLORENCE, SANTA MARIA DEL FIORE, TRIBUNE

cupola that it has always been uncertain that it is not a later replica of Brunelleschi's model. Without wishing to dismiss completely this possibility, it should be pointed out that it displays certain details which in stylistic terms suggest it dates from the time between 1400 and 1420. The broad balustrades which wrap round the corner verticals of the drum like a crows-nest, have been given long string courses. Far from being reminiscent of even a shortened classical profile, these recall the endless string courses running across the entire surface of the marble plates of the facing, and round the piers such as those found on the tribune chapels. The whole finish of the model of the cupola matches that of the tribune model, also found in the Museo dell'Opera. Individual details were carved fairly crudely from wood. Here, too, a cornice with superimposed string-courses runs round the top of the clerestory. As below the cupolas of the chapels, the balustrade wraps its way round the piers. By way of simplification the multiple arches of the console cornice were omitted. This form matches the lower balustrade of the cupola model. The ribs of the cupola are without crockets. Instead of this, to match the balustrades, thin ledges have been superimposed on the flat ribs. Brunelleschi ratained this detail, but linked the grooves of the ribs with moulding which opens out laterally. But, more than these details, it is the oculi of the drum which provide evidence of an early creation. The outer size of these oculi is smaller than on the finished drum and they do not expand to touch the balustrades which run above and below the wall space.[76] The model – aimed at establishing the general proportions and motifs – would have admitted of no inaccuracies in the main shapes and outlines. The model of the tribune was similar: it largely matches in all respects the finished building. So we may safely assume that the oculi of the drum were originally intended to have a smaller diameter, and were intended to match those of the upper nave. It was under Giovanni d'Ambrogio that they received their massive width. A maximum amount of light was to penetrate into the area beneath the dome. Even Brunelleschi had to take note of a petition to the consuls of the Arte della Lana requesting that the cupola itself should be given large openings to let in the light.[77] All the evidence suggests that the model of the cupola in the Museo dell'Opera came into being before Brunelleschi's involvement, possibly at the time of the building of the tribunes. This would demonstrate most clearly that Brunelleschi – as has always been stressed – took up an already existing form for the dome which dated from the Trecento.

15. The Baptistry in Pisa

An example of a Tuscan dome which was planned largely in terms of its outward appearance is furnished by the Baptistry of Pisa. It was already being built at a time when in Florence the final 1367 model for the cathedral was not yet in existence. Along with the Duomo Nuovo in Siena, the cathedral in Lucca, the Florence tribuna and the Loggia dei Lanzi, it is one of the major works of architecture produced during the second half of the Trecento.[78] When the Pisa dome was completed towards the end of the century the Baptistry, started in 1152 by Diotisalvi, could already look back on two hundred and fifty years of history. During this long period many alterations had of course been planned, including the rebuilding of the upper storey and vaulting. Even from 1278 to 1299, when the vaulting of the galleries was being added under the supervision of Niccolò Pisano, there must have been a radically different plan for alterations; for in 1358, when the model for the completion of the baptistry was ready, this vaulting was taken down again as it clearly did not fit in with the new finish being given to the building. In 1359, work started on the upper storey. Zibellino da Bologna was the leading light, for it was according to his plans that the canopies and pinnacles were produced in white and black marble '... per bellezza estetica, misura e somiglianza, tali quale il frontespizio e ciborio che già aveva consegnato e eseguito m. Zibellino da Bologna. E che la serie dei frontespizi fosse cominciata dal suo prototipo ...'.[79] In 1381 the final work ('estremi lavori') began, and by 1394 the dome must have been finished. For in that year a Pisan goldsmith left his entire fortune for the completion of the tabernacles (i.e. the window tabernacles), which surround the dome ('per di tabernacoli circondanti la Cupola').[80]

The very outward appearance of the dome betrays the unusual construction of the vaulting: the uppper third of the cupola which rises above the line of the window canopies turns sharply upwards and forms a cone capped with a semi-circular miniature cupola. It is only when one studies the cross-section that the heterogeneous nature of the vaulting becomes clear: the seemingly one-piece cupola is revealed as consisting of two parts: a cone which rises steeply above the circle of the galleries, and the fins which run across from the outer drum wall providing shoulders to support the cone. At the same time with their curved backs they support an outer shell. It is only the combination of the central cone and the outer shell which makes up what, from the outside, is seen as the complete cupola, consisting of the sum of the internal vaulting elements. On the inside all that can be seen is the shaft-like chimney of the central cone, so that the impression of a genuine cupola which extends upwards in its full breadth cannot be given. Thus when the 'cupola' of the Pisa Baptistry is discussed what is meant is the entire composite construction of this 'apparent' cupola.

This complex form was, however, as closer examination of the building reveals, the result of a new departure. It was only towards the end of the Trecento that completely new views came to the fore which ensured that the Pisa Baptistry would receive the form it finally did.

To appreciate what the original plan was and to gauge the far-reaching changes introduced by the later cupola, it is sufficient to examine the interior wall of the gallery which still today reveals the old imposts of the original vaulting. The peak of the ribbed vaulting would have reached the height of the top cornice which runs round the window canopies, whereas the present flying buttresses, which start from the same point but run at an angle, carry high stonework above them which reaches up into the cupola. The upper windows run well into what was originally the vaulting zone and disturb the symmetry below them. These are the twenty windows of the upper storey, whose axis relates again to the ground floor axis of the external composition. However, as the windows do not lie along the same axis as the configuration of arches the designer of the dome was forced to set the flying buttresses which run from the piers to the external wall at intervals that do not coincide with the windows. One can also see clearly the way the exterior wall has been extended from the layers of dark stone at the top. Above the windows, at the height where the inner vaulting of the cone starts, the barrel vaulting of the gallery encircles the cone, supporting its base and at the same time providing a surface from which the outer shell can rise up. The function of this vaulting becomes

clear from Rohault de Fleury's famous cross-section.

It sits, with its compact stonework, and its slightly angled roof around the base of the cone and rises far above the original limit of the top storey, which ran at the level of the arcade ledge. From the outside, too, one can discern where the vaulting runs; running behind the window canopies and pinnacles and providing a base for the cupola there is a broad band of marble which breaks off abruptly at the top. Thus the exterior of the building receives a third storey, even if it is not a genuine one. The ledge at the bottom of it runs in sharp points over the tops of the windows as if to draw the eye away from this storey, an effect heightened by the canopies and pinnacles. This is why the wall merges into the cupola itself without any delineating ledge. Thus there emerges a certain ambiguity about the line between the main building and the dome, and what might have been a division becomes more of a transition.

So the change undergone by the original plan has also left its mark on the exterior of the building. It was an alteration which only became necessary when the decision was made to create the steep cone of the cupola. This necessitated a supporting ring of barrel vaulting which rose above the level of the old storey.

The extremely steep line of the central cone was intended as far as possible to direct the lateral pressure downwards, where it could be taken up by the buttresses which ran slightly diagonally to the base. However, with such a high cone some sort of shoulder support was also necessary. The buttresses rise up for two thirds of the height of the cone and are themselves carried by the flying buttresses of the gallery. The fin-line supports sitting against the cone serve the double purpose of taking up the lateral pressure created by it and also providing a support for the outer shell of the lower half of the cupola.

This construction resulted from the problem of how to create on top of a broad drum a high dome which would be visible from all around. Height was achieved by the inner cone, breadth by the curved shell which runs into it. The total size of the dome was a product of the dividing up of functions and dimensions: the use of the inner arcade circle to support the height, i.e. the cone, and the outer drum wall to support the breadth, i.e. the cupola shell.

Thus the first 'extroverted', double-shelled dome in

PISA, BAPTISTRY, INTERIOR VIEW

PISA, BAPTISTRY, RIB OF DOME

PISA, BAPTISTRY, UPPER STOREY WITH START OF DOME

PISA, BAPTISTRY, SHELL OF DOME WITH BUTTRESSES

FLORENCE, BAPTISTRY, PASSAGE BELOW DOME BUTTRESSES

PISA, BAPTISTRY, DOME BUTTRESSES

FLORENCE, BAPTISTRY, DOME BUTTRESSES

Tuscany was created – a highly original if imperfect construction. The 'fins' which, on the Florence Baptistry remain hidden behind the attic storey and the pyramidal roof, now stretch high up, curving on the outside and determine the outline of the cupola. These buttresses, elongated beyond any normal proportions, supporting the cone and shell alike, create a very wide space in between. Its extent is not just a result of constructional necessity, but rather – and this is the decisive factor – results from a calculation of the *visual* effect. This is not to say that the space is calculated because of its own visual effect; on the contrary, as in the Florence Baptistry, it remains invisible, and can be 'viewed' neither from inside nor outside. What could be the point of such a huge area of lost space if it was not for constructional reasons? If one is to believe the reconstruction of the original plan by Rohault de Fleury[81] then the same cone did not require any supporting fins; this is, however, unlikely. According to him the later outer shell was only intended for optical effect, to allow the full curve of the cupola to be achieved, and the entire area between the shells was only created in order to obtain such a massive external profile. Nothing could be a better confirmation of an interpretation which stresses the optical effect. However it is hardly imaginable that such a chimney-like stone cone was part of the original plan. It is doubtful whether the vaulting of the gallery would have been of sufficient strength to withstand the pressure of the cone.

One probably has to imagine an entirely different sort of vaulting, perhaps a shallower, single-shelled cone, on the inner circle of supports.[82] Even the original ribbed vaulting of the gallery could not have been intended as a support. The inner cone only became necessary when a great external cupola was planned, on a drum which was not intended for such a dome. If the Florence Baptistry was intended to be double-shelled, even when the drum was constructed, and was given narrow galleries whose diagonal walls could serve as the substructure for the angled fins of the dome, the broad galleries of the Pisa Baptistry would have made such a double-shelled structure impossible. Only the relatively narrow inner circle of arches offered a high cupola any internal support. The cone helped create height, was supported by and gave support to the fins, so that an outer shell became possible. Only now was the decision made to create a third storey which raised up the barrel vaulting

as a support for the shoulders of the cone. The dome which emerged was a compromise, the result of a decision to take as a base a construction which was basically unsuitable for such a type of dome. The Romanesque building changed its character with the addition of a dome which distinctly catches the eye. Inside a narrow chimney remained, but outside the dome shape came into its own; indeed the external effect of it was the chief consideration. This is why the buttresses are curved to create the broad arc of the outer shell.

If this dome is compared with the dome of Florence Cathedral the enormous technical and aesthetic gulf between them becomes clear, and Brunelleschi's achievement is put into perspective. And yet among all the earlier domes in Tuscany the Pisa dome is, in terms of its external effect, closest to the Florentine one. And it did indeed immediately predate the latter, having been constructed at a time when work on the tribune in Florence was already under way.

The most important structuring elements in the outer shell of the Pisa dome are the narrow ribs with their crockets which subdivide the cupola. Unlike in Florence, they do not mark the sides of a polygon, but rather seem to create sectors in the dome at random. Nevertheless they reflect the inner structure, for they run above the supporting fins, so that the latter take on the role of ribs. The heavy ribs of the Florence dome contrast strongly with these thin, vertical ribs and crockets. Such a detail alone demonstrates not just a difference in rank but also the gap between Gothic and early Renaissance. On the other hand both are linked by the idea of running lines of white marble through a red tiled roof.[83]

16. The Dome of S. Petronio in Bologna

Remembering that Zibellino, who was responsible for the models of the Pisa canopies and ciboria and possibly also devised the structure of the Pisa dome, came from Bologna, it is interesting to examine the surviving wooden model of S. Petronio. It strikes one immediately that on the model the drum of the dome has a row of canopies which are almost identical to those of the drum in Pisa. In both cases a broad cornice wraps round corner pillars and travels up to the tips of the canopies; double sharp-pointed 'ciboria' sit side by side at the corners. A number of conclusions can be drawn from this:

1. The Bolognese, who took Florence Cathedral as the

model for S. Petronio wished to use Zibellino's experience for the decorative elements and possibly also for the vaulting of the dome. The rows of canopies in the side aisles of S. Petronio are based on the Pisa model.

2. In that case the Bologna wooden model, which differs from the later sixteenth-century designs by virtue of its elements of Trecento style, could be a replica of the great stone model of 1390.[84]

3. As there can be no doubt that the Bologna model and the Pisa baptistry, which was still under construction in 1370 are related stylistically, it would seem likely that the 1390 design for S. Petronio is contained in the wooden model.

4. In that case the Bologna model can also be compared with the Florence Cathedral dome, the plan for which is reflected, thirty years before work commenced on it, in the dome of the Bologna model; for it is not just the Pisa canopies which were repeated; the Bolognese also took over the nave system and the dome, which had already been designed. Its external profile and broad polygonal ribs are clearly recognisable. In addition to this there is the highly characteristic lantern which, however did not, as in Florence, take the form of a classical 'pilaster half-column aedicule' with volute buttresses, but rather a Gothic canopy with flying buttresses.

Accordingly in Bologna the jagged cornices of the Pisa baptistry and the new dome shape of Florence Cathedral were combined. In Florence such a row of canopies was out of the question. Andrea da Firenze in his (c 1350) fresco in the Cappella degli Spagnoli provided a horizontal division between the drum and the start of the cupola. In Bologna Gothic verticality was required, a crown of canopies which hid the base of the cupola.

The cupola is a Gothic ribbed one. Engaged columns rise up and continue as ribs. In Florence the Baptistry model has been repeated and a ribless cupola retained. And yet the Bologna model – as was customary in the Trecento – had a ribbed construction.

The Bologna model also enables an important observation to be confirmed which close examination of the Florence model revealed: the outline of the cathedral dome existed before Brunelleschi's creation, in the Trecento, and moreover broad external ribs and a lantern with flying buttresses were also planed.

17. The Volterra Baptistry

On 13th November 1427[85] Brunelleschi was called to Volterra as a consultant for the roofing of the baptistry. The building, started in the thirteenth century and continued around 1320, still had no dome. On the wall containing the portal one can make out Trecento striped cladding which stops just above the window. At the same height on the inside a double ledge with consoles runs round the octagonal room, with its engaged columns at the corners which stop abruptly where the cupola begins. Originally they were intended to continue upwards as vaulting ribs, but this function was dropped as soon as it was decided that an unribbed dome of the type found in the Florence Baptistry would be created. The console ledge provides a strong horizontal motif which separates the octagonal room from the cupola itself. This displays the influence of the Florentine school of architecture. The double consoles are a simplified version of the gallery in the high nave of Florence Cathedral.

On the exterior of the building one can see how the cladding of plain stone blocks without any stripes matches the attic storey of the Florence Baptistry and hides the base of the cupola, probably surrounding a framework of buttresses. The octagonal cupola sinks deep into the surrounding wall. In contrast to the Florence Baptistry and the one at Pistoia which was given a pyramidal roof in 1350, the Volterra dome curves up from the drum in the form of a rounded tiled roof. At the start of the Quattrocento, with Brunelleschi's advice, the influence of the Florence Baptistry, the great model for medieval Tuscan domes was once again felt. The construction of this dome matches every detail of the original model.[86] On the exterior, however, new ideas were expressed: the profile of the dome was to be visible; the shallow sides of the pyramid offered a perfect link to the outer wall of the drum. But they prevented the curve of the dome from being visible, an effect which in a tiled roof such as this, has not been completely lost, despite the base of the cupola being deeply embedded in the wall of the drum. In the long tradition of Tuscan dome-building the Volterra baptistry stands at a historical turning-point, though in a different way from the Pisa Baptistry; and it is not insignificant that Brunelleschi was involved in the creation of this building.

VOLTERRA, BAPTISTRY

VOLTERRA, BAPTISTRY, INTERIOR VIEW

FLORENCE, OLD SACRISTY, LANTERN (AFTER SANPAOLESI)

FLORENCE, BAPTISTRY, LANTERN

PISTOIA, BAPTISTRY, LANTERN

18. The Lantern

The wooden model of the Florence dome found in the Museo dell'Opera demonstrates how blunt and inelegant it would have looked without a lantern. The arches of the lantern are slim and elongated, with the pilasters spaced close together. It is only by running the polygonal sides of the drum up into the elongated arches of the lantern that the dome gains height. The buttresses, with their broad volutes that fan out at the sides, continue the line of the marble ribs upwards. The lantern could not be better proportioned: if it were smaller it would lose its elegance and would not offer sufficient counter weight to the curve of the cupola – if it were larger it would take on too much of a life of its own.

That fact that the form it takes was not laid down from the start is proved by Andrea da Firenze's lantern. The tiny cage with its biforia perches rather forlornly on the octagonal platform. The bizarre decorated ribs break off before they reach the rather demure little lantern.

The lantern actually created offered a new solution. Relations were set up by using optical links. The intention was not to emphasise the independence of individual forms but rather to create strong lines stressing the connection between the ribbed cupola and the buttressed lantern. The Gothic ribs of the dome are continued directly by the buttresses of the lantern. Instead of a simple aedicule with columns a complex buttressed construction was created which, despite its classical decor clearly reflects the Gothic concern with transcending forms and framing elements.

It seems hardly likely that Brunelleschi only started to develop his ideas for the lantern when his prize-winning model of 1436 was finally drawn up and work on the lantern actually started. The great stone model of 1420 must have crowned the dome with a lantern. Documents are largely silent about details of this model. However the memorandum of 1420, reproduced in Manetti, mentions the lantern.[87] Certain details were probably only thought out later, in 1436: the high attic storey of semi-circular arches with ornamental cones in between, or the form of the buttresses themselves with their niches, which reproduce the basic layout of the ring of chapels in Santa Maria degli Angeli.[88] But one cannot say with any certainty that Donatello's Tabernacle (1423) on the bishop's staff of Saint Luke or other examples of this type were the models for Brunelleschi's lantern. It is

equally possible that Donatello's tabernacle is based on an earlier design by Brunelleschi for the lantern.[89] Simple buttresses with slanting roofs – not volutes – run up to the pilasters. The same motif is found on a reliquary in the Museo dell'Opera in Florence.[90] Here too steeply sloping flying buttresses stand against unusually steep pilasters which carry a classical cornice with a cupola with ribs and crockets. The reliquary owes its particular style to the combination of Gothic and antique forms: the buttresses themselves have become pilaster-like fluted strips which carry roofs which are reminiscent of the buttresses on the exedra of Florence Cathedral. They take the form of thin tongues which are pierced by slim arches. This suggests that the reliquary, and probably also the top of Donatello's tabernacle, preserve the basic structure of the lantern as originally envisaged by Brunelleschi. The first step away from the Gothic had been taken. Gothic rods are replaced by pilasters and struts while what was actually the real Gothic form, the flying buttress, retains its traditional appearance. On the final version of the lantern the thin tongue becomes a heavy buttress, the arch becomes a niche and the slanting roof becomes a volute.

There is enough evidence to believe that the model of the cathedral of 1367 already had a lantern and provided the immediate inspiration for Brunelleschi's first design. However the antique forms of the pilasters and struts cannot be expected to appear yet, though the buttresses themselves, which Brunelleschi retained to the end, probably did.

It is significant that there is, on the wooden model of S. Petronio in Bologna which we can assume to have preserved the design of 1390, a lantern which is designed as a Gothic construction. The individual canopy arches are supported by genuine Gothic flying buttresses which rise up from the lines of the dome's ribs.

There are more examples of similar lanterns in paintings of the architecture of the late Trecento, for example the tabernacle dome in Piero di Puccio's Coronation of the Virgin in the Campo Santo in Pisa.[91] Interestingly enough the struts run straight up out of crocketed ribs and support the lower storey of a canopy lantern.

Even though the developments leading to Brunelleschi's lantern cannot be traced exactly, the evidence suggests that the final version was preceded by earlier stages and that the particular form of the lantern was dictated by the assumption that the dome would be ribbed; it was, however, probably not inspired by goldsmith's reliquaries,[92] but rather these and the lanterns one finds in pictures of buildings in the late Trecento are based on the great stone model of Florence Cathedral of 1367.

Since the building of the baptistry the lantern of the dome has remained a specifically Florentine form; domes in neighbouring cities were given Venetian onions.[93] One exception is the baptistry in Pistoia which may be regarded as a Gothic replica of the Florence Baptistry. The detail reveals many highly significant changes for the Gothic: there are no pilasters – these are replaced by cladding with continuous stripes.

But the lantern too has a new appearance. Instead of a simple aedicule with columns there is now a Gothic structure. The corners of the octagon are marked by buttress-like piers with dripstones, flanked by three-quarter columns which carry the arches. At first glance one recognises the Trecento pier-column system which we have analysed earlier[94] – a continuous ledge forming a frame for the arches and spandrels and separating them from the piers/columns. The bases of the columns, which link up with the piers in between, point towards the characteristic linking of half-columns and pilasters which, after Brunelleschi, became customary in the early Renaissance.

In the Barbadori Chapel Brunelleschi changed the Gothic system and differentiated between the rising pilaster and the arcade column which remains below. This system returns in the lantern of the cathedral dome, applied to an octagon.[95] As in the Barbadori Chapel, the formal classical vocabulary of the lantern of Florence Cathedral should not prevent us from recognising that the basic structure is built up on Gothic principles: the pilasters have the same function as the struts in the Pistoia lantern. They support the heavy cornice above. The attached half-columns carry the arches which fill the gaps between the piers. If one ignores the buttresses and volutes of the Florence lantern, then it is possible to see the Pistoia lantern as providing the prototype.

The three lanterns of the Florence Baptistry, the Pistoia Baptistry and, finally, Florence Cathedral, exemplify the contrasting styles of the different periods: the Romanesque brought the Roman aedicule with columns, the Gothic brought the composite framework, and the Renaissance took the Gothic system and gave it classical decor. With this lantern Brunelleschi is much closer to the Gothic lantern of Pistoia. But his other lanterns, where the Gothic structure of ribs is not so highly developed as on the dome of the Cathedral, he resorted to the classical aedicule and columns of the baptistry.

DONATELLO, TABERNACLE OF ST. LUKE, FLORENCE, OR SAN MICHELE

FLORENCE, SANTA MARIA DEL FIORE, LANTERN

FLORENCE, OSPEDALE DEGLI INNOCENTI, LOGGIA WITH VIEW OF THE PIAZZA SS. ANNUNZIATA

V THE OSPEDALE DEGLI INNOCENTI

FLORENCE, OSPEDALE DEGLI INNOCENTI, FACADE

1. History of the Building

Apart from the cathedral dome there is no other work of Brunelleschi's about the building of which there is such detailed information extant as the Ospedale degli Innocenti. However, while interpretation of the documentation on the building of the dome has left few questions unanswered, there are several aspects of the history of the Ospedale which remain unclear to this day, even though Fabriczy, who evaluated the *Libri della muraglia* of the Ospedale, brought out all the most important points and gave a brief account of the correct reconstruction of Brunelleschi's original plan.[96] Despite the wealth of documentation available, despite Manetti's unambiguous criticism of the distortion of Brunelleschi's original plan, and despite Fabriczy's correct reconstruction of the facade, it has been the appearance of the building in its present form which has determined the ideas of more recent researchers right up to the present day.[97]

In these circumstances it is necessary to give a brief reconstruction of the history of the building of the Ospedale as revealed by all the sources and published documents at present available.

Manetti, who in his role as *operaio* for the Ospedale in 1466[98] had Brunelleschi's original design in mind, claimed that he found it in the Udienza of the Arte della Seta.[99] This describes in detail the subsequent alterations undertaken by the later *operaio*, Francesco della Luna. According to his account, Brunelleschi ended the row of columns of the portico with only one pilaster field. Documents prove that a total of only four pilasters was created. Moreover there is no bill for the columns inside the pilasters and the arches above these. In Manetti's report, too, there is no mention of these added arches: '. . . ciascuno de' lati del portico uno spazio solo, che era messo in mezzo tra due pilastri di macigno, accanalati. . .'[100]

The large payment made in 1422[101] to Albizzo di Piero and Betto d'Antonio who created the workshop

107

elements for the portico was for the remaining nine columns, four pilasters, ten wall capitals and five great doorways; three of these are the main entrances under the loggia ('tre insulporticho'), the other two being low doorways ('alentrate deglabituri'). In addition two 'porticciule piccholine cioe a ogni testa del porticho' are mentioned; in other words two small doors at the ends of the portico. This means that the two fields within the pilasters had one door each.

When, in 1426, an emergency roof ('tetto salvaticho')[102] was put on the lower part of the building as Brunelleschi had planned, it was complete: an arcade of nine arches with side fields framed by pilasters, between each pair of which a small doorway led into the interior.

As it was not until 1439 that a bill was presented for the work on the upper storey,[103] it would appear likely that the portico stood incomplete for some time, covered with a temporary roof of its own. The bill for tiling the roof was not paid until 1429, when the roofing of the (now complete) church and the hospital, i.e. the two side wings of the internal courtyard, was being paid for[104]

It was in 1430 that the addition on the right, next to the pilasters was made. A precise account was presented for each individual element involved. Even the section of architrave which passes round the outer pilaster and descends to the plinth, and the pilaster added on the outside, are mentioned.[105] According to Manetti, this addition with its vertical section of architrave, which destroys the symmetry of the building, was strongly criticised by Brunelleschi.

The matching section on the left side was not added until 1843,[106] while it was in the sixteenth century that the creation of the opening for the Via Colonna removed Brunelleschi's originally closed pilaster field.[107]

The upper storey of the portico was completed in 1439: on 26th January 1438,[108] the ledge under the windows was contracted out, and in the following year the other elements were paid for.[109] Responsibility for carrying out the work lay with Francesco della Luna, who is named as *operaio* between 1435 and 1445.[110] Manetti criticises details of the upper storey just as strongly as he did the right-hand pilaster field added to the portico; he dislikes the ledges and architraves, and in particular misses the pilasters between the windows which, in Brunelleschi's plan, were to have run from the architrave up to under the ledge of the roof.

It is possible that Brunelleschi intended a different frame for the two outer windows, for Manetti only found that two windows had been wrongly created. When he immediately goes on to criticise the lack of 'membri di pilastrelli' we can conclude that it was only the two outer windows which were to have been separated from the central section of the facade by wall pilasters, which would have created a link with the pilasters below.

Such a plan would seem to be plausible because the outer fields (in the original plan) matched the slight extra width of the pilaster fields below by being marginally further away from the next window along. This barely perceptible difference in spacing would be justified if framing pilasters were created for the outer fields only.[111]

2. The Continuous Architrave

Despite this documentary evidence provided by Fabriczy, Folnesics and Willich[112] persisted in ascribing to Brunelleschi the architrave which descends next to the pilasters creating a sort of outer framework for the facade. The analogy with the attica field in the Baptistry is clear, and the comparison was a tempting enough opportunity to offer an example of Brunelleschi's indebtedness to the Florentine Romanesque. However the descending piece of architrave, together with all the other elements for the added outer field, would not have been ordered as late as 1430 if, under Brunelleschi's control, the inner pilaster field had already received such an architrave framework. Francesco della Luna would have merely needed to transfer a piece of architrave which had already been cut to the outside.

Manetti is no doubt correct when he speaks of Brunelleschi, on his return after a long period of absence, regarding the alteration as a distortion. Manetti's account is invaluable proof that Brunelleschi's critical faculties were such that he did not accept everything that the Baptistry offered him in the way of models. If the *operaio* who replaced Brunelleschi was capable 'per arroganza' of regarding himself as 'non essere di meno autorità di Filippo', and claimed to have followed exactly the classical example in correcting Brunelleschi's plan, and moreover expected to be praised by Brunelleschi for so doing ('stimando, che Filippo lo lodassi'),[113] then here we had, at the very start of the Renaissance, the conflict which was to erupt again and again: to what extent was one to take the recognised authority of antiquity literally;

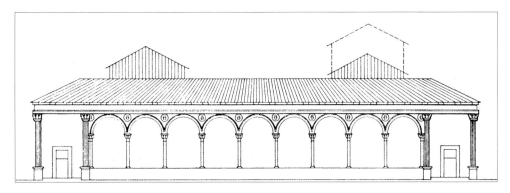

FLORENCE, OSPEDALE DEGLI INNOCENTI, SECTION OF LOGGIA IN 1429

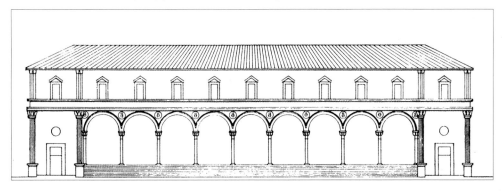

FLORENCE, OSPEDALE DEGLI, INNOCENTI, RECONSTRUCTION OF BRUNELLESCHI'S PLAN

FLORENCE, OSPEDALE DEGLI INNOCENTI,
ARCADE OF LOGGIA

FLORENCE, OSPEDALE DEGLI INNOCENTI,
OUTER FIELD OF FACADE

109

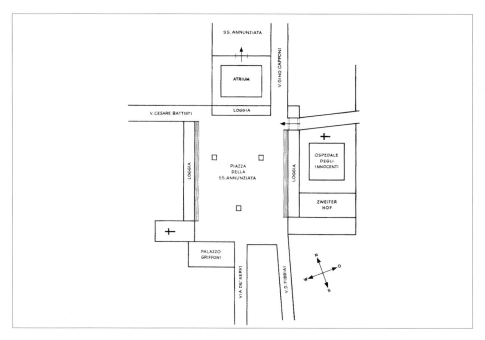

FLORENCE, GROUND PLAN OF PIAZZA SS. ANNUNZIATA

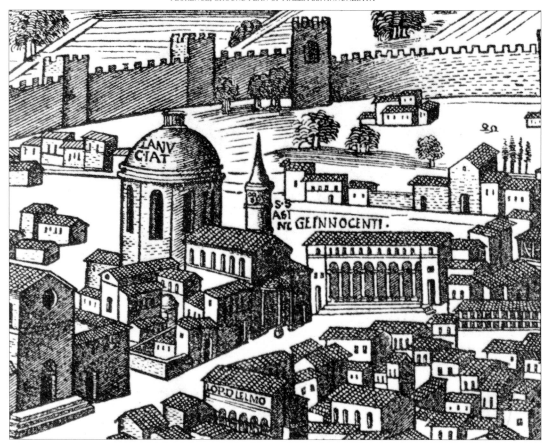

FLORENCE, PIAZZA SS. ANNUNZIATA, DETAIL OF PLAN (c. 1480)

to what extent should it be regarded as absolute? In not regarding the vertical architrave of the upper floor of the Baptistry as a model which he was duty-bound to imitate, Brunelleschi was displaying a highly developed degree of discrimination, seeing the architrave as no longer being a framing but rather a horizontal element in architecture. He was thus coming out against the medieval multivalence of a basically tectonic form which had been reduced to being a mere decoration. When Vasari later elaborates Manetti's report and has Brunelleschi saying that Francesco della Luna had taken over the one mistake which the Baptistry contained, then such an anecdotal hyperbole encapsulates the force of the conflict: Brunelleschi did not adopt all aspects of his great model uncritically, but rather tried to recognise mistakes which it contained, reserving the right to make the final judgement himself.

The authenticity of Manetti's report is supported also by the fact that he does not mention the name of the *operaio*. Manetti himself was involved with the building. The tortured way in which he talks round the indentity of the *operaio:* 'non parendo a qualcuno di quegli Operai',[114] is in itself significant enough. Vasari names names: Francesco della Luna, who, according to records, was in charge of the work between 1435 and 1445. Before that he had also worked on it between 1427[115] and 1430 and only relinquished his post 14 days before the contract for carrying out the work for the side field was given to the craftsmen. The final plan must thus have already been in existence.[116]

3. The Piazza di S. Maria dei Servi[117]

The entire complex of the Ospedale can only be properly understood in conjunction with the extension of the Piazza SS. Annunziata. Information is incomplete about the original layout. Documents relating to the purchase of the ground for the Ospedale[118] reveal that previously the area had been virtually devoid of buildings, thus allowing the Ospedale complex to be freely aligned. The north side of the square was determined by the facade of SS. Annunziata, which is identical with the present day facade which lies behind Michelozzo's atrium.[119] Thus the old Piazza dei Servi stretched further towards the north; it was only when Michelozzo's atrium and the sixteenth-century loggia were built that it moved closer to the side of the loggia of the Ospedale. At the beginning of the sixteenth century the loggia of the Confraternità dei Servi was built under Antonio da Sangallo the Elder and Baccio D'Agnolo, and the west side of the square was thus closed. And in the mid-sixteenth century the southern limit was created by the building of the Palazzo Grifoni.[120]

The only proof, albeit persuasive, that Brunelleschi reckoned with a regular shape for the square can be adduced from the alignment of the Ospedale with the already existing church of SS. Annunziata. Brunelleschi placed the portico exactly parallel to the axis of the church. By shifting it eastwards from the continuation of the line of the church and creating a side for a square which undoubtedly already existed ('Piazza dei Servi') he created a relationship between the church and the Ospedale which demanded a matching element on the other side, thus containing the seed of the idea for the loggia of the Confraternità.[121] The alignment of the portico of the Ospedale and that of the Servi speaks very clearly of Brunelleschi's having planned a symmetrical piazza to be flanked by two loggias, one opposite the other. These lead to the head of the square, where the centre of the entire complex is to be found: the facade of SS. Annunziata. At the other end the Via dei Servi, which already existed in the Trecento, enters the piazza and almost continues the central axis of SS. Annunziata to the choir of the cathedral. Thus there was here an alignment determined already in the Trecento.

The Via dei Servi, which points almost at the centre of the facade of the church, became, after the building of Brunelleschi's loggia, a definite central access to the piazza. In its role as marking the side of the square the portico of the Ospedale received a specific form: the facade is elongated and ranges along the entire length of the piazza, its ends actually extending beyond the square of the internal courtyard.

Thus the eye travels from the piazza to the Ospedale, whose ground plan shows the same astonishing symmetry displayed in the layout of the piazza. The regularity of the Ospedale buildings is perhaps the most convincing argument for Brunelleschi's having the same intentions as regards the piazza itself. What had been achieved in the layout of the Ospedale could not be entirely forgotten when the building was being related to its environment. Brunelleschi was confronted with a virtually empty area of land which he was able to plan as he liked. The lines which were offered to him were the street which led into the square and the line of SS. Annunziata. He established the ground plan of the Ospedale complex parallel to these lines and in doing so laid the foundations for the first clearly aligned square of modern times.

4. The Ground Plan

For any attempt to reconstruct the layout of the entire Ospedale an evaluation of the cellar vaulting recently restored by Morozzi is crucial. In particular the parts of the building at the rear, whose cellars were radically altered in the seventeenth century and whose upper walls date largely from the end of the sixteenth century, make it difficult to extrapolate Brunelleschi's original plan. Morozzi himself ended up with a ground plan which sought to revise the usual idea of a closed inner court-yard.[122] As his plan of the ground floor shows, he limited Brunelleschi's share to the portico (1) with the entrance buildings (2, 3, 7) and the two side wings of the church (8) and hospital (9). Thus a U-shaped layout emerges, open towards the back. Undoubtedly the entire complex had not advanced any further by 29th January 1427,[124] the time when Brunelleschi left. But by drawing the conclusion that this represented the 'first nucleus' of the complex, Morozzi is raising what was a passing stage in the development of the building to the level of a plan by Brunelleschi which can never have existed in this form. Even during Brunelleschi's period of office, on 9th August 1426, the order for the foundation work for the 'Chiostro degli uomini' had gone out.[125] Payment for the work completed occurred in April 1427, together with payment for the foundations 'del fabricato verso l'orto, in cui attualmenta è l'archivio, e di quello attiguo al chipostro delle donne'.[126] Thus Brunelleschi himself had laid down the closed complex of the 'Chiostro degli uomini' and had had the foundation work carried out. Even if the buildings at the rear had not been built at the time of his departure, this is of no great significance. The documents mentioned above reveal that even the foundations for the buildings which adjoin the 'Chiostro delle donne' (E) had already been laid.

We can thus be certain that Brunelleschi had planned a complex which would have enclosed the entire court-yard. The newly restored cellar vaulting corroborates the documentary evidence.

The two main buildings, the church and the hospital wing (C, D) each were given a two-aisled undercroft. The flat, broad arches of the vaulting rest on six simple square piers. The frescoes revealed by Morozzi on the piers and walls make clear what the function of the undercroft below S. Maria dell'Ospedale was: it served as a lower church. The undercroft of the hospital wing was also originally a single room which was only later divided by internal walls. The symmetry of the entire complex comes out very clearly in these two matching undercrofts, one opposite the other. The undercrofts below the buildings to the rear (E-H) were radically altered in the late sixteenth and seventeenth centuries. The substance of those below the buildings to the north-east (F, G) have also been completely renewed. On the other hand the basic ground plan of the south-east undercrofts has been largely preserved (E, H), as the piers have remained visible in the dividing walls which were added later. In contrast to the main buildings the vaulting rises above piers spaced out at rather smaller intervals. But the individual forms match those of the large undercrofts: the vaults fan out from simple piers without imposts, constructed of stone blocks across to the walls, which they join without any supporting consoles. The exact ground plan of this area of the building cannot be reconstructed with any certainty, in particular the transverse corridor which leads to the 'Chiostro delle donne' (J). The great vault would seem not to belong to the first plan. On the other hand, the pier standing on the other side of the corridor, should be included in the original building. Similarly the large room at the rear of the building (H), above which there now rises the six-teenth-century building, belongs to the Quattrocento. Even if we cannot say with any certainty that it was part of Brunelleschi's plan, we can at least establish that there already existed in the fifteenth century at least the under-croft of a second wing of a building at the rear which was possibly constructed in connection with the rear build-ing of Francesco della Luna's 'Chiostro delle donne'.

5. Symmetry

A sense of axially aligned buildings had never been lost in the Middle Ages. The very position of the Baptistry for the old S. Reparata proves this. The Ospedale in Siena, which was built in the thirteenth and fourteenth centuries, leaves a great area of square between it and the

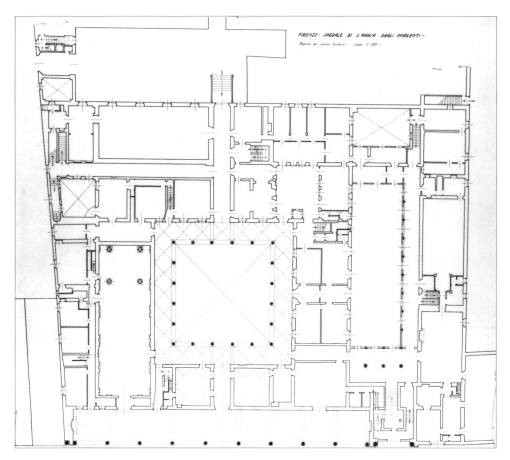

FLORENCE, OSPEDALE DEGLI INNOCENTI, GROUND FLOOR PLAN BEFORE RESTORATION (AFTER MOROZZI)

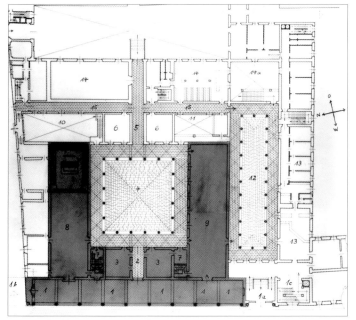

FLORENCE, OSPEDALE DEGLI INNOCENTI, GROUND FLOOR PLAN AFTER RESTORATION
(AFTER MOROZZI)

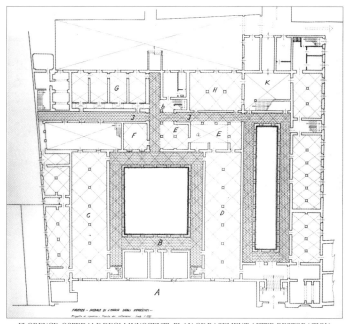

FLORENCE, OSPEDALE DEGLI INNOCENTI, PLAN OF BASEMENT AFTER RESTORATION
(AFTER MOROZZI)

113

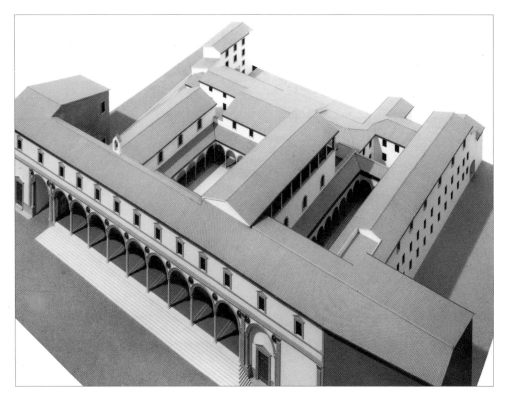

FLORENCE, OSPEDALE DEGLI INNOCENTI, MODEL OF RESTORATION ORIGINALLY PLANNED (AFTER MOROZZI)

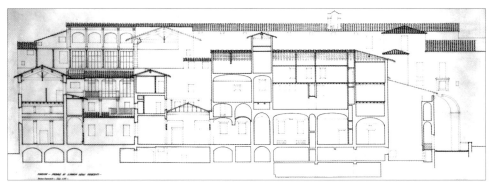

FLORENCE, OSPEDALE DEGLI INNOCENTI, CROSS-SECTION, BEFORE RESTORATION (AFTER MOROZZI)

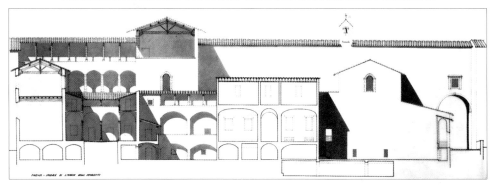

FLORENCE, OSPEDALE DEGLI INNOCENTI, CROSS-SECTION, AFTER RESTORATION (AFTER MOROZZI)

FLORENCE, OSPEDALE DEGLI INNOCENTI, CHIOSTRO DELLE DONNE

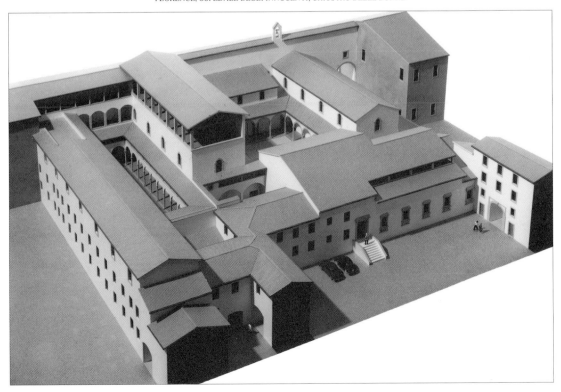

FLORENCE, OSPEDALE DEGLI INNOCENTI, MODEL OF RESTORATION ORIGINALLY PLANNED (AFTER MOROZZI)

FLORENCE, OSPEDALE DEGLI INNOCENTI, WINDOW IN CHURCH ON STAIRCASE

FLORENCE, OSPEDALE DEGLI INNOCENTI, WINDOW IN CHURCH

FLORENCE, OSPEDALE DEGLI INNOCENTI, DETAIL OF LEFT

front of the cathedral, but still attempts to establish a relationship with the latter by placing the main entrance exactly on the line of its central axis.

Nevertheless it was an entirely novel approach to plan a complex, consisting of several individual elements, to be symmetrical *in itself*. The plans for a reconstruction of the Ospedale recently produced by Morozzi[127] display the original layout of the complex. Gone are the later alterations which considerably changed Brunelleschi's work and, as in the case of the attic storey arcade on the roof of the facade, severely distorted it.[128] After reconstruction the whole complex presents a much more regular picture. The reception building behind the portico, with its square rooms divided by the entrance hall, is matched by an entrance building of similar size on the opposite side of the courtyard (5, 6). The line of rooms at the front has been extended by narrow access rooms at either end (7), so that a connection is created with the longitudinal line of the church (8) and the hospital wing (9), which themselves adjoin low, later heightened, horizontal arms (10, 11).

One important change of the overall appearance of the building after reconstruction is the way the hospital wing has been joined directly on to the portico (1). Originally there was no horizontal connection with the second courtyard. Today this has its main entrance on the front of the facade (1a), although it could naturally also be reached through doors leading from the south-west corner of the courtyard (4), through the hospital wing. The doorway in the southern pilaster field of the portico possibly led, like the former doorway in the northern pilaster field, to the doorway on the front of the portico, from whence one could pass into the colonnaded hall.[129]

The entire complex is aligned east-west with the portico. The main doorway with its broad corridor (2) leads into the inner courtyard and the line is continued in the corridor to the rear (5). Thus the centre axis is emphasised. It is accompanied by the two wings of the church and the hospital which are also reached from the portico through large doorways[130] and further emphasise the line of alignment. Only the square of the courtyard offers a counterbalance to this and lends breadth to the complex. From the southern arcade entrances lead into the church and hospital from the side. But even here the alignment from front to back dominates, for the arcades of the north and south sides penetrate the horizontal line of the

entrance building, and the division of the latter into rooms echoes the width of the arcade, with a small, elongated room on the right and the stairway on the left (7). In contrast to the elongated shape of the church and hospital, the rooms either side of the great through-line of the corridor are square (3, 6). It is only in the section of the complex to the rear that a horizontal corridor leading to the second cortile cuts right across the entire building (15) and echoes the line of the portico. The various elements with their front-to-back alignments run between these two horizontal axes.

This layout with its symmetry and alignments was only disturbed by the building of the second courtyard and the outer wing to the south (13). A second pilaster field at the southern end of the facade became necessary in order to give the extension a facade. This destroyed the symmetry of the portico. Interestingly enough Manetti directs his criticism at the extension built on the south side which appears on the external facade; by this he meant the second added pilaster field: '. . . un' aggiunto di muramento fatto dallo lato verso mezzodi, che apparisce di fuori lungo la faccia del portico, nel quale e' s' esce delle proporzioni di Filippo. . .'[131] The serious accusation of having thereby destroyed the proportions laid down by Brunelleschi makes it quite clear that symmetry was seen as a virtue in itself.

The elevation also is different after reconstruction. The extension of the rear wing (to the east) had only occurred in the late sixteenth or seventeenth century. Only the roof loggia of the hospital wing which, open to the wind, served as a drying area for clothes, rises above the other buildings. Finally at a later date were added the passages, lit by windows, above the pillared halls of the central courtyard, which adjoin the upper storey of the entrance buildings. Originally the roof sloped upwards directly from the architrave of the colonnades, so that the walls of the church with its elongated windows and the flanks of the hospital building with its similarly high windows, stood out. But the second storey of the rear entrance building also stood clear above the arcades; on both sides there were large gaps.[132] The buildings did not form a solid line, but rather the individual elements stood apart from each other and made a loose ensemble linked only by the square of the colonnaded courtyard. Thus the original plan allowed the compositional principles involved to be clear to the eye, each element to speak for itself; whereas the present plan assumes a tight unity of all the elements and forces the four wings of the courtyard into a square. The ruthless stereometry of the sixteenth century had defeated the loose symmetry of the building and replaced it with the uniform shape of the upper corridors.

6. Symmetry in the Trecento

Brunelleschi's symmetrical layout for the Ospedale and the symmetrical piazza it stands on, marked the final arrival of a tendency which could be found already in the Trecento.

The need even in secular architecture for regular, geometrical basic forms appears to have been a criterion even towards the end of the fourteenth century, when Villani wrote his history of the city of Florence. He could not express total enthusiasm about the Palazzo Vecchio, built after 1299: 'In order that the Palazzo should not be built on the area where the houses of the Uberti had once stood, those responsible built it crooked ('il puosono musso'); but this was unsatisfactory, because the palazzo should have had a square or rectangular form'.[133] The Uberti were banished members of the Ghibellini clan, whose houses had been razed to the ground to create in the centre of the town, an open space, the Piazza della Signoria, on which the Palazzo Vecchio was built. There was therefore sufficient space for a regularly shaped building to be created. But the ground had been sullied by Ghibellini and it was preferred to use 'pure' ground. The irregular ground plan of the Palazzio Vecchio displays clear attempts to create symmetry which were thwarted by the prudence of supersitition. Even at the start of the Trecento such reasons were strong enough to prevent this, the most important municipal building, from being given a rational layout. It could be said that the modern age only began when such beliefs ceased to weigh so heavily on people's minds, the need for a regular geometrical form took precedence over superstition, and a piece of ground became nothing more than a surface for which architects could plan a building.[134] It would seem unthinkable that Brunelleschi would have allowed such considerations to influence his planning of the Ospedale.

As early as the thirteenth century one finds planned towns laid out on symmetrical lines along defined axes[135], but regular layouts for buildings are more uncommon.

When they did occur they were based on the square courtyard as in the atrium set against the west doorway of churches, found even in Early Christian times, or later also the rectangular or octagonal castle with its corner bastions brought by Frederick I to Italy.

The Collegio di Spagna in Bologna, created at the end of the fourteenth century, provides a link between the atrium and the church. Here, however, the courtyard opens out to both sides so that, appropriately for its function, it gives the impression of having been there first and the chapel, a later addition. Its facade rises above one of the twin-storeyed wings of the arcade; the church stands in the axis of the courtyard, forming a counterbalance to the main entrance. The intentional symmetry creates an ensemble which is easily comprehensible, although the spacing of the arcade is not in alignment with the flanks of the chapel. Such a link between two basically independent buildings goes beyond the usual combining of church facade and atrium. The latter was merely a continuation of the actual main building, whereas here an arcaded courtyard draws the large and accentuated facade of a chapel towards its central axis. Segmental arches drawn across the corners of the courtyard lead the eye towards the facade and provide the outer balance for this central composition.

7. The Villa of Paolo Guinigi in Lucca

The building of the villa for the ruler of Lucca, Paolo Guinigi, started in 1407 or 1413, marked the beginning of a new era for villa and palazzo architecture.[136]

In the Ducento, and particularly in the Trecento, the custom had established itself among the richer families of building country houses outside the gates of the city; these were often angular buildings with irregular courtyard loggias and added towers at the sides.[137] The summer was spent in the cooler air of the mountains surrounded by gardens. The very situation of the Villa Guinigi differs from that of the usual country houses. It stands directly before the old walls of the city, opposite San Francesco, in a situation which is reminiscent of the villa surburbana. Accessible from all sides, the palazzo extends across an open space. The proportions of such a villa which spreads unrestricted into the surrounding countryside were unusual. There are no signs of any protective elements beyond the garden wall which encircles the entire area. Sercambi, the court chronicler

BOLOGNA, COLLEGIO DI SPAGNA, COURTYARD

LUCCA, VILLA GUINIGI, LOGGIA

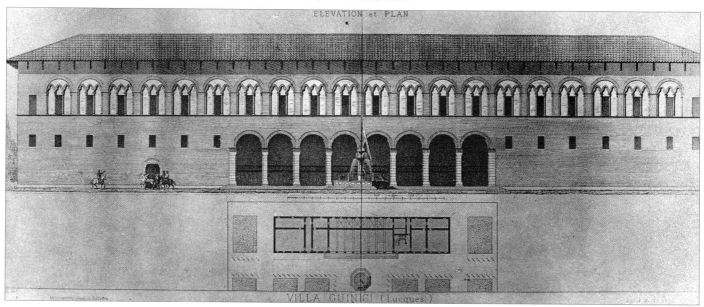

LUCCA, VILLA GUINIGI, FACADE (AFTER ROHAULT DE FLEURY)

of the Guinigi, mentions this garden: 'un nobile palagio con uno bellissimo giardino'.[138] Unlike the town house of the Guinigi, this villa exudes a spirit of openness and relaxation. The ground-level loggia opens invitingly towards those arriving from the town and makes the entire complex extend its arms towards the outside world. Only a prince who felt utterly sure of his position and power could have chosen to live in such an open villa surrounded by gardens. It retains the forms of the Trecento as a brick construction with Gothic triforium windows, and, as such, points forward to the type of building which was to reach its high point in the era of princely absolutism: the palace. In sharp contrast to the palazzi of the Trecento and even the early Renaissance, the Villa Guinigi is not oriented inwards with four wings around an internal courtyard, but is rather elongated, opening its arms into the surrounding gardens. The great villas of the Medici such as Trebbio, built by Michelozzo, retained the cortile and the external appearance of castelli, with a tower and a heavy row of consoles. But what makes the Luccan villa so remarkable in the present context is the symmetry of its plan and elevation.

The two-storey facade, which itself was a contrast to the town palazzo with its several storeys, uses the simple contrast of a ground floor which is closed to the side and open in the middle and the *piano nobile* which is structured symmetrically by a close row of windows with great triforia. At ground level the openings in the wall are concentrated on the centre, ie the loggia, while the row of windows extends right across the entire front of the building almost to the edges, where the row of triforia is finished off and framed by smaller rectangular windows. Only in the course of recent restoration work were these end windows wrongly walled up. Such an apparently unimportant window motif centres the whole building, bracketing the line of windows in the same way as the areas of wall with their smaller windows at either end of the ground floor, hold the loggia in the centre. The triforia above and the arcades below are axially related to each other; even the little side windows of the ground floor retain the same spacing as those above. In other words the entire elevation is based on symmetry and axiality. With the exception of one side door, there is no single detail, not even the smallest window, which disturbs the symmetry.

The rational principles of the elevation are repeated in the ground plan, which reflects the facade in its differentiation of the central section from the two sides. The loggia extends far back and provides a bridge even beyond the continuous horizontal line of the wall. The elongated passage is structured by vaulting – here, too, the centre differs from the sides – and leads through the axially connected ante-rooms, providing a sort of gallery connecting the whole sequence of rooms in a line. On the opposite side, towards the facade, there is a corresponding line of doors connecting the rooms with each other. The symmetry of the plan is only marginally disturbed by the lateral connections and the stairway in the right hand wing which leads to the upper floor. It is significant that the one-sided siting of the stairway brought with it a loss of symmetry. But the astonishing rationality of the sequences of rooms, with their consistent lines of doors, leaves us in no doubt that here we are witnessing the principles of layout which were to remain right down to the Baroque palaces.

Thus, some years before Brunelleschi started the symmetrical planning of the Ospedale, this prince in Lucca was presiding over an approach to architecture which already contained the seeds of the modern age: a carefully planned use of axes to produce symmetry and a new openness of the palazzo towards its surroundings.

Two of the master builders involved in the construction of the villa came from Germany: Engherardo di Franconia and Corrado di Verdena o d'Alemagna. They were among the large number of German architects who received important commissions from south of the Alps during the fourteenth century, and exerted a strong influence on the Italian Gothic. The third master mentioned, in 1410, was a Venetian: Niccolò da Venezia.

Paolo Guinigi had good political connections with Venice, which at the time was the most important power in northern Italy besides Milan.[139] In Venice since the eleventh or twelfth centuries a number of palazzi had been created under oriental influence which all shared the characteristic of having facades consisting of extended symmetrical loggias. It would appear that the above-named Niccolò da Venezia was heavily involved in the planning of the elevation of the Villa Guinigi and that he used this opportunity to introduce traditional Venetian forms to the Tuscan villa. The loggia framed by walls at either end and opening onto the canal, such as is found in the Fondaco dei Turchi, was repeated, albeit in more modest brick, in the Palazzo Guinigi. And, like the latter, the extended Romanesque palazzi of Venice are restricted to one upper storey which was structured by a row of open arcades, the models for the triforium storey of the Villa Guinigi, which retained the traditional window form for Lucca instead of the arched arcade. The framing effect of the ground floor at either end was peculiar to the Venetian palazzi.

8. The Ospedale Loggia in the Trecento

In Tuscany the ground had been prepared for such a transfer of architectural ideas from Venice. All that was required was for the Venetian palazzo to break through the established formal traditions for the facades of *ospedali* in Tuscany.

Brunelleschi's portico continues the Trecento tradition for such facades. The Loggia di San Matteo in Florence (c1390) has already been cited as an example. Above an arcade of seven segmental arches run the thin ledges dividing the window area from the arches, and creating a wide, smooth band of wall separating the floors from each other. This is basically the same elevation as that which applies to Brunelleschi's portico; a two-storeyed facade with a loggia and row of windows above.

The smaller front portion of the Ospedale of Lastra a Signa, created in 1406, only differs from this elevation in that the arches of the arcade are narrower and reach up higher, so that the upper floor under the roof is that much lower.[140] These are daring proportions resulting from an attempt to make the small facade as monumental in effect as possible by giving the arcades maximum height and importance. As in the Villa Guinigi, the arches curve in a semi-circle from the capitals; the first evidence of the new formal language.[141] The Ospedale in Volterra on the other hand, shows similarities with the elevation of San Matteo; it is a third example of how a traditional form had emerged for *ospedale* loggias in Tuscany in the Trecento.

In the Florentine and Volterra porticos the arcades end in broad piers of cut stone.[142] In the loggia of San Matteo these form a sort of frame round the arches with the result that at the corners of the upper floor there is a broad expanse of wall next to the end windows which can carry coats of arms in relief; these themselves then form, like the small end windows in the Villa Guinigi, a beginning and end to the row of windows. The Florentine facade also centres the entire ensemble, emphasising the middle window by placing reliefs on either side of it as well; the interplay of forms and emphasis, which helps to achieve perfect symmetry on the facade, brings out the central axis in particular. The seven bays which match Brunelleschi's uneven number of arches make possible a differentiated harmony by assigning two sets of three windows to either side of the centre. But at the extremities the massive corner piers provide a bracket for the entire facade and influence the division into bays. Thus by creating a beginning and an end they achieve a balance, with broad vaulting towards the centre framed by narrower arches at the sides. This rhythmical quality of the facade is echoed by the wall carrying the columns of the arcade, which is open below the outer arches and in the centre: in other words at the points where portals lead into the interior. This is the same layout of portals as in Brunelleschi's loggia. Thus, despite its modest intentions, the Trecento building, though far removed from Brunelleschi's elevation in individual detail, has been given a very fine symmetry, resulting not so much from a desire for uniformity as from a subtle use of accentuation. It is only the outer brackets which stand out massively and provide a solid framework for the broad arches in between. The same is true of Brunelleschi's loggia, which, instead of rough stone end-piers, has a clearly delineated area of wall framed by pilasters which gives it a new independence from the rest. The narrow outer vaulted bays of the Ospedale di San Matteo are replaced by closed side rooms which frame the loggia.

Palo Guinigi's villa proves that such a division of rooms and facades, the framing of arches which broaden in the middle with closed blocks of wall and rooms at the outsides, had traditional roots.

A construction which spread so generously in all directions was the most suited to a symmetrical approach, but this was achieved not just by repetitious rows, but rather by accentuation, by outer blocks which emphasise the arcade in the middle.

In Trecento painting, which often produced imaginative views one step ahead of actual developments in architecture, a pupil of Giotto had already thought up a similar structure. The remarkably classical palazzo reminiscent of Roman villas to be found in a fresco of the legend of

FLÓRENCE, OSPEDALE DI SAN MATTEO

VOLTERRA, OSPEDALE, LOGGIA

LASTRA A SIGNA, OSPEDALE, LOGGIA

FLORENCE, OSPEDALE DEGLI INNOCENTI, WINDOW IN FACADE

GIOTTO (SCHOOL), ST. FRANCIS TAKING LEAVE OF HIS FATHER, SANTA CROCE, BARDI CHAPEL

Saint Francis in Santa Croce (The Saint takes leave of his father) to a certain extent pre-empts the facade of Brunelleschi's portico.

9. Entablature, Architrave and Wall Strip

Keeping in mind the framing function discussed above, it becomes all the more understandable that Francesco della Luna felt the need, as in the Baptistry, to draw the architrave of the Ospedale loggia down the sides of the outer pilasters, so that once again – this time much more clearly – the frame was made obvious. It travels down the side of the facade outside even the pilaster fields which run like broad feet down the side of the loggia from the closed window storey, fulfilling a similar function to the corner piers of the loggia of the Palazzo Comunale in Pienza. But here the old, late classical motif was still recognisable, linking the free colonnade with the closed wall. It ultimately also determined Brunelleschi's elevation, which anchored the colonnade to the pilasters but placed the end columns next to them, apparently independently.

Francesco della Luna's realisation of the architrave – despite Manetti's criticism that it had been given the wrong architectonic content – expresses by its 'unclassical' function all the more strongly the need for linking; its medieval form brings out the hidden medievalism which pervades the structure of Brunelleschi's facade.

Even the architrave itself was given by Brunelleschi the character of the type of Trecento ledge which runs in a thin line across the surface of a wall. Like the latter, it is uninterrupted and retains the smoothness of the Gothic wall surface. It runs cleanly and without further links across the row of arches and above the pilaster fields and expanses of wall and can all the more easily be diverted into the vertical.

It is Alberti who comes up with a criticism here which also applies to Brunelleschi. He objects to the high walls of St Peter's in Rome, which for many years were in danger of collapsing, and criticises the lack of any reinforcement of the walls: '. . . in St Peter's in Rome it struck me – and should strike all who observe it – that the building has been constructed in a very irresponsible manner, for above the various openings an excessively high and broad wall has been created which is supported neither by curves nor by piers.'[145] Previously Alberti, citing the Romans, had made a theoretical demand:

'They were careful to avoid drawing any straight line on the ground plan up the outside without interrupting this in places with angled extrusions or corners let into the wall.'[146]

Alberti was all the more careful in his buildings to ensure that the architrave extruded over the columns so as to create sections in the wall, structuring it as in classical antiquity. It was only now that the 'shooting' architrave, which translated the Trecento ledge into a classical form, but did not overcome its smoothness, was completely discarded.

The ledge below the windows of the loggia, which Manetti also objected to, is an open reference to the Trecento ledge. It consists of two lines of reversed cornice each of which starts and ends with powerful convex moulding; a plastic expression of a traditional form of ledge for the Trecento as found frequently in the secular palaces of the city. At the corners the window ledge changes into the vertical, like the architrave below it, runs down to the latter, and travels back again. Thus it creates a remarkable, almost endless, framed expanse with a wave frieze at either end, which quickly breaks off and does not even begin the long journey across the facade. However, even these short pieces of frieze serve to emphasise the sides and to balance the ends.

A genuine entablature as created by Brunelleschi for the Sacristy and the Palazzo di Parte Guelfa was not created. Instead of this we have here an unorthodox combination of a classical architrave with a Trecento profiled frame which still fits the form of the traditional window-ledge.

But this form was not the product of the architect's imagination. When the window storey of the arcade was added a new problem must have emerged: how to convert the Trecento stretch of wall delineated by twin ledges running one above the other, which divided the windows from the arches, in to the language of Classicism; for now it was an entablature which was the unit structuring the divide between the arcade and the windows, its architrave resting on the arcade and its upper ledge serving as the bottom line for the windows.

Francesco della Luna solved the problem by isolating Brunelleschi's architrave, consigning it to the arcade and replacing the wreath cornice with the old throat cornice, making it into a frame and thus creating a frieze effect. This very imaginative and original form which nevertheless transcended the classical canons and, in Manetti's opinion, combined contradictory elements with each other.

Brunelleschi himself must have felt that the smooth, extended architrave was too insubstantial, for he supported it with leaf consoles, as in the Old Sacristy, and the interior and exterior of San Lorenzo. In the Pazzi Chapel there are only two consoles in very significant positions. In the central fields of the side walls and on the choir walls the continuous line of pilasters is interrupted so that instead of a pilaster, a console is used to support the architrave, thus replacing the supporting element in the order of columns.

10. Detail

In contrast to the portico the detail of the courtyard building has largely retained Trecento forms. While the facade was devoted to classical decor, the interior has retained much more modest and traditional forms of decoration. The loggia was the important external facade on which the new classical forms were realised for the first time. The interior did not need to be so elaborate, and has the simple, straightforward detail of the Trecento.

The cellar vaulting below the church and the hospital building, with their broad segmental arches, were like the traditional cellars of the fourteenth century. The undercroft of San Lorenzo has similar vaulting. In both cases there is no connection at all with the work of Brunelleschi. Thus the first building of the new age of architecture started off using old forms; local builders without any great ambitions, concerned instead with what was traditional and appropriate, created the basis for Brunelleschi's revolutionary construction.

Even the windows of the church and the hospital do not display anything of the classical style; they have heavy frames of stone blocks with the traditional shallow arches and angled corners. It was only the impost ledges which sit under the arches which were relatively uncommon in the Trecento.

Even the roof consoles above the later Baroque arches of the church are in the traditional style. The volutes are smooth and roll into a spherical form. Their similarity with the roof consoles of the great hall in the Palazzo Busini suggest that the same carpenters worked on both buildings between 1427[147] and 1429[148].

Brunelleschi then introduced a very different form of console which not only differed in the detail of the scrollwork from those of the Trecento, but also received greater supporting strength by a change in direction; he set the volute sideways under the load, so that the hanging volute now became a standing volute which could extend in a broad curve under the protruding architrave and run back into the wall at the bottom.

These can be found in unornamented form in the Ospedale in the connecting passage between the upper portal storey and the outer southern tract, which was built between 1430 and 1436. Brunelleschi's new type of console had now been established, but in places inaccessible to the public had been simplified.

In the same place there is a return to the Trecento type of pier made of square-cut stones with a thin impost and a flat arch. Brunelleschi's elaborate classical forms seem to have been kept for important positions, while the more simple functional elements do not appear to have taken on classical forms. The two styles are kept separate and mark the difference between the 'public' elements and the more functional ones. Similarly the heavy piers of the drying area above the hospital tract were, as befitted the position, simple and in Trecento style. The columns were kept for the courtyard.

* * *

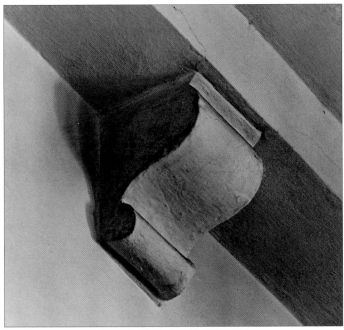

FLORENCE, OSPEDALE DEGLI INNOCENTI,
CEILING CONSOLE IN ENTRANCE ROOM OF SOUTH WING

FLORENCE, OSPEDALE DEGLI INNOCENTI,
ROOF CONSOLE IN CHURCH

FLORENCE. OSEPEDALE DEGLI INNOCENTI, CRIPT OF CHURCH

FLORENCE, OSPEDALE DEGLI INNOCENTI, ENTRANCE ROOM IN THE SOUTH WING

FLORENCE, OLD SACRISTRY

VI THE OLD SACRISTY OF SAN LORENZO

FLORENCE. OLD SACRISTY. CHOIR

1. Memorial Building in Florence

After Giovanni d'Averardo de' Medici, called Bicci, had given Brunelleschi the commission for San Lorenzo, interest was concentrated initially on the extension of the Old Sacristy. This was started in 1420 and completed in 1429, in which year Giovanni de' Medici was himself interred there. It can be regarded as the first major construction completed by Brunelleschi. The portico of the Ospedale had been covered with a temporary roof in 1424. Only the small Barbadori and Ridolfi Chapels had been finished at an earlier date.

The reason for the Old Sacristy, as an annexe of San Lorenzo, being built before the choir itself can only have been that a burial place for Giovanni de' Medici was required; in other words a private chapel for the Medici family. It could not yet serve as a sacristy for Christian services.[149]

It is interesting to note that there was an element of competition involved in the creation of this memorial.

Two years earlier, in 1418, Palla Strozzi had commissioned the building of the sacristy of Santa Trinità according to the wishes of his dead father Onofrio Strozzi and as a burial place for him. A plaque gives the year of consecration as 1421 and declares that only the offspring of the Strozzi family shall be buried there;[150] in other words this too was a family chapel (. . . 'ut nemo praeter descendentes eorum in ea seppelliri possit'). The Strozzis' claim to the building is declared in the great coats of arms in the tondi on the exterior and those in the windows and in the interior.[151]

The tradition had developed during the thirteenth century of using the chapels of the churches of the religious orders as burial places for the great families. The patrons were thus creating their own memorials. To endow an altar meant that one acquired the chapel for one's family. Thus the main church had attached to it a series of 'individualised' memorial chapels. The public, in paying tribute to the saint of the chapel,

129

was also paying tribute to the patron saint of the individual family.

The sacristy's assumption of the same function as the chapels – that of a family memorial – meant that a closed room had been given a separate function. It still remained connected with the main church but now what had already been a separate side room took on the role of an independent endowed chapel which stood out clearly from the row of family chapels which already existed in Santa Trinità.

The Santa Trinità sacristy also finally received its own facade. This bore the coat of arms of the Strozzi and also had two high windows which were given a surprising classical frame with a billet frieze and pediment. The marble portal in the interior which leads from the transept into the sacristy was also distinguished by its antique decoration; the columns were given fluting, the tympanum became a semi-circle framed with richly antique ledges; all in all an early classical vocabulary which differed clearly from that of the Trecento, and suggests, even before Brunelleschi's great works, a tendency towards a 'rebirth' of classical antiquity. The classical decor further served the goal of celebrating the Strozzi and their individualised memorial.

It is significant that in addition to the great creations Brunelleschi made for the guilds (the Ospedale of the Arte della Seta, the dome of the cathedral, produced for the municipality under the supervision of the Arte della Lana, and the Palazzo di Parte Guelfa), three of his early works were private commissions, the three family chapels created as memorials for individual citizens: the Old Sacristy, the Ridolfi Chapel and the Barbadori Chapel. The Strozzi sacristy served the same purpose and was the first memorial building to link the Early Renaissance of classical decor, the language of Rome, with the fame of an individual family name. The claim of the public corporations and the city itself to be the successors of the Romans had been transferred by the individual to himself and his house. The Barbadori Chapel, too, remained open to the rest of the church and had a part in the normal religious ritual. But it stood separately all the same, demanding only a corresponding chapel on the other side of the nave, and, with its square shape clearly defined by pilasters and crowned with a dome, it had its own integrity. But the family chapel acquired even greater independence by taking over the sacristy of the church. Even the Pazzi Chapel is in the last analysis a part of the general church space occupied by a family memorial; it had been the chapterhouse of the Franciscans of Santa Croce and had been constructed as such, but instead of bearing the coat of arms of the Franciscan order it bore that of the Pazzi.

The creation of the octagon of Santa Maria degli Angeli, the family chapel for the offspring of Pippo Spano, marked the emancipation of the memorial chapel from the main church. Here it was sufficient for it to be within the precinct.

During the second half of the Quattrocento the Strozzi, with their great palazzo in the Via Tornabuoni, had competed with the palazzo of the Medici; prior to this Onofrio and Palla Strozzi had provided an example, with their building of Santa Trinità as a family memorial, which had evidently spurred Giovanni de' Medici to do something similar which would outshine his rivals. The architects of the Strozzi sacristy were probably Ghiberti and Michelozzo,[152] but Giovanni de' Medici chose Brunelleschi, and in doing so destined his family chapel, the Old Sacristy, to have a new, well-formulated architectural language – that of Classicism. By declaring his willingness to pay for the building of the choir and the crossing of San Lorenzo, he secured himself a position of eminence among the other eight great families; tradition had it that they received the chapels to the side of the choir, but the Medici were able to lay claim not only to one of the transept chapels but also to the sacristy.

2. Type and Composition

Its additional role as a memorial meant that the traditional sacristy now gained in importance and became a building in its own right, rather than just an annexe providing space for the preparations for the church service. Traditionally the sacristy had not been a very substantial affair; in the Trecento it opened out from one of the transepts and consisted of a simple vaulted room connected to a smaller vaulted choir chapel. A good example is the sacristy of Santa Maria del Carmine. Any comparison of such simple rooms with Brunelleschi's Sacristy would merely serve to prove how different the latter is. Little is left of the traditional sacristy save the basic principle that it is linked with a shallow little choir.

Brunelleschi gave both rooms a dome, and this in itself was a fundamental innovation. The very form of

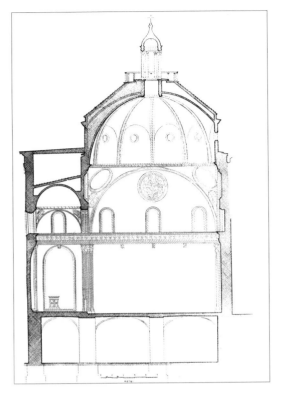

FLORENCE, OLD SACRISTY, CROSS-SECTION (AFTER SANPAOLESI)

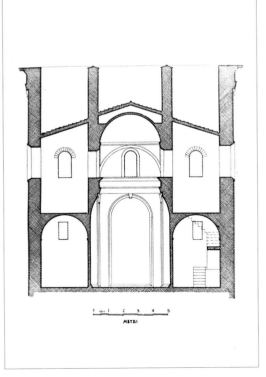

FLORENCE, OLD SACRISTY, SIDE VIEW (AFTER SANPAOLESI)

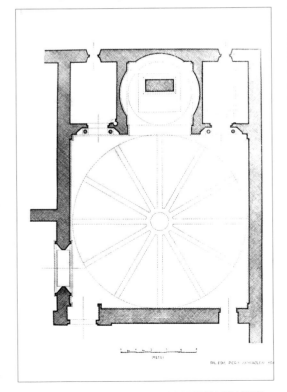

FLORENCE, OLD SACRISTY, GROUND PLAN (AFTER SANPAOLESI)

FLORENCE, OLD SACRISTY, SECTION OF CHOIR (AFTER SANPAOLESI)

FLORENCE, OLD SACRISTY, ARCH WITH DOME

FLORENCE, OLD SACRISTY, MAIN AREA AND CHOIR

FLORENCE, OLD SACRISTY, ARCH BELOW DOME

the dome gives rise to various questions: how could this dome, reminiscent as it is of Byzantine constructions, have reached Florence; or was it entirely the product of Brunelleschi's inventive imagination? None of the Roman examples, such as the domes of the Hadrian's Villa,[153] with their sharply contoured segments, which some would see as providing models, had the pendentives which are so typical of Byzantine domes. Others have cited as models Islamic examples, such as the side domes of the Green Mosque in Bursa (Anatolia). But Brunelleschi's dome, with its ribs and the webs in between, has retained a Gothic element. It is better not just to concentrate on a detail such as the dome in isolation if one wishes to establish formal and historical links, but rather to look at the construction as a whole.

In its totality the building, in its double role as sacristy and family memorial, is such a unique construction both in form and content that it is tempting to see it either as an invention without precedent or to search for an example which itself represents a unique entity.

The idea of dividing a square room into three zones was an unusual and surprising one for Tuscany: the lower wall with its corner pilasters, the semi-circular areas above the architrave with interpolated pendentives, and the dome with its clearly defined ribs descending to a full semi-circle. The semi-circular arches rise above the four wall areas and above these sits the circular dome, its shape echoed by the tondi below, the row of oculi running round its base, and, at the top, the circle of the lantern. It all makes for a well-balanced composition of basic geometric forms which support and complement each other and create an impression both of stability and, at the same time, movement. The pendentives which open out towards the dome lead down into the corners where the broken pilasters provide the only supports for the architrave. The supporting function is made clear for the eye to see by the fact that the only visible supports are at the points where the lines of the arches converge and lead downwards. The supporting strength of the building develops from the corners and spreads upwards and outwards through the pendentives to the dome itself. The walls themselves have no pilasters, for above them the arches stretch upwards, each with a tondo at its highest point. Only the windows provide an element of weight. Three consoles support the architrave, instead of pilasters running up

from below. In the centre the forms expand freely, whereas in the corners, in the pendentives, the tondi are tightly contained by the lines of the arches. And as though to emphasise the impression of support and tightness the Medici coats of arms are squeezed in between the arches and the frames of the tondi. These are forms which grow out of the concave surface, filling in the space available and linking the supporting elements in the corners. In this ensemble of basic geometrical forms their distinctive shield-like shape stands out.

The wall of the choir is the only elevation which differs; the ledge runs round into the adjoining chapel and is held majestically by the two pilasters of the chancel arch. The great arch runs concentrically with the one above it; one semi-circle above the other. The side walls are unexpectedly clearly defined, with Donatello's portals and the relief arches above. These echo the barrel vaulting of the interior which runs on both sides to the canopies of the choir niches.[154]

The square choir basically repeats the composition of the main room, but here Brunelleschi has introduced a slight variation in the geometry by not just repeating the dome but rather creating a perfect hemisphere, and putting shells in place of the tondi in the pendentives, so that the geometrical shapes receive a different realisation and form.

As though to broaden the small choir and to create a majestic setting for the altar there are niches with semi-circular arches in the walls, which create a degree of movement where in the main sacristy there is the severity of smooth surfaces. The echoes between the great cube of the sacristy and the little choir, the extensive ribbed dome and the smooth hemispherical dome are tangible, but at the same time the variety comes out, the contrast between the two linked spaces.

3. The Baptistry in Padua

Surprisingly enough it is in the Veneto, a region where, since the construction of San Marco in Venice, there had been a continuous tradition of Byzantine ideas in architecture right up to the High Renaissance period (San Salvatore in Venice, Santa Giustina in Padua), that one can find a building which is very similar to Brunelleschi's Old Sacristy: the Baptistry in Padua.

The interior of the building, which was completed in 1260, was decorated with frescoes in 1376 by Giusto de'

Menabuoni. Important decorative details were added which enriched this already unique interior with special motifs. These display close links with the Sacristy in Florence.[153]

The square main room is delineated by four broad expanses of wall which rise up into semi-circular arches which touch the base of the dome. The round dome is set on four pendentives. Corner piers link the sides of the walls and support the points of the pendentives. Towards the choir there is a triple arcade, the central arch of which leads into the choir, which itself has a pendentive dome, while the two side ones lead into shallow side-rooms which have diagonal double vaulting, but open into the choir via low arches.

Many essential aspects of the Padua Baptistry anticipate the basic design of the Old Sacristy. The combining of a square main room with pendentive dome and a choir with a similar dome, linked through a triple arcade with a higher central arch, recurs in the Florence building. Brunelleschi replaces the open side rooms of the choir with closed rooms whose barrel vaults support the canopies of the niches, which themselves carry the dome.

The exterior of the baptistry displays the inner structure. On the cube-shaped rump block sits the main cupola with its drum; linked with the main building is the smaller choir chapel with its own drum and cupola.[156] Brunelleschi linked the elements differently, bringing the outer wall of the main room round the choir so that only the drum of the great dome is visible. This created separate high rooms above the side rooms. Thus the exterior of the building would hardly lead one to believe that there was any connection between it and the Padua Baptistry.

But the similarities in the interior are all the more striking. Giusto de' Menabuoni's frescoes, which cover the walls with such a rich layer of pictorial material, at first seem heavy by contrast with the austere simplicity of Brunelleschi's creation. But they also bring out certain architectural motifs which must have supplied Brunelleschi with a host of ideas.

The small choir, with its imaginative frescoes could have given Brunelleschi the model for his dome composition. Even the unusual division of the Padua cupola into sections, as a result of the painter's portrayal of pointed baldaquins running from the Apostles' seats up to the centre, provided the principles for the composition of Brunelleschi's dome. In his eyes the posts became actual ribs, linked with each other by small semi-circular arches like the arched canopies of the Apostles' seats. Similarly the circle of concave arches round the figure of Christ could be changed into the circular rib of Brunelleschi's central lantern.

The lines incorporated in the pictorial decoration here became, in Brunelleschi's hands, architectural structure. Above all the tondi in the pendentives which are touched at three points by opposing arches supplied a significant idea. If one includes the mandorla of the choir wall then we already have here the tondi which circle the edge of the dome in Florence. What forced the artist to apply architectural principles despite the richness of the pictorial decoration was the need to create frameworks for it all. These run as thin light lines round the expanse of the wall arch, round the tondi and round the circle of the dome, providing the basis for Brunelleschi's stone frames; thus the play of geometrical shapes of the Old Sacristy was already created here as a *disegno*. And Brunelleschi's architectural lines have a pictorial effect because they were actually taken from pictures – the frescoes.

In this Duecento room with its Trecento decoration there are other motifs which are so original that the connection with the Old Sacristy is undeniable. The pendentives of the main room were given a complicated decoration of arches. Larger niches for the Evangelists, who recur in the Old Sacristy in the wall tondi, are flanked by smaller niches for the Prophets. But here too there are tondi, in the bottom points of the pendentives, and these are supported and framed by shapes stretching far into the spandrels, thus taking on the same function as the Medici coats of arms in the pendentives of the Old Sacristy. Thus in the Padua Baptistry the same position was destined for the coats of arms of the patrons as in Florence. A closer look reveals that small coats of arms with helmets on top have been added to the edging of the framework. The detail on the shield has been scratched out but one can just discern the remains of the coat of arms of the rulers of Padua – the *carro*, the Carrara carriage with four red wheels. This is also found in the smaller spandrel tondi at the sides. This detail of the coats of arms on the pendentives in itself makes it impossible that there could have been parallel models for the Old Sacristy in Byzantine or Islamic traditions. But this does not mean that certain Byzantine forms have

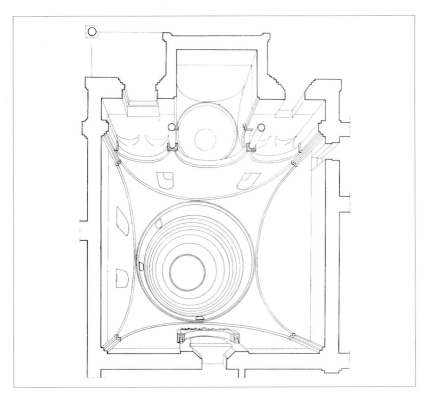

PADUA, BAPTISTRY, ISOMETRIC (AFTER BELLINI)

PADUA, BAPTISTRY, WALL IN MAIN AREA

PADUA, BAPTISTRY, DOME OVER MAIN AREA

PADUA, BAPTISTRY, PENDENTIVE SPANDREL

PADUA, BAPTISTRY

PADUA, BAPTISTRY, CHOIR DOME

PADUA, BAPTISTRY, CHOIR

PADUA, BAPTISTRY, PENDENTIVE

FLORENCE, OLD SACRISTY, RIBBED DOME

PADUA, SAN ANTONIO, VAULTING IN CHOIR

not left their mark, via intermediaries, on the Padua Baptistry. The pendentive dome of San Antonio in Padua, a massive version based on the model of San Marco in Venice, was the leading model of Byzantine architecture. Other details of the Old Sacristy reveal Byzantine influences; for example the group of three windows above the architrave. The arch walls of the Hagia Sophia were pierced by similar sets of windows. In San Antonio there is only a pair of windows, which recurs in the Padua Baptistry on one of the side walls. The horizontal window ledges are on the same plane as the imposts of the pilasters. In the Old Sacristy Brunelleschi separated the lower expanse of wall from the arch area by an entablature, at the same time providing a broad base for the windows. Significantly enough in the Padua Baptistry Giusto de' Menabuoni ignored the division, painting across the architectural line between the pilaster imposts and the window ledge, which nevertheless remains. Brunelleschi emphasised them all the more, strengthening a division which was already hinted at in the basic architectural structure of the Padua building.

The two windows to the sides of the choir sit slightly above the line of the imposts. But the way they are set to the side just under the arch is similar to the position of the windows in the wall of the chancel arch of the Old Sacristy.

It is easy to establish that in both buildings the proportions of an expanse of wall are similar: they contain roughly the ideal proportions of a full circle; in each building there is one element which upsets the proportions – in Florence it is the height of the architrave, which prevents the circle drawn from the assumed centre from reaching the ground, and in Padua it is the height of the choir stalls. The geometry of the circle is thus roughly confined to the optically important fresco wall. (Significant for the symbolism is the matching of meaning with central proportions: the centre point of the entire wall, i.e. the centre of the circle, is Christ's navel). The relationship between Baptistry, Baptism of Christ and Cross is expressed in the proportions themselves.[157]

Finally the similarities also stretch to the absolute dimensions themselves. In both buildings the width of the main room is 11.5 metres. In the more abstract language of architecture this similarity gains a special significance, just as, on a pictorial level, did the similarity between the pendentive coats of arms. The two buildings are closely related. The question therefore arises as to whether the passing on of forms could have occurred in any way other than on the basis of direct study of the earlier building. Brunelleschi must not only have been in Rome but also in Padua,[158] which is initially a rather confusing idea, given that this fact is not documented in the sources at present available.

4. The Ribbed Dome

One of the main indicators that Brunelleschi had visited Rome at an early stage was the 'Roman' form of his domes, although the 'Gothic' skeleton with its webbed canopies has always made the assumption that they were derived from Roman or Eastern models highly dubious. The ambiguity of the style of his domes is demonstrated by the fact that the origins of Brunelleschi's dome have also been sought in the very antithesis of the classical world, in the birthplace of the Gothic. The vaulting of the crossing of the cathedral of Coutances in Normandy has much in common with the dome, but such examples surely lay outside Brunelleschi's sphere of experience.[159] And one does not find here the characteristic motif of the arch rising into the dome with oculi, which is reminiscent of Byzantine examples.

The choir vaulting of the Padua Baptistry, with its frescoes, might have aroused certain associations and have been the inspiration for the fan shaped ribbed sections, but the picture in itself was not a basis for any construction.

Brunelleschi had found the structure of the dome in that great Paduan church, the Santo (S. Antonio). In contrast to the smooth cupola of the nave the dome in the choir had ribbed sections running up to a central stone. On all sides the ribs rise up out of the engaged columns. Slightly pointed steep arches rise into each section. Below the typical little Byzantine windows in the dome there is a string of broad oculi letting in the light which runs right round, stopping only at the chancel arch which separates the choir vaulting from the nave.

Thus the Gothic choir vaulting of the Santo provided the decisive model for Brunelleschi's dome. But, in line with the fresco of the Baptistry, his ribs run less sharply into the centre, curving back concavely when they reach the lantern. Similarly the ribs gently join the ring of the cupola and no longer rise up from engaged columns.[160]

It was not the vaulting of the Florentine Baptistry

which was the model for Brunelleschi's domes but the Gothic ribbed cupola of the Santo in Padua. But the Florentine cathedral tribuna would never have taken such a finely structured construction as this. On the other hand the vaulting of the Baptistry, with the hardly visible edges to its sections was too heavy to match the elevation Brunelleschi had given the Old Sacristy and the Pazzi Chapel. The lines of ribs were missing, the elements which brought out the structure of the building in line with his 'membri et ossa' approach to the wall elevations.

For the construction of the ribbed dome Brunelleschi took over principles from the dome of the Baptistry: above every rib he put a strut which ran right up to the lantern; this was not just in order to heighten the external line of the cupola and give greater strength to the ribs and intervening webs, but also in order to carry the ring and lantern which had replaced the Gothic centre stone. By linking the different worlds of the Florentine tradition and the Paduan Gothic he created a new form. In drawing the struts of the Baptistry dome right up to the top he followed the line of the ribs and thus came close to the Gothic skeleton framework. But the ribs were altered by linking them with the struts, which radiate out from the centre. At the same time the ribs are held from above by hidden arched struts rather than being supported on engaged columns from below. The inner structure and the visible forms which are thus produced are neither Romanesque nor Gothic.

5. The Side Rooms of the Choir

The new role of the Old Sacristy as an independent element is underlined by the fact that this annexe to the church has, itself, had side-rooms attached, on either side of the choir. It was these that made it possible for Donatello to develop the richly decorated facade of the choir wall of the Sacristy, for the doorways to these rooms make it possible to create a frame out of the whole side-field and decorate it with terracotta reliefs. The doorways were given columned aedicules and the doors were cast in bronze, which was a luxurious material to be used on the interior of a sacristy.

These side-rooms themselves acquire the nature of sacristies, an impression which is strengthened by Verrochio's lavabo in the left-hand room. Again one can see here the influence of the Padua Baptistry, which also had a sacristy attached, with a lavabo which bore the initials

of the patron. A surviving wooden door with four panels and cable moulding was possibly the inspiration for the doors created for the side-rooms of the Old Sacristy, although these are more richly decorated. But initially, before Donatello's bronze doors were added, wooden doors had been planned.[161]

The barrel vaulting of the side-rooms is the first of its kind in the Renaissance. Such vaulting was unusual in fourteenth-century Florence. In one building Brunelleschi has created three different kinds of vaulting: the semi-circular dome, the ribbed dome, and the barrel-vaulting which seemed to fit naturally onto the elongated rooms and offered support to the side walls of the choir. Significantly, Brunelleschi made a clear line of demarcation between the walls and the vaulting by drawing a continuous cornice around all four walls of the room. The profile of the cornice was the customary type for the Trecento. Thus here, in a side-room, Brunelleschi deviated from the classical language of the Sacristy. The cornice acts as a delineation, not a decoration; this simplification recalls Trecento forms and can also be observed in the Ospedale degli Innocenti.[162]

Michelozzo was the first person to follow Brunelleschi in using barrel vaulting and to remember at the same time Brunelleschi's predilection for a thin ledge running round the walls. The corridor leading to the steps up to the library in the monastery of San Marco repeats Brunelleschi's barrel vaulting. The ledge is extremely thin and delicate and creates a rectangular shape which seems to hover above the room. The Trecento Gothic lives on. But soon such simple forms were to be rejected; in the anteroom of the Sacristy of Santo Spirito, Guiliano di San Gallo sits the barrel vaulting on an arcade, adds a substantial entablature and decorates it with coffering and reliefs. One can see here a predecessor of the entrance gateway of the Palazzo Farnese in Rome.

6. The Baptistry in Padua as a Memorial Building

The addition of frescoes by Giusto de' Menabuoni (completed 1376) was part of the alteration process of the baptistry of Padua Cathedral, which had been in existence since 1260, into a building with a different purpose. On the one hand it remained what it always had been: a place for the ceremony of baptism, (a new font was placed in the centre of the room and the frescoes had as their centrepiece a portrayal of the baptism of Christ).

FLORENCE, OLD SACRISTY, VAULTING IN CHOIR SIDE ROOM

FLORENCE, SAN MARCO, ENTRANCE CORRIDOR

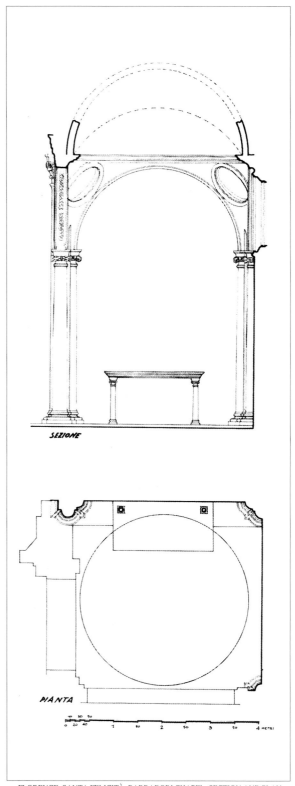

FLORENCE, SANTA FELICITÀ, BARBADORI CHAPEL, SECTION AND PLAN
(AFTER ZANETTI)

FLORENCE, SANTA TRINITÀ, FACADE OF SACRISTY

But, on the other hand, the ubiquitous paintings of the coats of arms of the Carrara family bring a personal, individual note to the universality of the scenes portrayed. Fina Buzzaccarini, the wife of the ruler of Padua, Francesco da Carrara, had the baptistry converted into a burial place for herself and her husband. Thus, even though the building retained its general function and purpose, it was also a memorial to an individual. Integrated into the great Christian cycle of baptism, burial and resurrection,[163] an individual human being awaits the Last Judgement and *his own* resurrection. The appearance of the Carrara coat of arms below and beside the symbols of the Evangelists on the main dome signifies an unusual 'highjacking' of Christianity by an individual. The Baptistry retained the general 'public' significance of the story of Christ, but at the same time an individual had been emphasised and had taken over this world for himself. A family memorial in the interior of a church, a single sarcophagus or grave-stone had possessed the necessary Christian *humilitas;* already a different note was struck by the placing of the coat of arms of the patrons at the peak of the arch of the chapel; but here it was an integral part of the picture, directly under the dome and in the centre of the whole cycle.

In the Old Sacristy the coat of arms of the Medici appears in the same position. Admittedly the liturgical importance of the Old Sacristy was much less than that of the Baptistry. It only really gained significance when it was extended in height by its patron, whereas the Baptistry had, from the very start, been a building of considerable weight and importance. It was an independent sacred building with a public role and was not built specifically as a memorial chapel, but was rather diverted for this purpose by the Carrara family. In Giotto's Arena Chapel the patron of the building, Enrico Scrovegni, appears in the Last Judgement in an attitude of humility below God. He did not permit a coat of arms to appear at any point in the fresco cycle. Between this work, completed at the beginning of Trecento, and the Carrara family's baptistry there lies an enormous change in people's ideas of the importance of the individual.

Brunelleschi considered the architecture and the fresco decoration of the Padua Baptistry to be closely linked into a unified whole. Just as he followed the proportions, forms and dimensions of the architecture, so, too, he respected the frescoes; not so much the rich detail of the pictures as the main lines, the frameworks of the whole composition; in other words the architectural elements. The lines of the choir, with its thinly drawn semi-circular arches, its tondi and the ring of the cupola reappear in stone in the Old Sacristy. The architectural elements in the frescoes have now been translated into real architectural forms, but retain some of the pictorial qualities of the framing elements in the Padua Baptistry from which they are derived. This also explains the position of the pilasters in the Old Sacristy which are drawn round the corner just like the narrow corner piers of the Padua Baptistry. Brunelleschi translated all these forms into the new classical language of architecture, changing a Trecento system of frames into *membri et ossa* and the rich pictorial language into purely architectural forms. A new ordering relates the forms to each other: the great semi-circular arch of the choir wall and the rather uncertain chancel arch of the Padua Baptistry are given a direct relationship with each other by Brunelleschi by virtue of their geometrical concentricity. The enormous change which has taken place, despite all similarities, can be seen alone in the heavy entablature which separates the lower wall from the arches in Brunelleschi's Sacristy, bringing a sense of weight and organisation into the building. With its asymmetrical frescoes and its direct transition from one room to the next the Padua Baptistry was rooted squarely in medieval tradition.

But the fact that Giusto de' Menabuoni, like his fellow-countryman Giotto before him, had created an unusual feast for the eyes of the citizens of Padua is underlined by Michele Savonarola in *De Laudibus Patavii,* written in 1440; he singles Menabuoni out from all the other artists and praises his frescoes as 'so magnificent that on those days when access was granted it was crowded with people, none of whom wished to leave the building'.[164]

*   *   *

FLORENCE, SANTA FELICTÀ, BARBADORI CHAPEL, ARCADE SPANDREL

VII THE BARBADORI CHAPEL

FLORENCE, SANTA FELICITÀ, BARBADORI CHAPEL, INTERIOR VIEW

It was in Padua that Brunelleschi was able to visit the Monument to Antenor, which, with its pendentive dome resting on four arches, was reminiscent of the Barbadori Chapel. But Brunelleschi's creation differed from this rather heavy monument in many ways. The former is based on a framework of Gothic piers/half-columns while the latter retains a Romanesque structure: the baldaquin rests on four individual columns. But what both buildings have in common is the combination of a pendentive dome and a roughly square supporting structure.

Brunelleschi pays the price for the contradicting supporting elements and the heavy dome on top. The corner pilasters, which appear to lie flat against the facade and rise up to the architrave, are in fact square piers supporting the dome. On the inside of the baldaquin, i.e. where the engaged columns meet, the edge of the pier runs into the pendentive and disappears – a somewhat unsatisfactory solution! This fact was used to attribute the building to someone other than Brunelleschi, who was thought incapable of such lack of clarity. But what we have here is a more general problem of combining the main bulk of the building with the structuring elements. There is a similarly unfortunate combination of pilasters and wall in the Ospedale portal. Here the last columns of the arcade stand on their own next to the pilaster; here, too, what appears to be a pilaster set against the wall is revealed to be a supporting pier. Its lower half rises side by side with the columns, though independently, and runs directly into the spandrel, in other words is swallowed up by the wall.[165]

The Loggia di San Paolo also reveals an inability to resolve this problem. In fact it is increased because, as in the Barbadori Chapel, two sets of arches meet at a right-angle, so that the corner pier stands free. The body of the pier was bevelled between the two columns. It runs into the arch in much the same way as the corner pilasters in the Barbadori Chapel run into the dome. In principle the same problem had occurred with the pilasters of the

Ospedale, but had been more easily solved as a wall at right angles absorbs the pilaster so that the free-standing column supports both arches. Behind the capital of the column the fluting of the 'pilaster-pier' – the name itself expresses its ambivalent function – runs without any clear horizontal definition into the arch. The capital and abacus hide the end of the pilaster almost by chance. Had not the wall of the loggia held the pier, in other words, if the arcade had been open at the end of the loggia, then Brunelleschi would have been forced to find a solution similar to that used in the Barbadori Chapel and the Loggia di San Paolo. The corner of the 'pilaster-pier' would have presented a similar challenge.

In such places where two opposing principles clashed – the structuring elements and the undefined main mass of the building – Brunelleschi found no absolute solution and had to be content with a certain lack of clarity. This was a legacy of medieval architecture.

The small but important chapel in Santa Felicità contains other details which aroused criticism and led to doubts about Brunelleschi being the creator of the building. An example is the Corinthian capital used for the pilasters which differs from all other Corinthian capitals by Brunelleschi in the way the grooves of the upper row of leaves are drawn right down to the base of the neck. One can also point to the wide variety of models which were on offer. The capitals of San Miniato and San Giovanni are by no means uniform in their detail. The Florentine Renovatio offers examples both of capitals with grooves which stop short and of ones where they run right down to the base.

A comparison with the basic forms which served as models for Brunelleschi can clear up many misunderstandings. Of more critical significance was the form given to the architrave, which was unusual for Brunelleschi. The architrave of the Palazzo di Parte Guelfa had established a basic form from which Brunelleschi subsequently did not deviate. The upper ledge of the cornice is followed by three panels each of which ends in a convex moulding.[166] But the architrave of the Barbadori Chapel has a line of moulding below the upper cornice as well, which has an effect on the entire appearance of the architrave. The cornice takes on a role similar to the panels below and forms a link which points to the elements beneath. The Baptistry offered a model; its architrave has a similar moulding under the cornice and the panels below.

The architrave of the Barbadori Chapel is particularly close to the original model. It also shows Brunelleschi's metamorphosis of his model. In contrast to the architrave in the Baptistry, where from top to bottom the panels become narrower, Brunelleschi chose to maintain equal width of panels for the Palazzo di Parte Guelfa. To maintain the balance, he gave the lower panel a line of moulding, where the Baptistry architrave has a sharp edge. All these changes are found in the architrave of the Barbadori Chapel, which thus is mid-way between the model and the final version.

Thus these details should not be judged against the criterion of Brunelleschi's final fully developed style, and classified as the work of a poor imitator who has misunderstood Brunelleschi's intentions, but should be seen as stages in the development of a master who was gradually developing away from his original models;[167] in other words Brunelleschi himself. What we have here is the flexibility of forms for which strict rules have not yet been laid down. No other building by Brunelleschi displays so clearly the signs of his development. These include the soft curve of the bases of the columns with their rounded plinths, which are reminiscent of the bases of the columns in Orcagna's Tabernacle.

A final indication of Brunelleschi's involvement in the chapel is given by documents on the building of the dome of Florence Cathedral. Manetti had already stated that the vaulting for the Ridolfi Chapel had been demonstrated in a model without ground-scaffolding.[168] There is no similar indication of this for the Barbadori Chapel, but it is no coincidence that later both the Ridolfi family and a Barbadori were chosen for the important task of overseeing the building of the cathedral dome.

Bartolomeo Ridolfi held this office in 1423 and 1425,[169] and in 1426 Manetti names Schiatta Ridolfi[170] as responsible for the Ridolfi Chapel.[171] At the same time the influential position of consultant and representative of the Arte della Lana during the building of the cathedral dome was given to Gherardo Bartolomeo Barbadori.[172]

We can take the involvement of the Ridolfi and Barbadori as a confirmation of the fact that through the erection of their own family chapels by Brunelleschi they had gathered sufficient experience to be able to be involved in the decisions of the team building the cathedral dome.

FLORENCE, SAN LORENZO, PILASTER CAPITAL, SIDE-AISLE

FLORENCE, SANTA FELICITÀ, BARBADORI CHAPEL, CORNER CAPITALS

FLORENCE, BAPTISTRY, CAPITAL ON OUTER BLIND ARCADE

FLORENCE, BAPTISTRY, CAPITAL ON OUTER BLIND ARCADE

PADUA, MONUMENT OF ANTENOR

VIII FLORENCE AND PADUA

PADUA, MONUMENT OF ANTENOR, DOME

After Giotto's decoration of the Arena Chapel in Padua the artistic links between Florence and Padua continued well into the fourteenth century. As early as 1343 documents mention a certain Domenico da Firenze who worked for the Carrara family and was responsible for building the Loggia of the Carraras' palace,[173] which has survived, albeit in a heavily restored condition.

About 25 years later Giusto de' Menabuoni appears as the court artist for the Carrara. He was given a number of commissions in addition to the decoration of the Baptistry, and dominated the artistic scene in Padua until the rise of the Verona School under Altichiero and Avanzo. Even then, though, a Florentine artist, Cennino Cennini, whose name appears in a document of 1398, remained active in the service of the Carrara.

During the Early Renaissance Florentine artists came back into their own. In 1430 Pietro Lamberti and Nani di Bartolo (il Rosso) created the Monumento Fulgioso in San Antonio. In 1433 Filippo Lippi appeared and painted not only a tabernacle in the Santo but also the Capella de Podestà. These artists prepared the way for the appearance of Donatello in 1443. One of his main works, the high altar in San Antonio, was created during his residence in Padua. Under his guidance a Paduan school of sculpture emerged. Not least Mantegna was influenced strongly by Donatello. But among all these names of Florentine artists in Padua an unknown one deserves particular attention – Niccolo Baroncelli, who came to Padua in 1434 with Palla Strozzi. He was a pupil of Brunelleschi.

The close artistic connections between the two cities were also based on political links. Both Florence and Padua were under continual threat from the ambitions of the Visconti. In 1390 the Florentines had openly supported Francesco II against the Visconti and helped him to return to Padua from imprisonment in Milan. Caught between Milan and Venice Padua had become a buffer state; in 1404 it and Verona, under the Scaligi, were

149

conquered by Venice. Francesco II and Francesco III were executed, but the Carrara sons, Ubertina and Marsilio, escaped to Florence. Thus the heirs of the house of Carrara were in Florence from 1405 onwards.

Later on, when the city already belonged to Venice, Padua became a popular exile for the great families of Florence. Cosimo de' Medici was banished there for four years by the Balia, but soon moved to Venice.[174] In 1434 Palla Strozzi was exiled to Padua, and among his followers was that pupil of Brunelleschi's, Niccolo Baroncelli.

It was against this background of political events that the artistic links between the two cities developed. As part of this exchange of ideas, started in the Trecento, Brunelleschi will have become aware of Paduan buildings such as the Baptistry and the dome of the Santo choir. All the evidence suggests that he went himself to Padua and studied carefully what he acknowledged to have been models for him. The only report linking Brunelleschi personally with Paduan culture comes from Vasari, who mentions Paolo dal Pozzo Toscanelli as Brunelleschi's teacher. He returned to Florence at the age of 27 or 28 after studying in Padua, and was said to be a learned Astrologer and Mathematician who also had a knowledge of perspective.[175]

But another document points to a close link even at the conceptual stage between the Old Sacristy and the Padua Baptistry: if there was any church in Padua which was known to the Florentines, then it was the Baptistry, dedicated as it was to the patron saint of Florence, San Giovanni. The Florentines living there had therefore been coming to worship in the Baptistry since the fourteenth century.[176] Just as Michelangelo was later to build a church for the Florentines in Rome, San Giovanni dei Fiorentini, so too the Paduan Florentines had selected the Baptistry as their official place of assembly.

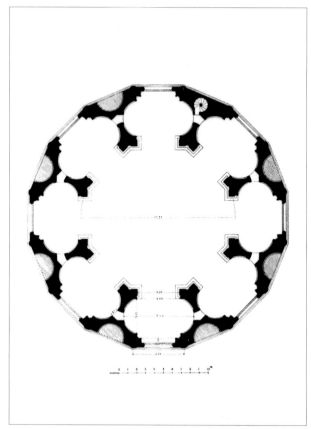

FLORENCE, SANTA MARIA DEGLI ANGELI, GROUND FLOOR PLAN
(AFTER SANPAOLESI)

FLORENCE, SANTA MARIA DEGLI ANGELI, ELEVATION
(AFTER SANPAOLESI)

FLORENCE, PAZZI CHAPEL, END WALL

PADUA, SAN ANTONIO, CHOIR, EXTERIOR

IX THE EARLY RENAISSANCE IN PADUA

PADUA, SAN ANTONIO, SAN FELICE CHAPEL, BLIND ARCADE

It is significant that even Jacob Burckhardt did not see fit to mention the humanistic culture of Padua. Yet it was there that in the early days of the Renaissance, between the tyranny of the Carrara and the rise of the bourgeoisie, that a Renaissance movement developed. Though not comparable to its Florentine counterpart, it had many similarities with the latter, and yet has been largely ignored by art historians.[178] Interest has been concentrated on Florence. A figure such as Giovanni Dondi, who went to Rome in the 1370s and made measurements of antique Roman buildings, was regarded as an exception.[179] It was not possible to ignore the court of the Carrara entirely, as Petrach spent much of his later life there under the patronage of Francesco Novello. But if one puts together all the individuals a picture begins to emerge of the importance of the early Paduan Renaissance.[180]

If Brunelleschi found his model for the Old Sacristy in Padua, then the road there had been prepared by more

than just the political links we have already mentioned. The conflict between the Cararra and the Visconti had made the rulers of Padua into natural allies of the Florentine Republic. After the expulsion of Francesco I it was with crucial help from the Florentines that his successor Francesco II was established and rapturously welcomed by the city as a guarantee of their further independence from Milan and Venice. It was in these years that the link between Coluccio Salutati and the Paduan humanist Vergerio bore fruit. The latter was the first person outside Florence to take up and defend the Florentine interpretation of Roman models as offering *libertas* to the *respublica*. After his return to Carrara he wrote a history of the House of Carrara and was probably the tutor of the young prince Ubertino who was later exiled to Florence.[181] There developed in Padua a strange mixture of humanistic tendencies which hovered between advocating tyranny and support for republican ideas; Giovanni Conversino sided with the princes and,

153

in his *Dramalogia* provided an exaggerated formulation of the conflict between the general usefulness of a tyrannical regime and the disadvantages of the communal movement.[182] The humanistic tradition in Padua can be traced back further than the presence of Petrach. As early as 1300 Albertino Mussato, a contemporary of Dante, had formulated the first civic humanism.

But how is the late fourteenth-century Paduan interest in Antiquity reflected in the art of the period? Giovanni Dondi, mentioned above, who took measurements of old Roman remains, mentions in a letter written in 1375 a sculptor who praised the old statues and apparently said of them that 'if they were not lifeless they would be better than the living, as though he wished to say that nature had not just been imitated but actually surpassed by the genius of the great artists'.[183] This statement contains in essence of the theory of art of the Renaissance.[184]

But Giovanni Dondi was not the only person in Padua to admire the monuments of ancient Rome. Ghiberti mentions as worthy of study certain antique statues which had been found in Rome, Siena and Florence during the late fourteenth century.[185] A statue of Venus discovered in the cellar vaulting of a house in Florence was brought to Padua by Seta di Lombardo, a courtier of the Carraras', and set up in his house. This offers us a further hint of a link between Brunelleschi and Padua, for the Florentine Venus acquired by Seta di Lombardo was, interestingly enough, discovered under one of Brunelleschi's houses.[186] It is perhaps also worth mentioning that Brunelleschi's father, Brunellescho di Lippo Lapi, in his function as notary and ambassador of the Florentine Republic, had been in several cities in Lombardy, including Padua, which at the time did not yet belong to Venice. This was probably around 1384, about seven years after the birth of his son Filippo.[187]

Monuments in Padua which adopted this late Trecento imitation of antique models were confined to those erected by the Carrara family and their followers.

In the portrayal of the Last Supper which makes up part of the Baptistry cycle the disciples are seated in a semi-circle around Christ. The table appears to follow the curve of a round building which, without any arcading, encloses the disciples. Above the outside wall, which is pierced by biforia, there is vaulting divided into unusually broad coffers of a kind which could only have been familiar from the Pantheon. The generous curve of the building leaves us in do doubt that this was a Trecento reinterpretation of the Roman building. During the entire Middle Ages it had been depicted on seals and maps as a trademark of the city of Rome, but never before had an attempt been made to represent the interior in a situation removed from the special associations with Rome. Giovanni Dondi's interest in Roman architecture is without artistic parallel.

The Carrara family themselves had expressed their interest in forms derived from imperial Roman culture when they had coins minted depicting Francesco I and II. These were created by an unknown artist towards the end of the Trecento, laying the foundations for the development of a form very typical for the Renaissance period: the medallion portrait.[188] It was thus not one of the great families of the time but the Carrara family, relatively insignificant in politics, who returned to this form, with its appeal to *aeternitas,* and created the first Italian medallions.

Petrarch himself very probably contributed to this Paduan study of ancient classical forms. He was a collector of Roman coins, and a personal friend of Giovanni Dondi.

It is even possible that Brunelleschi, on the visit to Padua which he presumably made in order to study the Baptistry and the dome of San Antonio, took in certain other, less obvious details. This would seem to have been the case if we look at the decoration of the spandrels in the arcades of the Capella di San Felice. These have six points which, like the tondi of the Ospedale degli Innocenti, are cut at the top by a horizontal ledge and contain depictions of human figures in their centres.[189]

Fabriczy also used an architectural detail to argue in favour of Brunelleschi's having visited Padua. He argued that the narrow gaps between the columns of balustrades,[190] e.g. in the Palazzo Pitti, were derived from the loggia of the Palazzo della Ragione. Such close placing of balustrade columns had become customary in the Veneto towards the end of the Trecento. In addition to this, the inspiration for the unusual inclusion of such a balustrade between the main columns, as in the entrance to the Pazzi Chapel, could be found in the same loggia and elsewhere. What Brunelleschi did not transfer were the Gothic capitals; he chose instead the Corinthian and Ionic 'orders'.

PADUA, BAPTISTRY, GIUSTO DE' MENABUOI, LAST SUPPER

PADUA, BAPTISTRY, VAULTING OF SIDE ARCADES IN CHOIR

X CONCLUSION

FLORENCE, PAZZI CHAPEL, INTERIOR

If we summarise the results presented here, two basic aspects of Brunelleschi's works emerge:

Firstly, the customary interpretation of his position *vis à vis* tradition will have to be reassessed. His link with the architecture of the Trecento go beyond mere similarities of certain forms such as a cornice or a wall console.[191] It is much more concrete than comparisons of a general nature, such as that the broad gap between the arcade columns in the Gothic churches of Florence are echoed in the nave of San Lorenzo.[192] The identification of such links is undoubtedly correct, but the realisation that an essential element of Brunelleschi's style, such as the composition of his walls, is derived directly from the composition of the walls of Florence Cathedral,[193] helps to explain the development of this style. In the light of this it seems to have been almost an aberration to concentrate only on individual classical forms and not to recognise the close link between his style and the Florentine Gothic.

Because the form and structure of the cathedral dome had been laid down at a time when Brunelleschi was not even born, in other words because they were conceived in a period which predates the dividing line used to separate the Medieval from the Modern period, they have had to suffer classification as 'Gothic' works, from a master who is otherwise classified as belonging the the Renaissance.[194] If one wished to take this attitude to its logical conclusion and erase all Gothic elements from his works then hardly anything would remain. A 'modern' ideology which measures the Renaissance purely by the classical elements it contains would end in absurdity.[195] The traditional element in Brunelleschi's works is usually sought in those areas where the name Renaissance was already heralded, namely in the 'Proto-Renaissance', the creations of the Florentine Romanesque period in the eleventh and twelfth centuries. Medieval Classicism is used to legitimise the traditional element in the Classicism of the

156

Renaissance.[196] Such a reference to the architecture of the Romanesque period implies a leap-frogging over the most recent traditions which Brunelleschi's works were seen as having 'transcended'. It is a very naive approach to history which sees change only in terms of a revolution which rejects all that went before, as though it was possible to break completely the continuum of history. The question of the extent to which a revolution retains elements of the system it wished to change is a general methodological problem for the historian. As far as Brunelleschi's works are concerned it can at least be said with some certainty that he did not simply brush aside the immediate past but rather took up important elements of it, changing them but also on occasion even retaining them.

His Classicism – the revolutionary aspect of his work – is much more independent and therefore radical than can be explained simply by reference to the medieval Renovatio (Proto-Renaissance). Brunelleschi made only very limited use of the rich source of classical forms found in the Florentine buildings of the eleventh and twelfth centuries. Although the first to give these forms a canonic value by his use of them, he seems to have deliberately selected the most typical and simple forms: the simple plinth, attic base, Ionic and Corinthian capital and the Corinthian pilaster, always with six rows of fluting. As soon as the frieze above the architrave received any decoration, Brunelleschi consistently used the egg and tongue and the billet design,[197] although this was one area where the imagination of the Florentine Romanesque had known no bounds. The architrave, too, with its lines of rounded moulding subdividing it became, apart from certain initial exceptions, a consistent form for Brunelleschi, and reappears always with the same structure and the same spacing between the lines of moulding; geometrical regularity replacing the optical impression of load-bearing created by a graded composition.

Brunelleschi did not primarily use the structural elements of classical architecture primarily to illustrate the tectonic principles involved. What he did frequently was link them with the wall, creating an almost figurative pattern against the surface. That is why his early elevations create such an impression of lightness. Yet the elements, unlike in the Romanesque period, have definite bulk and are not 'flattened' by the wall but rather stand out independently with their contrasting material.

What separates Brunelleschi both from the Renovatio and from his successors is his strict systematisation. The way in which he selects only certain elements from the vocabulary available to him from the past reveals a clearly defined intention. What he aimed at was not frivolous ornamentation, nor did he intend to offer the eye a diverting feast of decorative variety, but rather he wished to create a language which leaves nothing to chance, which establishes a reliable set of standards. In this aspect Brunelleschi is diametrically opposed to the Florentine Renovatio of the Middle Ages and is closer to the theoretically-based architectural rules reminiscent of Vitruvius and his sixteenth-century admirers. Brunelleschi later had supporters who emphatically defended his rules, among these Manetti. But it is not as though Brunelleschi became a dry classicist; however strictly consistent he was with individual forms, his creations as a whole display great imagination.

Such a new start in architecture must have tempted him to demonstrate the entire formal variety of the newly discovered classical antiquity. Only a clearly defined plan prevented him from doing so. An important aspect of Brunelleschi's innovatory approach is the way in which he systematically limited himself, thereby giving his works a hitherto unknown degree of individualisation. When craftsmen such as Albizzo di Piero and Betto d'Antonio created the ornamentation of the columns, capitals, architraves, entablatures and tondi of the Loggia degli Innocenti according to Brunelleschi's models, not the slightest element of any personal style of their own remained.[198] In Gothic buildings the individual stonemason was given considerable scope to incorporate spontaneous inspiration into his carving (even Talenti's model for the capitals of Florence Cathedral was not spared individual variation). But Brunelleschi, allowed no possibility of inspiration on the part of the individual craftsmen, but rather forced them to submit to his strict rules. This resulted in a consistency of style both in detail and in the whole which clearly bore the hallmark of the architect's personality. The massive, monumental architectural creation, which from time immemorial had been a product of the close co-operation of many different artists and craftsmen and had displayed all the characteristics of such a genesis, had now become the work of one single artist.

NOTES

Part I: Brunelleschi's Style

1   Vitruvius, *De Architectura Libri Decem*, ed and trans Curt Fensterbusch, Darmstadt, 1964, Vol 4, I, pp 166-174.

2   The term 'Classicism' ('classical') is used here and elsewhere to denote not the romantic classicism of the nineteenth century but rather a general stylistic approach which took the architecture of classical antiquity as its inspiration (cf Kurt Bauch, 'Klassik – Klassizität – Klassizismus' in *Das Werk des Künstlers*, Stuttgart, 1939/40, pp 429-40.

3   Leon Battista Alberti, *Ten Books on Architecture*, trans Max Theuer, Vienna and Leipzig, 1912, Vol 6, XIII, p 333.

4   Walter Paatz, *Werden und Wesen der Trecentoarchitektur*, Burg b M 1937, pp 70 ff and Notes 300, 309.

5   The capital and the base, which were temporarily added to the shaft during excavations probably come from a different source, as they hardly fit the octagonal column.

6   Similar examples are: the loggias of the *Ospedali* of Volterra and Lastra a Signa (see page 122).

7   The relief coat of arms of the Arte della Seta was only created by Francesco della Luna in 1439. It was originally positioned in the southern section of wall between the pilastres above the portico. Cf Cornel von Fabriczy, *Filippo Brunelleschi*, Stuttgart, 1892, p 576. The second relief was added during alterations in 1843.

8   Alberti assigned the plinth to the column from the outset: 'The elements of a column are the bottom plinth, above this the base, on the base the column, then the capital. . .' L B Alberti, trans 1912, Vol 7, VI, p 360.

9   Heydenreich already interpreted it thus. See: 'Spätwerke Brunelleschis', in *Jahrbuch der Preuss. Kunstsammlungen*, L II, 1931, p 14.

10   Cf. Howard Saalman, 'The Palazzo Comunale in Montepulciano', in *Zeitschrift für Kunstgeschichte*, XXVIII, 1965, pp 1-31; Gosebruch says very aptly of Michelozzo that 'he was able to change his formal language like a chameleon'. See: 'Florentinische Kapitelle von Brunelleschi bis zum Tempio Malatestiano und der Eigenstil der Frührenaissance', in *Römisches Jahrbuch für Kunstgeschichte*, VIII, 1958, p 129.

11   Martin Gosebruch, 'Varieta bei Leon Battista Alberti und der wissenschaftliche Renaissancebegriff', in *Zeitschrift für Kunstgeschichte*, XX, 1957, pp 229-38.

12   'But the most superb element in the decoration of the walls and ceilings is the incrustation itself, apart, of course, from the columns.' L B Alberti, trans 1912, Vol 6, V, p 308.

13   Heydenreich, 'Gedanken über Michelozzo di Bartolomeo', in *Festschrift für Wilhelm Pinder*, Leipzig, 1938, p 267, brings out most clearly the contrast between Brunelleschi and Michelozzo: ' . . . in Michelozzo's works we meet a treatment and use of architectural decoration which is in strong contrast to that of Brunelleschi, for while the latter displays a minimum of variation, the former uses a maximum'.

14   Cf Fabriczy, 1892, p 342.

15   The capitals of the Ospedale portal differ from all other capitals by Brunelleschi by virtue of the egg and tongue decoration of the calathos lip; they thus take on a composite character.

16   Howard Saalman, 'Filippo Brunelleschi: Capital Studies', in: *Art Bulletin*, XL, 1958, pp 113-137; Martin Gosebruch, 1958; Euginio Luporini, *Brunelleschi*, Milan, 1964, pp 170-95. It is not necessary to add a fourth interpretation and chronology to these existing studies. On the other hand the claim made by Martin Gosebruch 1958, p 78, that two of the capitals in the left-hand entrance hall of the cathedral of Pistoia are the real precursors of Brunelleschi's volute capitals, requires reassessment. To my mind they do not, as Gosebruch assumes, date from 1200 but rather were created when the portal was renewed in 1449. In the cloisters of S Francesco in Pistoia, together with a Gothic-type capital, one can find one volute capital which repeats Brunelleschi's Corinthian capital in a rather coarsened form, but can no more have been its precursor than the capitals of the cathedral portal. Brunelleschi's volute capital was used as a model throughout Tuscany in the first half of the Quattrocento, but was frequently simplified and coarsened. In the cathedral of Arezzo, whose main arches were built up towards the middle of the century, Brunelleschi's capital even reappears on a composite pier. Apart from the above objections the stylistic characteristics of the capitals in Pistoia suggest they were not created around 1200. The fleshy leaves, whose veins are ill-defined, as though they had been carved in soft clay, suggest the capital carving of the Trecento supplied the models. The helix volutes are revealingly close to Brunelleschi's Ospedale capitals, although the 'stem' which grows up out of the middle row of leaves is missing. Instead of these one finds the ornamental lines which virtually cut through the stems and emphasise the calathos surface. On the capital of San Francesco the same lines serve rather better as grooving for the stems. This translation of what was originally an organic form into an ornamental one strongly suggests that Brunelleschi's capital already existed as a model.

17   Saalman, 1958, p 115, in contrast to Gosebruch, points specifically to the established type of capital for Brunelleschi: 'This passion for reduction and regularisation of forms and the absolute uniformity of identical details comprise the novelty and distinguishing characteristics of Brunelleschi's style. . .'

18   Gosebruch, 1957, specifically separates Alberti's *varietas* from medieval traditions as being a particular characteristic of the Renaissance and sees it as being something which all three architects of the Florentine Renaissance had in common. It seems to me, on the other hand, that in Michelozzo this variety of forms retains something of the medieval tendency merely to play with formal variants, particularly in the case of the change of capital decoration. Whereas Brunelleschi retains the Corinthian capital for all his buildings, even Alberti changed his decoration from one building to the next, although he does not go as far as Michelozzo, who presents four different types of capitals in *one* building: the Tabernacle of San Miniato al Monte. Alberti comes between Brunelleschi and Michelozzo in this respect; he was consistent in adhering to one type of decoration within each building, provided the interior of the Tempio Malatestiano is not ascribed to him. But when Gosebruch, 1958, pp 170-189, uses precisely this confusing variety of decoration as an example for his concept of a *varietas* peculiar to the Renaissance ('Here the *varietas* appears not to be a category subordinated to a superior statement, but rather the statement itself . . .', p 170; 'the programme is *varieta e copia*, p 189), he is undermining the concept won from Alberti's theory of art by referring to this real 'executed' example, whose variety of decoration may differ from the medieval 'randomness'; in the language of the decoration but not in the way it is used (like, for example, an 'unsystematic' variation of capitals in a basilica colonnade). See Heinrich Klotz, 'L B Alberti's *De re aedificatoria* in Theorie und Praxis', in *Zeitschrift für Kunstgeschichte*, XXXII, 1969, pp 93-103.

19   Saalman, 1958, and Luporini, 1964, ignore the throated capital. Martin

Gosebruch specifically stresses the high quality of the capitals in the Barbadori Chapel (1958, pp 82-4). To understand Brunelleschi's capitals it is important to be aware that in addition to the Corinthian capitals he also consistently repeated the Ionic capital; in other words he recognised a first general order and a second minor one.

20 On the ascribing of the Barbadori Chapel to Brunelleschi, see pp 24-31, 145-6.

21 Our illustration shows the interior with a smooth calathos. On the exterior there is egg and tongue moulding.

22 Brunelleschi's authorship is not certain. I assess this capital in connection with the building of the corridor which leads to the great hall (see pp 72 ff).

23 Under the supervision of Francesco della Luna, 1436. Fabriczy, 1892. pp 574 ff.

24 The date of the completion of the dome of the portal '1461 A DI 10 di Giugno'; Sanpaolesi, 1962, p 82. See also: G Laschi, P Roselli, P A Rossi, 'Indagine sulla Cappella dei Pazzi', in Commentari. XIII, 1962, pp 24-41. This raises the question of whether Brunelleschi had planned such a portal at all. As in other cases, his successors appear to have adhered largely to his suggestions. The facade of S Andrea a Camoggiano seems to repeat the facade originally planned for the Pazzi Chapel, as reconstructed by Folnesics, Brunelleschi. Vienna, 1915, pp 57-9; see Mario Salmi, 'Sant'Andrea a Camoggiano e la Cappella de' Pazzi, in Festschrift Ulrich Middeldorf, Berlin, 1968, pp 136-9.

25 In the discussion which follows, the balustrade capitals on the facade of the Palazzo Pitti have been ignored, on account of the uncertainty surrounding their authorship. On the balustrades inside the cathedral dome (see page 22) which definitely go back to Brunelleschi's plan, a simplified form of the Ionic throated capital returns at a later date, when the floor slabs of the parapet were laid in 1441 (see Fabriczy, 1892, p136).

26 Cf note 25.

27 Brunelleschi's authorship has more recently been put in doubt: Ursula Schlegel, 'La Cappella Barbadori e l'architettura fiorentina del primo Rinascimento', in Rivista d'Arte, XXXII, 1957, pp 77-106. Cf, by contrast, pp 145-6.

28 M Gosebruch, 1958, p 82, correctly refers to the columns as 'secondary' column. The question has often been asked whether Brunelleschi was familiar with Vitruvius' treatise. Francesco Pellati, 'Vitruvio e Brunelleschi', in La Rinascita, II, 1939, pp 343-65, offers compelling evidence that this was the case, and retracts his statement in his monograph on Vitruvius (Rome 1938) that Brunelleschi completely ignored Vitruvius. Fabriczy, 1892, p 40, Note 1, also makes remarks which suggest that Brunelleschi was familiar with Vitruvius: 'But if the architectural treatise in the Magliabechiana cobbled together from Vitruvius' writings... were, as some researchers would have it, the work of Lorenzo Ghiberti, then it would hardly be possible not to allow also for Brunelleschi, his contemporary and colleague, to have been familiar with the Roman writer. Those voices which ascribe the code to Lorenzo's grandson, Buonaccorso, are the ones which really deserve to be heard.' On the other hand, since Schlosser's research we have known that Lorenzo Ghiberti quoted Vitruvius at length in his Memorabilia. Ghiberti even mentions Vitruvius as his sourse: 'Dice Vitruvio...' (I Commentarii, Berlin, 1912, I, p 19); cf also the large number of passages parallel to Vitruvius' treatise, ibid, II; Julius von Schlosser unquestioningly assumed that Ghiberti knew Vitruvius, cf ibid, II, 12 passim. An important passage in Gombrich also confirms that Ghiberti was in close touch with the humanists of his age and borrowed the newly discovered classical manuscripts, including the illustrated manuscript

by Athenaeus on siege machines. The owner of the book, Aurispa, wrote on 2nd January, 1430, to the humanist monk Ambrogio Traversari that he wished to swap with Ghiberti a Virgil manuscript which he had borrowed from him, for the Athenaeus (see E H Gombrich, 'The Renaissance Conception of Artistic Progress', reprinted in: Norm and Form, Studies in the Art of the Renaissance, London, 1966, p 5). Alberti, of whom Manetti said he was the first to record the modern rules of architecture, studied Vitruvius while Brunelleschi was still living, as can be noted from his treatise Della Pittura. completed in 1435 (see L B Alberti, Kleinere kunstthe oretische Schriften, ed H Janitschek, Vienna, 1877, p 113, 137). This, too, provided Fabriczy, 1892, p 345, with a source of far-reaching conclusions: 'As this work was dedicated by its author, who had only just returned to his homeland, to Brunelleschi, one may assume that the two great minds knew each other already, and that Alberti would have discussed some of the Vitruvian problems with his older contemporaries. But this late, indirect and unsystematic familiarisation with the teaching of the Roman writer will have without doubt had no influence on Brunelleschi's work...' The list of Vitruvian manuscripts put together by Carol Herselle Krinsky ('Seventy-eight Vitruvius Manuscripts', in: Journal of the Warburg and Courtauld Institutes, XXX, 1967, pp 40 ff) shows that long before the St Gallen manuscript was discovered by Poggio in 1416 at least two Vitruvius manuscripts were available in Florence. In 1359 Nicola Acciainoli left his books, including a Vitruvius manuscript, to the library of S Lorenzo (see R Sabbadini, 'I libri a la stampa', Bulletino Ufficiale della Società Bibliografica Italiana, 1907, pp 33-5, 37, 39). Boccaccio left his Vitruvius to a monk of S Spirito (1374). The manuscript remained even after the latter's death in the 'parva liberia' of the convent (see Arthur Goldmann, 'Drei italienische Handschriftenkataloge', pp VII-XV, in Centralblatt für Bibliothekswesen, IV, 1887, pp 139, 151).

29 Alste Horn-Oncken, 'Über das Schickliche, Studien zur geschichte der Architekturtheorie I', Abh der Akademie der Wissenschaften in Göttingen, Phil-Hist. Klasse 3, Folge, 11.

30 The earliest examples are the arcades of Diocletian's camp in Spalato. Gustavo Giovannino, 'Leptis Magna e l'architettura del Rinascimento', in Palladio, I, 1937, pp 3-16, proved the existence of arcades with rounded arches in Servian architecture, ie some hundred years earlier than Spalato. For a summary of this problem see Hans Sedlmayr, 'Spätantike Wandsysteme', in Epochen und Werke, I, Vienna and Munich, 1959, pp 31-79.

31 Alberti, trans 1912, Vol 7, XV, p 396: 'In the case of arcades the columns must be quadrangular.' However in the first book Alberti is less emphatic: 'Closely spaced columns are linked with a beam, widely-spaced ones with an arch.' Vol 1, XII, p 61. It is therefore not true that Alberti 'speaks out in principle against combining columns and arches': Heydenreich, 1931, p 14, Note 3. We can assume that in the first volume Alberti is reflecting Florentine traditions, and is thinking both of Brunelleschi's closely-spaced colonnade with architrave above in the Pazzi portal in Santa Croce, and of the broadly spaced colonnade with archivolt in the Ospedale; later, in the seventh volume, he is referring only the Roman model, cf Klotz, 1969, pp 98 ff.

32 The authorship has recently been confirmed by Manfred Wundram, 'Albizzo di Piero', in Das Werk des Künstlers, Festschrift zum 60. Geburtstag für Hubert Schrade, Stuttgart, 1960, pp 169 ff.

33 See p 145 ff.

34 In the Ospedale the outer columns stand independent of the pilasters, as also in Donatello's Tabernacle of Or San Michele. But the motif of the transcending pilaster and the column which carries the archivolt is not put in question.

35 Cf Note 34.

36 Fabriczy, 1892, p 172.

37 Heydenreich, 1931, p 14, refers to the ring of chapels in S Trinità

38 'The continuous base linking half-column and the corners of the piers still retains something of the transcending shapes of the medieval period, such as the quatrefoil.' Gosebruch, 1958, p 83.

39 Antonio di Tuccio Manetti, *Filippo Brunellesco*, ed Heinrich Holtzinger, Stuttgart, 1887, pp 41-3, first names the Ospedale and then immediately afterwards the Barbadori Chapel. I am quoting the edition edited by Holtzinger, as the edition prepared from a second manuscript by A Chiapelli is more difficult to obtain and does not deviate from Holtzinger's edition in the passages quoted here. 'In general, observations would suggest that the Capella Barbadori was created at an early stage, and if there were any documentary evidence available one could even place it *before* the foundling hospital.' Gosebruch, 1958, p 83. By contrast Ursula Schlegel, see Note 27.

40 Paolo Fontana, 'Il Brunelleschi e l'architettura classica', in *Archivio Storico del'Arte*, VI, 1893, pp 256-67.

41 Apart from those made of brick (the so-called 'Backsteingothik'), and the buildings of the mendicant orders, cf Richard Krautheimer, *Die Kirchen der Bettelorden in Deutschland*, Cologne, 1925.

42 The ledge divides the fronts of the buttresses into regular sections.

43 See Marvin Trachtenberg's work in preparation on the Florence Campanile.

44 Werner Gross, *Die abendländische Architektur um 1300*, Stuttgart, 1947, pp 148-300.

45 Folnesics, Vienna, 1915, p 36, points specifically to 'the ledge, which still protrudes very little'.

46 Cesare Gusti, *Santa Maria del Fiore*, Florence, 1887, p 299, Doc 425.

47 In a talk given in Göttingen (autumn 1968), Howard Saalman drew attention to the fact that the elevation of the side aisles did not match Brunelleschi's original plan. However the question remains whether the change in the plans was perhaps made by Brunelleschi himself, so that the architects who followed him, initially Michelozzo, based their work on the elevation determined by Brunelleschi. Leonardo Benevolo is preparing a monograph on S Lorenzo which will look into this problem in greater detail. I would prefer to reserve judgement until the works announced by Saalman and Benevolo have appeared in print. In any case the elevation of the wall of the side aisle in S Lorenzo can serve as an example of the lasting influence of Florence Cathedral.

48 The typical Italian elevation, with great arcade arches rising up without any horizontal divisions into the triforium, had been established since the thirteenth century, cf Renate Wagner-Rieger, *Die italienische Baukunst zu Beginn der Gotik I (Oberitalien)*, Graz and Cologne, 1956.

49 Which does not mean that all that occurred was a mechanical exchange of forms. It goes without saying that Brunelleschi's creation was more than just this.

50 Similar tendencies can be observed in the second half of the fourteenth century in other buildings in Florence, for example Or San Michele, where the tondi on the exterior have frames which penetrate the wall in a similar fashion.

51 Cf Heydenriech, 1931, pp12 ff.

52 Already in the Pazzi Chapel the niches and windows have fuller and heavier frames. The combination of cornice and torus brings a new effect to what initially had been much more delicate frames (Old Sacristy). Such details could suggest that the Pazzi Chapel stands at the transition to Brunelleschi's late works. See Heydenreich, 1931, esp p 2.

53 Ibid.

54 Even Manetti reports that Brunelleschi's first ribbed vaulting for the Ridolfi Chapel was referred to by contemporaries as consisting of 'crests and sails' ('che si dice ancora a creste ed a vela'). Ed Stuttgart, 1887, p 29.

55 Geymüller, 1885-93, I, p 17. Fabriczy, 1892, p 192, expresses agreement.

56 Geymüller, ibid, p 25.

57 The vehemence of the argument which flared up between Brunelleschi and his contemporaries about the decoration of the church is illustrated most clearly by the disagreement between Brunelleschi and Donatello, who, without Brunelleschi's agreement had decorated the choir wall of the Old Sacristy with portal aedicules and large terracotta reliefs. For this he was, according to Manetti, severely rebuked by Brunelleschi, who even wrote satirical verse attacking him ('certi sonetti'): 'Le quali cose sue della sagrestia e ciascuna di per se, e tutte insieme, non ebbono mai la grazia di Filippo, il che veggendo ed intendendo Donato, furono cagione di grande indignazione verso Filippo. . . Pure, dopo le molte, perseverando Donato nelle sue prosunzioni, e per purgarsi Filippo pe'tempi, che le porticciuole de'macigni, che hanno per usci i bronzi, non fussino sue, nè nulla, che fussi in quelle facciuole delle porticciuole tra pilastro e pilastro, dalla cappella alle mura de'canti, costrinse Filippo a fare certi sonetti, che ancora se ne truova qualcuno, che lo purgano di tutto.' Manetti, ed 1887, pp 49 ff. This argument reflects ultimately the contrast between Brunelleschi, concerned solely with pure architecture, and Donatello, who in his concern to achieve maximum plastic decorative effect converted all architecture into sculpture, covering his tabernacles, chancels and choir galleries with ornamentation which hardly allowed the purely architectural elements to exist independently.

58 Giorgio Vasari, *Le Vite*, ed Gaetano Milanesi, Florence, 1881, VII, p 691. '. . . La quale convenzione fatta, mi ricordai avere inteso che Filippo di ser Brunellesco architetto di quelle chiesa [S Lorenzo] avea data quella forma a tutte le cappelle, acciò in ciascuna fusse fatta, non una piccola tavola, ma alcuna storia o pittura grande, che empiesse tutto quel vano'. Thus Brunelleschi had planned a large picture for each chapel which would fill the empty space. No mention is made of any fresco.

59 Hans Kauffmann, *Donatello*, Berlin, 1935, p 38; cf also Hans Sedlmayr, *Epochen und Werke, I*, Vienna and Munich, 1959, p 222; cf also the statements made about Brunelleschi's purism in the essay shortly to appear by R Hatfield, 'Some Unknown Descriptions of the Medici Palace in 1459', in *Art Bulletin*, LII, 1970.

60 Cesare Guasti, *La Cupola di Santa Maria del Fiore*, Florence, 1857, p 39 (Doc 75, report of January 1425 included).

61 Guiseppe Marchini pointed out that the entire tribuna, including the front of the piers was intended to be painted (see 'Il palazzo Datini a Prato', in *Bolletino d'Arte*, XLVI, 1961, 212-218). On the other hand there is evidence to suggest that the choir tribuna itself was to retain the 'intonaco', ie uniform white or single-colour walls. Among documents relating to the construction of the tribuna published by Cesare Guasti, Florence, 1887, there are three which mention painting: of these two refer to the painting of the coats of arms at the tops of the great octagonal arches, (Doc 332, 1382, Coats of arms of Liberty; Doc 417, 1399, Lily coat of arms), and another (Doc 310, 1380) gives the commission to 'Jacopo Cionis vocato Robbiccia pictori, qui pinsit corum novum ecclesie Sancte Reparate, ad rationem soldorum duorum f.p. pro quodlibet bracchio quadro'. Thus the painting was calculated per square yard. If one considers how poor the payment of two soldi per 'bracchio quadro' is, it would seem beyond doubt that the passage referred to nothing more than a uniform one-colour wash. One might assume that this was intended to be temporary, to await the completion

of the building. But the coloured rendering of the *Libertas* coat of arms two years later speaks against this. Around 1430-40 all that was added was the framed frescoes of the saints below the windows of the chapels which sit entirely on their own on the wall and restrict the painting to a very limited area. They relate to the altar, so that the frescoes have a similar effect to the individual altar pictures in the side chapels of S Spirito. Thus, if in 1380 there was still a plan to paint the tribuna any further, it had undoubtedly been dropped by Brunelleschi's time – the years 1430-40 – when the individual frescoes of saints were put under the windows as isolated 'pictures'.

62 Ghiberti, *Memorabilia*, trans Julius von Schlosser, Berlin, 1920, pp 50 ff; also his *I Commentari*, Berlin, 1912, p 35.

63 Alberti, trans 1912, Vol 7, X, p 381.

64 Alberti, ibid. See Klotz, 1969 on this.

65 Although this is not to say that Alberti would have identified with such unrestrained richness. Nevertheless, the sculptors working here met Alberti's preference for 'plastic statues rather than pictures' for the decoration of the temple (cf trans 1912, Vol 7, X, p 381).

66 M C Mendes Atanásio and Giovanni Dallai, 'Nuove indagini sullo Spedale degli Innocenti a Firenze', in *Commentari*, XVII, 1966, Doc XVI.

67 The Roman origin of the Baptistry was clear for Salutati, who claimed to see in this building from the eleventh and twelfth centuries the former temple of Mars: '. . . et teplum olim Martis insigne quem gentilitas romani generis volebat auctorem; et templum non graeco non tusco more factum, sed plane romano.' Ernst H Gombrich was the first to draw attention to this statement by Salutatis and he added the (already known) description of the Baptistry from Giovanni da Prato's *Paradiso degli Alberti*, in which the so-called Roman qualities of the building are praised lavishly and rhetorically (see Gombrich, 'From the Revival of Letters to the Reform of the Arts', in *Essays in the History of Art Presented to Rudolf Wittkower*, 1967, pp 78 ff.)

Part II: Brunelleschi's Early Works

1 The diameter of the Pantheon dome is 43.50 metres, ie only 1.50 metres more than that of the Florence dome, for the planning of which the dimensions of the Pantheon undoubtedly served as a model. cf Fabriczy, 1892, p 130, note 1.

2 '. . . the contents of the programme of April 1420', (in which the principles for the construction of the dome were established), 'refer only to the constructional details of the building, laying down the strength, number and dimensions of vaulting, struts, retaining rings, passages, arches, rain channels, and the type of masonry and materials to be used. Only one of the points dealt with refers to an artistic detail. . .' Fabriczy, 1892, p 123.

3 'Fece pensiero di ritrovare 'l modo de'murari eccellenti e di grand' artificio degli antichi e le lore proporzioni musicali. . .' Manetti, ed 1887, p 16 '. . . vide 'l modo del murare degli antichi e il loro simetrie . . .' Ibid, p 8.

4 'Perch' egli appariva in lui. . . maraviglioso ingegno, molto era richiesto di consigli di muramenti. . . ' Ibid, p 8.

5 Ibid, p 41.

6 Fabriczy, 1892, p 609.

7 Guasti, 1887, p 316, Docs 473 and 475.

8 Giovanni Gaye, *Carteggio inedito d'artisti*, I, Florence 1839, p 545. Fabriczy, 1907, pp 609 ff.

9 Giuseppe Marchini, *Il Tesoro del Duomo di Prato*, Milan, 1963, p 102, No 41. Sottosezione dell'Archivio di Stato di Prato; archivio del patrimonio ecclesiastico, 62(pe), c 38v-39rv. Marchini gives the follow-

ing interpretation: '. . . quando nel 1412 si vollero riprenderne i lavori. Ed ecco allora le consultazioni con personalità fiorentine eminenti: con Nanni Niccoli. . . e sopratutto. . . col Brunelleschi, che venne in quell' anno due volte a Prato. Può esser questo un indizio del fatto che l'artista, abbandonata la practica del' orafo, avesse già dato quei saggi delle sue possibiltà di costruttore cui accennano le fonti. Ma si conferma come principale artefice della costruzione Niccolo di Piero Lamberti, detto il Pela, che risulta aver dato misure precise sul posto ed eseguito un disegno o un modello colorato (nonostante che esista notizia d'un modello avanzato da Giov. d'Ambrogio).' Ibid, p 62.

10 According to it, Nanni di Banco seems to have started to work with Brunelleschi as early as 1412, and in 1419 the two of them produced the great stone model for the new dome of Florence Cathedral. See Guasti, 1857, p 25, Doc 43.

11 Such a division of labour was customary on fourteenth-century Florentine – and indeed all medieval – construction sites. In Florence a differentiation was made between the 'magistri scharpelli' and the 'magistri chazzuole sive murandi'. Even the top position of *capudmagister* could be shared by two masters: 'duo capudmagistri: unus murorum, alter scharpelli'. See Guasti, 1887, p 262, Doc 334 (10th November 1382).

12 Ibid, p 299, Doc p 425.

13 Ibid, p 302, Doc 434; ie not 1406 as Fabriczy, 1892, p 543, states.

14 From 28th February 1400 to 19th October 1418 Giovanni d'Ambrogio was sole *capudmagister* in Florence. When Brunelleschi and Nanni di Banco are referred to as being 'capimaestri' during their work in Prato this does not reflect their true position; probably this was an attempt to justify their presence in Prato by underlining their particular qualifications – which itself proves that already in 1412 Brunelleschi was regarded as a 'magister muratorum'. This important document at last provides some explanation of Brunelleschi's sudden appearance in 1417 (ff) as an applicant for the task of constructing the cathedral dome, and thus makes his entrance into the centre of the artistic scene rather less surprising than it has been hitherto.

15 Manetti, ed Heinrich Holtzinger, Stuttgart 1887, pp 8 ff.

16 Ibid, p 9

17 'E quivi si può vedere ancora che, in quanto a' conci, quello, che s' usava a' sua di, e' non gli piaceva, e non vi poteva stare su, però gli usò altrimenti; e quel modo, che prese poi, non sapeva ancora, che lo prese poi ch'egli ebbe veduto e' muramenti antichi de' Romani'. Ibid, p 9.

18 Fabriczy, 1892, p 53.

19 Erwin Panofsky, *Early Netherlandish Painting*, Cambridge, Mass, 1953, p 412, note 2. On the following, the same author, *Renaissance and Renaissances*, Copenhagen, 1960, p 165: 'And as Brunelleschi's work reveals the influence of such pre-Gothic Tuscan structures as S Miniato and the Badia of Fiesole, so did the great Flemish painters of his time develope an interest in their indigenous Romanesque – an interest which in Jan van Eyck reached the proportions of a genuine revival, based upon systematic, almost archaeological study and extending from architecture and sculpture to the murals, niellos, stained glass and epigraphy.

'To a considerable extent this "Romanesque revival" was motivated by iconographical considerations. . . This does not, however, preclude but rather presupposes a purely aesthetic relevance of the phenomenon: the fathers of Early Netherlandish painting were evidently attracted by the Romanesque style *qua* style. . . the substantial sturdiness and poise of Romanesque structures (dramatically apparent in the use of circular rather than pointed or three-centred arches) were bound to appeal to Jan van Eyck in much the same way as they did to Brunelleschi. . . '

20 Panofsky, 1953, p 412, note 2.

21 It would not have been possible to create a link between the window consoles and a continuing wall of stone blocks.

22 Cf pp 98 ff.

23 Geymüller, 1885-93, I, 26, had already raised the question of whether the round-arched windows of the Sala dei Cinquecento could not be the work of Brunelleschi. Fabriczy, 1892, p 53, however, rejected this attribution, stating that the hall had only been built towards the end of the Quattrocento by Cronaca.

24 Vasari, ed Milanesi, II, 1878, p 366.

25 The three documents derive from an earlier common source, cf Fabriczy, 1892, p 53, note 3; ibid, pp 412-29.

26 Saalman, 1965, p 34, note 40.

27 The letting of the commercial rooms ('botteghe') in 1442 may have been a re-letting, and therefore does not necessarily relate to the date of completion of the palazzo. Saalman himself assumes the latest possible date (c1427) for the commencement of work (see op cit, list p 45) – which is hardly possible, given the size of the building and the fact that the twelve monolithic columns of the cortile themselves would have taken some time to produce.

28 Fabriczy, 1892, p 55, ruled out Brunelleschi for the palazzo: '. . . the unstructured archivolts and the extremely fragile ledges (in the court-yard) are so strongly redolent of the Gothic that we must rule out Brunelleschi as the author'. By contrast compare Hans Willich, *Die Baukunst der Renaissance in Italien*, I, Berlin, 1914, p 17: 'In my opinion the palazzo can be the work of none other than Brunellesco, and indeed is probably not even one of his earliest works. What speak against this are the particularly beautiful proportions of the arcades, which seem a more mature work than those in the Ospedale'. Sanpaolesi, *Brunelleschi*, Milan, 1962, p 93 ff, has been the most recent author to devote some brief remarks to the palazzo, but without looking at its historical position. Finally Saalman included the building in his exhaustive catalogue of Michelozzo's works (see note 27), an assumption which will have to be examined.

29 The staircases are, in their present form, products of the sixteenth century – originally a further doorway in the rear wall of the courtyard led into a garden.

30 Manetti, ed 1887, p 8.

31 Alste Horn-Oncken, 1967.

32 Michelozzo frequently used these forms of consoles and ledges, which we do not find in Brunelleschi's work. cf also the 'model collection' which Saalman, 1965, put together.

33 Cf note 37.

34 Manetti, ed 1887, pp 43 ff.

35 There is still uncertainty regarding the beginning of the work on the new palazzo by Brunelleschi. Jodoco del Badia, 'Il vecchio palazzo della Parte Guelfa', in *Bolletino dell'Associazione per la difesa di Firenze antica*, III, Florence 1902, pp 63-74, pointed out that as early as 1377 the site for the new palazzo had been acquired. However, the documents put together by Fabriczy, 'Brunelleschiana', in *Jahrbuch der Königlich Preussischen Kunstsammlungen*, XXVIII, supplement, 1907, pp 58-66, throw some light on the building process. In a document dated 17th September 1422 a reference is made to work on the palazzo having already started: 'Ut incepta pro honore dicte partis in hedifitio et constructione palatii partis eiusdem celeriter perficiantur' (p 58). The next document, dated 28th November, 1425, also gives no precise information on the state of the building: '. . . Incepta pro honore partis et perfectione novi Palatii Partis eiusdem ad celerem expeditionem reducere et recipere. . . ' (p 60). Fabriczy relates the first report to the basic bottom storey, and thus assumes that work on Brunelleschi's new

palazzo started around 1425. But this allows a relatively generous stretch of time between the dates. If one keeps in mind that the choice of the 'Offiziales Muraglie' must have occurred before 1418 (Fabriczy himself stresses this), then it is possible that the palazzo itself was begun before 1418. In the period of at least four years, betwen 1418 and 1422, the bottom storey could well have been built, so that it is possible, indeed more probable, that the document of 1422 is already referring to Brunelleschi's new building. Manetti counted the building of the Parte Guelfa among Brunelleschi's first works. According to him only the Barbadori Chapel and the Ospedale were started earlier; Ernst H Gombrich, 1967, pp 79 ff, probably goes too far when he assumes that this building marked the first introduction of the new formal language of classicism to Florence. The Sacristy of S Trinità, started by Ghiberti and Michelozzo in 1418 proves that this trend already existed before Brunelleschi's first buildings. New light is shed from another quarter on the activities of the Parte Guelfa around 1420. It is simply not true that the Parte – as is generally assumed in research on Brunelleschi – was already on the decline when the new palazzo was started as a symbol of power which they were already losing. The opposite is the case; in 1420 the Parte Guelfa – significantly enough – received new statutes and new important tasks as the official defender of the freedom of the city, the programmatic *libertas* pointed to by Hans Baron, *The Crisis of Early Italian Renaissance*, 2nd Ed, Princeton, 1966, pp 20 ff, and Gene A Brucker, *Florentine Politics and Society, 1343-1378*, Princeton, 1962, pp 99-100. The fact that this occurrence cannot have been without significance is indicated by the name alone of the individual who revised these statutes: Leonardo Bruni. It was Bruni who, with Coluccio Salutati in his *Laudatio* had invoked the republican city of Rome as the mother of Florence; it would seem a reasonable conclusion to draw that at the same time as the political programme was drawn up the decision was made to create a visible symbol, ie, to build a 'Roman', classical palazzo which would embody the new values in visible form. Political reform and architectural innovation were two sides of the same coin. Leonardo Bruni may have played an important role in the development of the new classical architecture, for he also figured largely in the creation of the Ospedale – it was his suggestion which led to the founding of this communal welfare institution (see Fabriczy, 1892, pp 246 ff).

36 Translation according to Fabriczy, 1892, p 293. Manetti, ed 1887, pp 44 ff.

37 The incomplete building cannot have been intended to be built much higher than the present wall coping, which was built at a later date.

38 Cf Pietro Toesca, *Il Trecento*, Turin, 1964, p 36, note: 'In questa (S Stefano) la parte superiore della facciata è del Trecento e nella finestra centrale preludia al Rinascimento.' The similarity between the moulding and the upper windows of Or San Michele makes it possible to ascribe it to Simone Talenti.

39 *Filarete's Treatise on Architecture*, ed John R Spencer, New Haven and London, 1965, II, fol 58v; cf also fol 120 r.

40 Vasari, ed Milanesi, II, 1878, p 380.

41 Gosebruch, 1958, p 92

42 Manetti, ed 1887, p 45.

43 Vasari, ed Milanesi, II, 1878, p 380.

44 Mario Salmi, 'Il Palazzo della Parte Guelfa de Firenze e Filippo Brunelleschi', in *Rinascimento*, II, 1951, pp 3-11.

45 Cf p 16.

46 The centre torus in the frame of the blind windows in the Pazzi Chapel is similar.

47 On the other hand Saalman, 1965, p 44, ascribes all parts of the palazzo

apart from Brunelleschi's main block to Michelozzo. Saalman's oeuvre-catalogue brings together the most heterogeneous buildings under Michelozzo's name. However many different aspects there may have been to his formal language, it would seem highly dubious to ascribe to Michelozzo virtually all the major Florentine palazzi whose authorship is uncertain. Saalman's important insight is to have recognised that in Brunelleschi's Florence there was a late-Gothic style which persisted right into the first half of the Quattrocento. But this does not mean that all Trecentoesque buildings were actually created in the later Quattrocento; some of them clearly belong to the transitional period around 1400. Saalman's oeuvre-catalogue of Michelozzo needs a more precise degree of differentiation.

48 The basic ones hitherto being: Cesare Guasti, *La Cupola di Santa Maria del Fiore*, Florence, 1857. A Nardini Despotti Mospignotti, *Filippo di Ser Brunelleschi e la Cupola del Duomo di Firenze*, Livorno, 1885. Josef Durm, 'Zwei Grossconstructionen der italienischen Renaissance I, Die Domkuppel in Florenz', in *Zeitschrift für Bauwesen*, XXXVII, 1887, pp 353-74. Piero Sanpaolesi, *La Cupola di S Maria del Fiore. Il progetto. La Costruzione*. Rome, 1941.

49 The actual model must be Bramantes' design for the dome of St Peter's and the Tempietto S Pietro in Montorio, as well as Christopher Wren's dome of St Paul's in London.

50 Folnesics, 1915, p 10.

51 Willich, 1914, p 9.

52 A drawing in the Uffizi, No 1330, which Sanpaolesi (1941, Fig 19), drew attention to, shows a Roman building with 'spina-pesce' masonry. But this type of masonry work seems to have already become known in Florence during the Trecento; Sanpaolesi also recently pointed to the 'spina-pesce' cupola of the chapel in the Badia Fiorentina; see Sanpaolesi, 1962, Fig 18.

53 Frank D Prager, 'Brunelleschi's Inventions and the "Renewal of Roman Masonry Work"', in *Osiris*, IX, 1950, p 492.

54 Ibid, p 468

55 Heinrich von Geymüller, *Die Anfänge der Architektur der Renaissance in Italien*, Munich, 1908, p 2.

56 Ibid, p 3.

57 Cf Gosebruch, 1958.

58 Guasti, 1857, pp 89 ff, Doc 259.

59 See note 58.

60 I am grateful to Martin Warnke for pointing this out.

61 The tempietti do not appear in Andrea da Firenze's fresco – just the domes of the apses.

62 Cf Willich, 1914, pp 71-3.

63 Hitherto the triforium of Siena Cathedral has been considered the work of Giovanni di Cecco and dated after 1377 (see Harald Keller, 'Die Bauplastik des Sieneser Doms', in *Kunstgeschichtliches Jahrbuch der Biblioteca Hertziana*, I, 1937, pp 139-221). However there is sufficient evidence to suggest that the triforium of the nave was built towards the end of the thirteenth century and the upper part of the facade immediately after this, c1305-15; see Antje Kosegarten 'Einige Sienesische Darstellungen der Muttergottes aus dem frühen Trecento', in *Jarhbuch der Berliner Museen*, VIII, 1966, pp 103 ff.

64 Renate Wagner-Rieger, *Die italienische Baukunst zu Beginn der Gotik*, II. Graz and Cologne, 1957, pp 294 ff, reconstructs some barrel vaulting which started under the balustrade of the dome and joined on to the crossing arch.

65 There are clear parallels with the arched balustrades of Romanesque crossing towers.

66 There is no need for me to examine in any greater detail the structure and architectural history of the Florence Baptistry here; it suffices to refer the reader to the excellent study by Walther Horn: 'Das Florentiner Baptisterium', in *Mitteilungen des Kunsthistorischen Instituts in Florenz*, V, 1937-40, pp 100-151. Horn not only gives a cogent account of the history of the building but also a convincing interpretation of it. In my opinion this work supersedes all the earlier literature on the Florence Baptistry.

67 Prager, 1950. p 468 and *passim*, sees 'neo-classical tendencies'; in the construction of the dome of the Baptistry and transfers this judgement to the dome of the cathedral, which he views largely in terms of its references back to the Baptistry dome, thereby failing to take into account the fact that the 'neo-classical' shoulder supports of the Baptistry have become a continuous rib-construction which contains as many Gothic elements as it does 'Classical' ones from the Baptistry dome. It should in any case be noted that the structure of the dome of S Giovanni itself deviates largely from the Roman model, the Pantheon.

68 Cf for example the views of Siena in the *Adoration of the Magi* by Bartolo di Fredi and in the painting of Pope Calixtus III by Sano di Pietro, in Enzo Carli, *Guide to the Pinacoteca of Siena*, Milan, undated, Figs 16 and 59. An early seventeenth-century copper engraving in the Museo del'Opera in Siena shows a cross-section view of the original construction of the dome prior to Bernini's alterations. The relatively flat inner cupola carried a framework of beams which supported a steep outer shell like that of S Marco in Venice.

69 For further detail see H Klotz, 'Deutsche und italienische Baukunst im Trecento', in *Mitteilungen des Kunsthistorischen Instituts in Florenz*, XII, 1966, pp 202 ff.

70 Nardini, 1885, p 17, was the first to point out the hardly visible drum of the Tabernacle: '... anche L'Orcagna (...) sottopone un tamburo altissimo alla cupola del suo tabernocolo d'Or San Michele.' Roberto Salvini, 'Arnolfo e la cupola di Santa Maria del Fiore', in *Atti del I⁰ Congresso Nazionale di Storia del'Architetturo*, 1938, p 27, stresses the theory that the dome of the tabernacle reflects the original forms of the cathedral dome as planned by Arnolfo di Cambio.

71 The helm roofs of the towers of St Maria Stiegen in Vienna and of Frankfurt Cathedral are, like Orcagna's dome, no longer pointed, as was customary for Gothic ribbed helm roofs, but rather rounded like domes.

72 It is hardly possible to doubt that this is a representation of Florence Cathedral, as the campanile, moved to the end of the choir, matches the Florence campanile in all details, The three apses also are those of the Florence building.

73 Wolfgang Braunfels, *Mittelalterliche Stadtbaukunst in der Toskana*, 2nd ed, Berlin, 1959, pp 172 ff, was able to prove with various examples the extent to which the distant effect of major buildings in a city was taken into account in the Trecento. The disagreement about the new model of the cathedral was largely an argument about the drum of the dome: 'Two points of view clashed. The masons took the view which lay behind the Gothic cathedrals. The entire exterior is only meaningful in as much as it serves the interior ... The artists (on the other hand) had in mind the outer effect of the church ...' 'Jacopo degli Alberti summed up the essence of the situation: the artist's model was more beautiful from the outside, the mason's model was more beautiful from the inside'. Ibid, p 173.

74 Prager, 1950, *passim*, specifically mentions the heated arguments about a high clerestory with struts visible from outside – as appear in Andrea da Firenze's fresco – and the fact that the proponents of a low triforium with struts hidden by the roof prevailed.

75 The cladding of the drum was only added by Manetti in 1451-60. It would seem probable that Brunelleschi had already planned such a

division into fields. The size of the oculi required fields of massive proportion. In addition to this, the proportions of the fields match those in the lower storey of the drum, whose absolute dimensions are smaller because of the inferior height of the latter. Sanpaolesi, 1941, p 12, supports such a view with his interpretation of the two drum models in the Museo dell'Opera. He too is of the opinion that the model with the marble fields (Tav IIIb) are identical to the drum described in Giuliano di Tommaso Gucci's programme (1420), while the model with pilaster fields (Tav IIIa) only came into being after Brunelleschi's death. Manetti appears to have taken up the earlier model by Brunelleschi and Ghiberti.

76 A closer examination of the relations between the breadth of the oculus and the wall fields, taking into account the distances between the ledges, reveals the different scale.

77 See Guasti, 1857, p 38, Doc 75 ff, Docs 194-6.

78 Up to the present no comprehensive account of late Gothic architecture in Tuscany has been produced. There is general uncertainty about its historical developments. Similarly there is no monograph on the building of the Pisa Baptistry.

79 Pèleo Bacci, *Per la istoria del Battistero di Pisa,* Pisa, 1919, p 15. Here also all further documents on the history of the building of the Pisa Baptistry.

80 Ibid, p 16.

81 Georges Rohault de Fleury, *Les Monuments de Pise au Moyen Age,* Paris, 1866, Plate 27.

82 Urs Boeck *(Das Baptisterium zu Pisa und die Jerusalemer Anastasia,* Bonner Jahrbuch, 1964, pp 146-56) gives a reconstruction of the original building according to the model of the Church of the Sepulcre in Jerusalem; cf also Dehio-Bezold, *Die kirchliche Baukunst des Abendlandes,* Stuttgart, 1887-1901, I, pp 43, 547a; Richard Krautheimer, 'Introduction to an Iconography of Medieval Architecture', *Journal of the Warburg and Courtauld Institutes,* V, 1942, pp 1 ff, Boeck assumes that 'the horizontal layering of the exterior' reflects 'precisely Diotisalvi's layout', and furthermore that 'the double-shelled wall and dome as they exist now' were already 'part of Diotisalvi's project' (p 149). The complete match of original plan and later realisation, which Boeck claims to see in the basic forms of the entire building, means that the lower part of Diotisalvi's building must already have been prepared for the double-shelled dome. But this is not the case. The flying buttresses which carry the supporting struts for the outer cupola totally break with the dimensions of the rest and even partly obscure the windows of the upper storey. They were clearly added later; the upper storey with its high drum which meets the inner vaulting at an angle, was also not planned in this form, but rather was only drawn up above the original height of the gallery when the outer dome was planned (see p 97). The model of the Jerusalem Church of the Holy Sepulcre would have suggested the reconstruction of a single-shelled, less pointed cupola, possibly also made of wood, which sits on the inner circle of arcading. This would have meant a much more faithful adherence to the basic form of the Jerusalem model.

83 The dome of the Pisa Baptistry was intended, like that of Pisa Cathedral, to receive a metal roof, but this was only partly finished, so that the dome largely retained its tiled roof.

84 On the history of S Petronio see Ludwig Weber, *San Petronio in Bologna,* Leipzig, 1904; see B Supino, *L'arte nelle chiese di Bologna,* Bologna, 1932, pp 317-49. The architect responsible, Antonio di Vicenzo, must at least have been familiar with Zibellino's storey of Pisa Baptistry.

85 Fabriczy, 1907, p 79.

86 Unfortunately there is not, as far as I am aware, any graphic cross-section of the Volterra cupola extant; in addition to this, access to it is difficult so that any attempt to examine it in detail faces great problems.

87 Manetti, ed, 1887, p 30. Further versions of the document are quoted by Gottschewski and Gronau in the German edition of Vasari, Strasburg, 1906, III, p 100, note 39.

88 Cf Heydenreich, 1931, p 16.

89 Ibid, p 17.

90 Ibid.

91 Illustration in Robert Oertel, 'Wandmalerei und Zeichnung in Italien', *Mitteilungen des Kunsthistorischen Instituts in Florenz,* V, 1937-40, p 289.

92 However see Heydenreich, 1931, p 17.

93 The same applies to the dome of Siena Cathedral. Its lantern is not, as Heydenreich (op cit p 17) assumes, medieval, but rather was built by Bernini and renewed in the late nineteenth century. (See Heinrich Brauer and Rudolf Wittkower, *Die Zeichnungen des Gianlorenzo Bernini,* Berlin, 1931, text volume, p 60, note 4.)

94 Cf pp 23-31.

95 Paatz, 1937, p 124, names the chancel by Giovanni Pisano in Pisa Cathedral as a model for Brunelleschi's lantern. This is, in my opinion, a comparison which is less than convincing – as indeed are the links Paatz sees between Brunelleschi and Giovanni Pisano, which do not go beyond the general classical tendencies which are discernible in both these masters.

96 Fabriczy, 1892, p 562.

97 Folnesics, 1915, pp 16 ff, and Willich, 1914, pp 21 ff, glossed over Manetti's report with the same ease with which they ignored the documents published by Fabriczy. Sanpaolesi, 1962, pp 91-3, simply assumes the existence of the present-day building in his description of the portal. Luporini, 1964, only makes marginal reference to the Ospedale without going into detail. G Morozzi, 'Ricerche sull' aspetto originale dello Spedale degli Innocenti di Firenze', in *Commentari,* XV, 1964, pp 186-201, in connection with preparations for restoration work, was the first to refer back to Fabriczy's reconstruction. Of particular interest are the new documents discovered by Mendes and Dallai, 1966, pp 83-106.

98 Saalman, 1965, p 35, note 47, announced a Brunelleschi monograph and referred to an important discovery of documents by Padre Mendes, 1966, p 105, XXVII; interestingly enough it emerges that Antonio di Tuccio Manetti worked as *operaio* of the Ospedale in 1466. Saalman particularly stresses that this supports the authenticity of the Brunelleschi *Vita.* However see Fabriczy 1907, pp 1-5. Here one finds the case against Manetti's authorship.

99 Manetti, ed 1887, p 42.

100 Ibid.

101 Fabriczy, 1892, p 561

102 Ibid, p 565.

103 Ibid, p 576.

104 Ibid, p 567.

105 Ibid, p 571.

106 Cf Mendes-Dallai, 1966, Figs 13 and 14.

107 Ibid, Figs 5 and 6. The great portal at the head of the arcades providing entry into the courtyard originally led into a closed space; since the sixteenth-century this has been the 'hatch'.

108 Fabriczy, 1892, p 575.

109 Ibid, p 576.

110 Ibid, p 582, Mendes-Dallai, 1966, Doc XIV.

111 In connection with this, attention should be drawn to an attempted

reconstruction made by Mendes and Dallai (op cit 1966, Ills. p 87, Fig 1), who see Brunelleschi's portal as a simple arcade without an upper storey. They base this interpretation on a number of newly discovered documents and on the stonework of a gable uncovered in the rear wall of the upper storey which could have formed the front of the hospital wing and which used to extend above the roof of the portal. Mendes and Dallai complete a matching gable on the side of the church facade. Such a picture of the portal facade had in any case to be assumed as a transitional stage in the construction process (1426-39). Now, however, Mendes and Dallai fixed this stage as representing Brunelleschi's original plan, which was only completed and, in the process, fundamentally changed in 1466-74/80 by the addition of the upper storey. The strongest argument in favour of such an interpretation is the brick gable which was uncovered, the shattered stonework of which is reminiscent of a billet frieze.

On the other hand the church opposite, which, with the hospital wing, was roofed in 1429, did not receive such a gable. (When the restoration work was being carried out the rear wall of the dormitorium was searched in vain for any such traces.) It seems possible that it was decided to decorate the hospital wing with a simple gable as soon as it emerged that the upper storey of the portal was not to be constructed at that stage because of the other building work which still had to be completed.

At any rate the documents cited by Mendes and Dallai would tend to prove the opposite of what they were intended to: the fact that the upper storey of the loggia was not started until 1466. It is true that in 1466 the start of building of a 'dormitorio nuovo' is mentioned, but this is not 'sopra il portico', as the authors quote (p 89), but rather 'dallo *lato* della chiesa' (Doc XXXIX), ie at the side of the church. This may be understood to have been an addition on the north side of the church which had to give way to the present building towards the end of the sixteenth century, erected when the road was taken through at that point. Mendes and Dallai link a second collection of documents from a later period (1474, Doc XXX; 1476, Doc XXXI; 1480, Doc XXXII) with the collection of 1466/7, and apply both to the building of the upper storey of the loggia.

In the document of 1474 the roofing work on the portal dormitorium is commissioned. If one keeps in mind the fact that as early as 1438/9 work had been being carried out on this storey and the 'finestre della faccia' are mentioned (see below), then the roofing referred to in 1474 may well have been the final roofing, which replaced a possible similar 'tetto selvaticho' (temporary roof) which covered the portal from 1426/9. The Documents of 1476 (p 89 and Doc XXXI) refer to the additional work on the windows. These were given new frames after already being moved in 1438/9 (see below). The 1480 document finally makes clear that in both cases the work carried out represented a completion or restoration. Payment is made for a tremazzo beam in the roof, which was clearly a replacement, as only one is mentioned.

The crucial document which refutes Mendes and Dallai's theory is dated 3rd November 1439 (libro della muraglia E, fol 30 v and 31 r). This makes reference to the upper loggia; it lists the payments 'per fare chornicj e cantonj per mattere nel fregio, per chornicie sopra alle finestre della faccia, per fare ifrontonj di sopra alle finestre dette (window pediments), per fare chornicie nella faccia della testa dellabituro dinnanzi, per fare le chornicie sotto i chorentj deltteto' (see Fabriczy, 1892, p 576). Of similar significance is the document dated 26th January 1438 (Libro D, fol 107 r), a bill for 'pezi quindici dj chornicie simisono nella faccia dello spedale el porticho. . . ' (see Fabriczy, ibid, p 575).

112 See note 164. Folnesics provides an exhaustive argument in favour of

Brunelleschi being the author of the continuous architrave. Ultimately what speaks against Mendes and Dallai's reconstruction is the traditional Tuscan form of the ospedale portal. The ospedali of Lastra a Signa and Volterra as well as the Ospedale di San Matteo in Florence itself are all two-storey buildings with a pillared portal and a closed upper storey. Such a strong tradition of a particular type of building should not be ignored.

113 Manetti, ed 1887, p 42.

114 Ibid.

115 Documents published by Mendes-Dallai (1966, Doc XII, XIII) mention F della Luna being involved as early as 1419/20 with the Ospedale.

116 Fabriczy, 1892, p 571.

117 Today 'Piazza della SS Annunziata'.

118 Fabriczy, 1892, pp 246 ff.

119 The old facade, with the Trecento portal, is still preserved today and can be seen inside the atrium. On the reconstruction of the first building see H L Heydenreich, 'Die Tribuna der SS Annunziata in Florenz', in *Mitteilungen des Kunsthistorischen Instituts in Florenz*, III, 1930.

120 Fig 190 shows that in the fifteenth century a private palazzo several stories high stood here. The buildings to the east of the Via dei Servi are nineteenth century.

121 Sanpaolesi, 1962, pp 91 ff also assumes that Brunelleschi planned a symmetrical layout which included a corresponding loggia on the opposite side.

122 Morozzi, 1964. See the shaded portions of his ground plan (p 110).

123 '. . . forma di U, di cui il porticato esterno era né più né menoche la facciata, e i due corpi ad esso normali e constituenti il primo nucleo dello spedale, destinati rispettivamente alla chiesa e agli alloggi per i fanciulli'. Ibid, p 187.

124 Brunelleschi did not leave his post as chief architect of the Ospedale in 1424, as has been assumed since Fabriczy, 1892, p 569, but rather is still mentioned in 1427 (January) in first place above the *operai*. He received a final payment 'per resto do uso salaro e provisione per insino a di detto, della faticha e tempo à messo nella edificazione di detto Spedale', ie only months before Francesco della Luna took over on 1st May 1427 (Mendes-Dallai, 1966, p 84 and Doc X).

125 See Fabriczy, 1892, pp 569 ff.

126 Morozzi, 1964, p 197.

127 Morozzi, see note 107. I was fortunate enough to be able to inspect the restoration model, which is preserved in the Ospedale itself.

128 As the later extensions can be clearly distinguished from the original building there can be no doubts as to the form of the reconstruction.

129 I am passing on here an assumption made by Mendes and Dallai, 1966, p 92. The pilaster fields at the side, together with the position of the portal at ground level, would thus gain a functional justification. And indeed the flight of steps was only moved in 1457 by Bernardo Rossellino (see op cit Doc XXV). Nevertheless it seems difficult to imagine that Brunelleschi did not originally allow for any steps.

130 The frame of the centre portal is sixteenth-century. But Brunelleschi had had three great portals created at the same place, according to a document of 1422: 'cinque portj grandj cioe tre insulporticho'; see Fabriczy, 1892, p 562.

131 Manetti, ed 1887, p 42.

132 Neither did the entrance building of the portal stretch up the high wall of the church. A window in the clerestory which was later walled up was discovered during restoration work.

133 Giovanni Villani, Cronica, ed Francesco Gherardi Dragomanni, Florence, 1844 ff, VIII, p 26. Braunfels, 1959, p 200, counters this statement by Vilani by stating that this intention of now allowing the

spirit of the Ghibellini to live on in the new palazzo '[was able to] influence only the position of the palazzo, not its basic form, which was dictated by the irregularity of the surrounding streets. And the shortcomings of the ground plan became obvious when the piazza was created round the palazzo.' Against this speaks the fact that this irregularity was already reflected in the asymmetrical placing of the columns in the inner courtyard, in other words it was obvious from the very outset. In any case the sober account by the contemporary chronicler, distinguished by its objectivity, cannot be weakened by mere conjecture.

134 I am not aware of any other text which interprets an asymmetry of medieval layout, which is widely regarded as 'artistic', not just in terms of typically medieval attitudes but actually as being clearly felt to be unsatisfactory.

135 For example Pietrasanta 1255, Manfredonia (1256), Citaducale (1309) and others, cf Ernst Egli, *Geschichte des Städtebaues*, II, Erlenback and Zürich, 1962, pp 35 ff. Figs 1a, 1b, 2.

136 The significance of the Lucca villa for the rise of the Renaissance has been neglected, especially any attempt to see it in a larger context. Paolo Guinigi's extensive library contains a collection of the most important authors of antiquity (see Salvator Bongi, *Di Paolo Guinigi e delle sue richezze*, Lucca, 1871, pp 74-82). He owned probably the first 'studiolo', decorated with inlaid wood (1414), perhaps the most characteristic attribute of the humanistic Renaissance prince. The fame of this *studiolo* caused Lionello d'Este in 1434 to order a 'studio di legno' from the same artist, Arduino (see Giovanni Poggi, *La cappella e la tomba di Onofrio Strozzi nella chiesa di Santa Trinita*, Florence, 1903, p 16 and Bongi, op cit pp 27, 48-50). Paolo Guinigi collected a circle of humanists and scholars around him; his chancellor Guido Manfredi da Pietrasanta had a continuous correspondence with Coluccio Salutati. Last but not least, the Lucca prince was the first to commission work from Jacopo della Quercia, who created the monument for Paolo Guinigi's deceased wife Ilaria del Carretto. Geymüller said of this monument that it was the very first work of the early Renaissance. See Bongi, op cit, pp 13 ff, on the start of work on the villa in 1407 or 1413.

137 See B Patzak, *Palast und Villa in Toscana*, I, Leipzig, 1912; Boccaccio, *Amorosa Visione*, Venice, 1531, cantos XXXVIII and XL.

138 Giovanni Sercambi, *Le Croniche di Giovanni Sercambi Lucchese*, ed Salvatore Bongi, Rome, 1892, III.

139 Bongi, 1871, p 14.

140 The fact that Brunelleschi's client may have known the *ospedale* at Lastra a Signa as a model can be proved by a visit in 1419 of the later master in charge of the construction, Francesco della Luna, whose name is mentioned in connection with the *ospedale* at Lastra a Signa. Creighton Gilbert, 'The Earliest Guide to Florentine Architecture', in *Mitteilungen des Kunsthistorischen Instituts in Florenz*, XIV, 1969, pp 36 ff, was able to show that Francesco della Luna was one of the group of builders who appointed Brunelleschi as master-builder.

141 After the building of the Duomo Nuovo in Siena the arcade with semi-circular arches spread and soon reappeared in the cathedral of Lucca and the Loggia dei Lanzi in Florence; however in these cases the massive arcades had composite piers which lead one to expect a pointed arch, while the ospedale loggias had retained the segmental arch.

142 In Volterra the arcade runs to the right into a wall against which it is supported on a simple console.

143 The outer arches of the loggia at Lastra a Signa were closed at a later date so that a similar framing effect seems to be achieved.

144 See page 31.

145 L B Alberti, trans 1912, Book 1, X, p 53.

146 Ibid, p 50.

147 In 1427 the Palazzo Busini is mentioned as already being in existence; cf notes 26 and 27.

148 The church was discovered as early as 1429. See note 168.

149 On Brunelleschi's death in 1446 not even the transept and crossing were complete, cf Manetti, ed 1887, p 50.

150 Poggi, 1903, p 12.

151 Ibid, p 15.

152 See Guiseppe Marchini, 'Aggiunte a Michelozzo', in *La Rinascita*, VII, 1954, pp 37-44.

153 Sanpaolesi, 1962, Ill 11, 'Le cupole e gli edifici a cupola del Brunelleschi a la loro derivazione da edifici Romani', in *Atti del 1° Congresso Nazionale di Storia dell'Architettura*, Firenz, 1938, pp 37-41, assumed that the models for Brunelleschi's ribbed domes were Roman domes on Hadrian's Villa (cf on this H Siebenhüner, 'Zur italienischen Baukunst des Quattrocento', *Zeitschrift für Kunstgeschichte*, VIII, 1939, p 88). Fabriczy, 1892, p 193, note, already put together the most important Roman examples for comparison including the domes of the Hadrian's Villa. Folnesics, 1915, p 40, isolated the inner barrel structure of the Florence Baptistry as fanned vaulting and saw in it a clear precursor of Brunelleschi's ribbed dome (also suggested by L Crema, 'Romanità delle volte Brunelleschiane', in *Atti del 1° Congresso Nazionale di Storia dell'Architettura*, Florence, 1938, p 134). Such an ideal model does not, however, match the actual morphology of the Baptistry dome. The radiating barrels do not extend as 'webs' up to the lantern, but rather, about half-way up, run into the shell of the dome, whose upper half is completely free. Of the genuine central domes that of the Parma Baptistry is closer to Brunelleschi's ribbed dome than that of the Florence Baptistry.

154 A description of the Old Sacristy is necessary here in order to offer a different interpretative perspective from the one taken hitherto by Geymüller, I, 1885-93, p 17, and Fabriczy, 1892, p 194, both of whom evaluated Brunelleschi's elevations largely in tectonic terms, playing down too much the supporting and load-bearing aspects and stressing the decorative characteristics. An idealised decoration of the Sacristy was intended to replace the missing tectonic qualities; particularly with Geymüller one has the impression that he assessed the architecture exclusively in terms of the supposedly missing decoration, finding those faults which should have been evidence of the real fault. Neither interpreter saw how consistently Brunelleschi brought out the tectonic qualities from the corners of the pilasters and allowed them to be contained in a seemingly purely decorative form: the pendentive tondo linked to the coats of arms in the spandrels. On the contrary they demanded tectonic-plastic elements even in places – for example in the frames of the great pointed arches – where Brunelleschi wanted nothing more than a pictorial-type composition.

155 Even Kurt Bauch, *Abendländische Kunst*, Düsseldorf, 1952, p 183, suggested this link with a brief remark: 'The Chapel (Old Sacristy) is in its composition and dimensions a pre-Gothic chapel, created after the model of the Baptistry in Padua, which is a product of Romanesque-Byzantine art.' On the other hand see Harald Keller, *Die Kunstlandschaften Italiens*, Munich, 1960, p 336, note 48: 'As far as we can determine medieval Italy only produced one pendentive dome, the Baptistry in Padua. It cannot be proved that Brunellesco was familiar with this.' As far as I am aware these are the only statements in which a link between the two buildings is discussed.

156 The portals to the choir, together with the side portal were only created in the Trecento. Originally the only entrance was opposite the choir.

157 It was customary for the builders of medieval cathedrals to link central dimensions of the elevation with central thematic ideas, cf H Klotz, *Der*

Ostbau der Stiftskirche zu Wimpfen im Tal, Munich, 1967, pp 48 ff and III XII.

158 Heydenreich, 1931, p 8, gives a convincing exposition of the arguments against the likelihood of Brunelleschi having undertaken a 'first' journey to Rome and for the probability that he only went there at a later stage in the period between December 1432 and July 1434.

159 L Crema, 1938, p 135.

160 The keystone relief with the monogramme of Christ is recognisably a work from the late Quattrocento. The dome of the choir was not completed until 1424, ie shortly before the completion of the dome of the Old Sacristy in 1429 (see B Gonzati, *La Basilica di San Antonio di Padova*, I, Padua, 1852, p 51, note 1). Given its size it would seem likely that the Padua dome was only completed after a long period of construction and was probably constructed according to a model which was already in existence (see Gonzati, ibid). At any rate its structure had already been prepared by the elevation of the choir wall. The capitals of the engaged columns are similar to those in S Francesco, Bologna, and it is there also that we find the closest parallel to the ribbed vaulting with oculi inserted into the pointed arches; both embody the stylistic characteristics of the second half of the Duecento. A similarly Duecento product, judging from the decorative details, is the gallery round the outside of the choir, its flying buttresses running from between the pairs of windows with pointed arches across to the vaulting, supporting the ribs of the dome from the outside. On the other hand painting in fourteenth-century Padua already reflects such a type of vaulting, for example in the two architectural paintings of the story of the Virgin Mary by Giusto de' Menabuoni in the Baptistry; in both frescoes of the *Annunciation* and the *Visit to the Temple* (to the right and left of the *Birth of Mary*) one can see indistinct representations of similar domes, which, interestingly enough, are closer to the ribbed domes than the model of the Santo vaulting, as the individual 'webs' are bordered at the bottom by a horizontal line which pre-empts Brunelleschi's dome ring. This important motif of a now semi-circular arch cut off horizontally at the base, recurs below the vaulting of the side rooms of the choir in the Baptistry. Here, unlike the pictures by Menabuoni, the decoration has the task of structuring the actual space.

161 Filippo Baldinucci, *Vita di Filippo di ser Brunelleschi*, Florence, 1812, p 346.

162 See pp 124 ff.

163 See Richard Krautheimer, 'Introduction to an Iconography of Medieval Architecture', in J*ournal of the Warburg and Courtauld Institutes*, V, 1942.

164 Quoted by Ludwig Volkmann, Padua, Leipzig, 1904, p 6, cf Julius von Schlosser, *Quellenbuch zur Kunstgeschichte des abendländischen Mittelalters*, Vienna, 1896, p 372.

165 I am grateful to Ulrich Krause for drawing my attention to this.

166 Not, however, the architrave above the arches of the Loggia degli Innocenti. Here the faces are cut with sharp edges and have no torus moulding; this too may be regarded as an early form as yet untypical for Brunelleschi's style.

167 Critical doubts as to Brunelleschi's authorship were expressed by Ursula Schlegel, 'La Cappella Barbadori e l'architettura fiorentina del primo Rinascimento', in *Rivista d'Arte*, XXXII, 1957, pp 77-106.

168 Manetti, ed 1887, p 29.

169 See Guasti, 1857, pp13 ff, Doc 6, 9.

170 Ibid, p 14, Doc 10.

171 See note 168.

172 See note 170.

173 M Checchi, L Gaudenzio, L Grossato, 'L'arte a *Padova* da Giotto ai nostri giorni', in *Padova*, Venice, 1961, CCLI.

174 Cavalcanti, *Istorie Fiorentine*, I, Florence, 1838, p 530.

175 G Uzielli, *Intorno ad un passo di Giorgio Vasari relativo a Paolo dal Pozzo Toscanelli quale maestro di Filippo Brunelleschi*, Rome, 1894.

176 See Checchi, Gaudenzio, Grossato, 1961, p 577.

177 Cf Jacob Burkhardt, *Die Kultur der Renaissance in Italien*, 10th edition, ed Ludwig Geiger, Vol 1, Leipzig, 1908, pp 8 ff. Burckhardt mentions the Carraras in passing in connection with Petrarch's princely upbringing.

178 Cf Julius von Schlosser, *Präludien, Gesammelte Aufsätze*, Berlin, 1927, p 54: 'Even the beginnings of the Renaissance reach much further back into the last decade of the fourteenth century. In particular these early developmental stages of an independent Renaissance in upper Italy have hitherto been largely neglected.' Schlosser's statement is as valid today as it ever was.

179 See Fabriczy, 1892. p 37.

180 As far as I can see, no detailed historical study of the early Renaissance in Padua around 1400 has yet been written.

181 Baron, 1966, p 131, note 20.

182 Ibid, pp 134-45.

183 J Morelli, *De Joanne Dondio, Operette*, II, 1820, pp 285 ff.

184 On this see Erwin Panofsky, *Idea*, 2nd edition, Berlin, 1960, pp 23-38.

185 See *Lorenzo Ghibertis Denkwürdigkeiten*, ed Julius von Schlosser, I, Berlin, 1912, pp 62 ff.

186 Ibid, p 62: 'Ancora uidi in Padoua una statua, ui fu condotta per Lombardo della Seta; essa fu trouata nella città di Firenze cauando sotto terra nella casa della famiglia de "Brunelleschi"' (there follows a more precise description of the statue and the circumstances of its discovery).

187 Baldinucci, ed 1812, pp 156 ff, note 2. The first visit by Ser Brunellesco Lippi to the signori of Padua, 1367. He is last mentioned in 1384 as 'Ambasciatore in Lombardia'.

188 Cf Schlosser, 1927, p 54: 'These are completely faithful imitations of Roman medallions: the copies are so exact that the portrait is not just draped in antique fashion but is an approximation of the well-known model of Vitellius.'

189 The atrium arcades of S Maria dei Servi in Bologna (c1390) were also decorated by having tondi with relief frames in the spandrels of the arches. This was pointed out already by Fabriczy, 1892, p 254.

190 Fabriczy, 1892, p 137.

191 Cf Folnesics, pp 21 ff.

192 Cf Heydenreich, 1931, pp 10 ff.

193 See pp 39-56.

194 See p 111.

195 The term 'Regotisierung' (Regothicisation) which is used for the style of the second half of the Quottocento remains very much in evidence, and assumes tacitly that there was such a thing as an 'absolute Renaissance'.

196 It is significant that even Geymüller, 1908, tried to see the Gothic element of the Renaissance in the classicism of the Gothic, ie in the Renovatio of Frederick II and in the works which were created in this area by Niccolò Pisano.

197 Only on the architrave of the Tempietti of the cathedral tribune does Brunelleschi use richer decoration which is reminiscent of Alberti.

198 See Fabriczy, 1892, p 561, 569.

BIBLIOGRAPHY

Alberti, Leon Battista, *Zehn Bücher über die Baukunst*, transl. Max Theuer, Vienna and Leipzig 1912.

——, *Kleinere Kunsttheoretische Schriften*, ed H Janitschek, Vienna 1877.

Bacci, Pèleo, *Per la istoria del Battistero di Pisa*, Pisa 1919.

Badia, Jodoco del, 'Il vecchio palazzo della Parte Guelfa', in *Bolletina dell'Associazione per la difesa di Firenze antica*, III, Florence 1902.

Baldinucci, Filippo, *Vita di Filippo di ser Brunelleschi*, ed Domenico Moreni, Florence 1812.

Baron, Hans, *The Crisis of Early Italian Renaissance*, 2nd edition, Princeton 1966.

Bauch, Kurt, 'Klassik – Klassizität – Klassizismus', in *Das Werk des Künstlers*, Stuttgart 1939/40.

——, *Abendländische Kunst*, Düsseldorf 1952.

Boccaccio, Giovanni, *Amorosa Visione*, Venice 1531.

Bongi, Salvator, *Di Paolo Guinigi e delle sue richezze*, Lucca 1871.

Brauer, Heinrich and Rudolf Wittkower, *Die Zeichnungen des Gianlorenzo Bernini*, Berlin 1931.

Braunfels, Wolfgang, *Mittelalterliche Stadtbaukunst in der Toskana*, 2nd edition, Berlin 1959.

Brucker, Gene A, Florentine Politics and Society, 1343-78, Princeton 1962.

Burckhardt, Jacob, *Die Kulter der Renaissance in Italien*, 10th edition, ed Ludwig Geiger I, Leipzig 1908.

Carli, Enzo, *Guide to the Pinacoteca of Siena*, Milan, undated.

Cavalcanti, *Istorie Fiorentine*, Florence 1838.

Cennini, Cennino, *Tractat der Malerei*, transl. Albert Ilg, *Quellenschriften für Kunstgeschichte*, I, Vienna 1871.

Chiapelli, Alessandro, *Della Vita di Filippo Brunelleschi*, Florence 1896.

Crema, L, 'Romanità delle volte Brunelleschiane', in *Atti del i° Congresso Nazionale di Storia dell'Architettura*, Florence 1938

Durm, Josef, 'Zwei Grossconstructionen der italienischen Renaissance, I, Die Domkuppel in Florenz', in *Zeitschrift für Bauwesen*, XXXVII, 1887.

Dehio-Bezold, *Die kirchliche Baukunst des Abendlandes*, Stuttgart 1887-1901.

Egli, Ernst, *Geschichte des Städtebaus*, II, Erlenbach and Zürich 1962.

Febriczy, Cornel von, *Filippo Brunelleschi, Sein Leben und seine Werke*, Stuttgart 1892.

——, 'Brunelleschiana', in *Beiheft zum Jahrbuch der Königlich Preußischen Kunstsammlungen*, XXVIII. 1907.

Filarete, *Filarete's Treatise on Architecture*, ed John R Spencer, New Haven and London 1965.

Folnesics, Hans, *Brunelleschi*, Vienna 1915.

Fontana, Paolo, 'Il Brunelleschi, de l'architettura classica', in *Archivio Storico dell'Arte*, VI, 1893.

Gaye, Geovanni, *Carteggio inedito degli artisti italiani*, Florence 1839f.

Geymüller, Heinrich von, *Die Architektur der Renaissance in Toscana*, I, Munich 1885-93.

——, *Die Anfänge der Architekture der Renaissance in Italien*, Munich 1908.

Ghiberti, Lorenzo, *I Commentarii (Lorenzo Ghibertis Denkwürdigkeiten)*, ed Julius von Schlosser, Berlin 1912.

——, *Denkwürdigkeiten*, transl. Julius von Schlosser, Berlin 1920.

Gilbert, Creighton, 'The Earliest Guide to Florentine Architecture', in *Mitteilungen des Kunsthistorischen Instituts in Florenz*, XIV, 1969.

Giovannoni, Gustavo, 'Leptis Magna e l'architettura del Rinascimento', in *Palladio*, I, 1937.

Goldmann, Arthur, 'Drei italienische Handschriftenkataloge S. VIII-XV, in *Centralblatt für Bibliothekswesen*, IV, 1887.

Gombrich, Ernst H 'The Renaissance Conception of Artistic Progress', reprinted in *Norm and Form, Studies in the Art of the Renaissance*, London 1966.

——, 'From the Revival of Letters to the Reform of the Arts', in *Essays in the History of Art Presented to Rudolf Wittkower*, London and New York 1969.

Gonzati, B, *La Basilica di San Antonia di Padova*, I, Padua 1852.

Gosebruch, Martin, '"Varieta" bei Leon Battista Alberti und der wissenschaftliche Renaissance-begriff', in *Zeitschrift für Kunstgeschichte*, XX, 1957.

——, 'Florentinische Kapitelle von Brunelleschi bis zum Tempio Malatestiano und der Eigenstil der Frührenaissance', in *Römisches Jahrbuch für Kunstgeschichte*, VIII, 1958.

Gross, Walter, *Die abendländische Architektur um 1300*, Stuttgart 1947.

Ghecchi, Gaudenzio, 'Grossato, L'arte a Padova da Giotta ai nostri giorni', in *Padova, Venezia* 1961

Guasti, Cesare, *La Cupola di Santa Maria del Fiore*, Florence 1857.

——, *Santa Maria del Fiore*, Florence 1887.

Hatfield, R, 'Some Unknown Descriptions of the Medici Palace in 1459', in *Art Bulletin*, LII, 1970.

Heydenreich, Ludwig Heinrich, 'Spätwerke Brunelleschis', in *Jahrbuch der Preussischen Kunstsammlungen*, LII, 1931.

——, 'Dei Tribuna der SS. Annunziata in Florenz', in *Mitteilungen des Kunsthistorischen Instituts in Florenz*, III, 1932.

——, 'Gedanken über Michelozzo di Bartolomeo', in *Festschrift für Wilhelm Pinder*, Leipzig 1938.

Horn, Walther, 'Das Florentiner Baptisterium', in *Mitteilungen des Kunsthistorischen Instituts in Florenz*, V, 1937-40.

Horn-Oncken, Alste, *Über das Schickliche, Studien zur Geschichte der Architekturtheorie*, I, Göttingen 1967.

Kauffmann, Hans, *Donatello*, Berlin 1935.

Keller, Harald, 'Dei Bauplastik des Sieneser Doms', in *Kunstges-*

chichtliches Jahrbuch der Bibliotheca Hertziana, I, 1937.

——, *Die Kunstlandschaften Italiens*, Munich 1960.

Klotz, H, 'Deutsche und italienische Baukunst im Trecento', in *Mitteilungen des Kunsthistorischen Instituts in Florenz*, XII, 1966.

——, *Der Ostbau der Stiftskirche zu Wimpfen im Tal*, Munich 1967.

——, 'L B Albertis "De re aedificatoria" in Theorie und Praxis', in *Zeitschrift für Kunstgeschichte*, XXXII, 1969

Kosegarten, Antje, 'Einige Sienesische Darstellungen der Muttergottes aus dem frühen Trecento', in *Jahrbuch der Berliner Museen*, VIII, 1966.

Krautheimer, Richard, *Die Kirchen der Bettelorden in Deutschland*, Cologne 1925.

——, 'Introduction to an Iconography of Medieval Architecture', in *Journal of the Warburg and Courtauld Institutes*, V 1942.

——, *Lorenzo Ghiberti*, Princeton 1956.

Krinsky, Carol Herselle, 'Seventy-eight Vitruvius Manuscripts', in *Journal of the Warburg and Courtauld Insititutes*, XXX 1967.

Laschi, G; Roselli, P; Rossi, P A; 'Indagine sulla Cappella dei Pazzi', in *Commentari*, XIII, 1962.

Luporini, Eugenio, *Brunelleschi*, Milan 1964.

Manetti, Antonio di Tuccio, *Filippo Brunelleschi*, ed Heinrich Hotlzinger, Stuttgart 1887.

Marchini, Giuseppe, 'Aggiunte a Michelozzo', in *La Rinascita*, VII, 1954.

——, 'Il palazzo Datini a Prato', in *Bolletino d'Arte*, XLVI, 1961.

——, *Il Tesoro del Duomo di Prato*, Milan 1963.

Mendes Atanásio, M C; Dallia, Giovanni, 'Nuove indagini sullo Spedale degli Innocenti a Firenze', in *Commentari*, XVII, 1966.

Morelli, J, *De Joanne Dondio, Operette*, II, 1820.

Morozzi, G, 'Ricerche sull' aspetto originale dello Spedale degli Innocenti di Firenze', in *Commentari*, XV, 1964.

Nardini Despotti Mospignotti, A, *Filippo di Ser Brunelleschi e la Cupola del Duomo di Firenze*, Livorno 1885.

Oertel, Robert, 'Wandmalerei und Zeichnung in Italien', in *Mitteilungen des Kunsthistorischen Instituts in Florenz*, V, 1937-40.

Paatz, Walter, *Werden und Wesen der Trecentoarchitektur*, Burg b. M 1937.

——, *Die Kirchen von Florenz*, III, Frankfurt 1952.

Panofsky, Erwin, *Early Netherlandish Painting*, Cambridge, Mass 1953.

——, *Idea*, 2nd edition, Berlin 1960.

——, *Renaissance and Renaissances*, Copenhagen 1960.

Patzak, Bernhard, *Palast und Villa in Toscana*, I, Leipzig 1912.

Pellati, Francesco, 'Vitruvio e Brunelleschi', in *La Rinascita*, II, 1939.

Poggi, Giovanni, *La cappella e la tomba di Onofrio Strozzi nella chiesa di Santa Trínita*, Florence 1903.

Prager, Frank D, 'Brunelleschi's Inventions and the "Renewal of Roman Masonary Work"' in *Osiris*, IX, 1950.

Rohault de Fleury, Georges, *Les Monuments de Pise au Moyen Age*, Paris 1866.

Saalman, Howard, 'The Palazzo Comunale in Montepulciano', in *Zeitschrift für Kunstgeschichte*, XXVIII, 1965.

——, 'Filippo Brunelleschi: Capital Studies', in *Art Bulletin*, XL, 1958.

Sabbadini, R, I libri e la stampa, *Bulletino Ufficiale della Societa Bibliografica Italiana*, 1907.

Salmi, Mario, 'Il Palazzo della Parte Guelfa a Firenze e Filippo Brunelleschi', in *Rinascimento*, II, 1951.

Sanpaolesi, Piero, 'Le cupole e gli edifici a cupola del Brunelleschi e la loro derivazione da edifici Romani', in *Atti del 1° Congresso Nazionale di Storia dell'Architettura*, Florence 1938.

——, *La Cupola di Santa Maria del Fiore. Il progetto. La costruzione.* Rome 1941.

——, *Brunelleschi*, Milan 1962.

Salvini, Roberto, 'Arnolfo e la cupola di Santa Maria del Fiore', in *Atti del 1° Congresso Nazionale di Storia dell'Architettura*, Florence 1938.

Schevill, Ferdinand, *History of Florence*, New York 1961.

Schlosser, Julius von, *Quellenbuch zur Kunstgeschichte des abendländischen Mittelalters, Quellenschriften N.F.*, VII, Vienna 1896.

——, *Präludien, Gesammelte Aufsätze*, Berlin 1927.

Schlegel, Ursula, 'La Cappella Barbadori e l'architettura fiorentina del primo Rinascimento', in *Rivista d'Arte*, XXXII, 1957.

Schmarsow, August, *Gotik in der Renaissance*, Stuttgart 1921.

Sedlmayer, Hans, 'Spätantike Wandsysteme', in *Epochen und Werke*, I, Vienna and Munich 1959.

Siebenhüner, Herbert, Zur italienischen Baukunst des Quattrocento, in *Zeitschrift für Kunstgeschichte*, VIII, 1939.

Supino, I B, *L'arte nelle chiese di Bologna*, Bologna 1932.

Toesca, Pietro, Il Trecento, Turin 1964.

Uzielli, G, *Intorno ad un passo di Giorgio Vasari relativo a Paolo dal Pozzo Toscanelli quale maestro di Filippo Brunelleschi*, Rome 1894.

Vasari, Giorgio, *Le Vite*, ed Gaetano Milanesi, Florence 1878-85.

——, transl. Gottschewski and Gronau, Strassburg 1906.

Villani, Giovanni, *Cronica*, ed Francesco Gherardi Dragomanni, Florence 1844.

Vitruvius, *De Architectura Libri Decem*, ed Val. Rose and Müller-Strübing, Leipzig 1867, – transl. Curt Fensterbusch, Darmstadt 1964 (with page numbers ed Rose and Müller-Strübing).

Volkmann, Ludwig, *Padua*, Leipzig 1904.

Wagner-Rieger, Renate, *Die italienische Baukunst zu Beginn der Gotik*, I and II, Graz and Cologne 1956, 1957.

Weber, Lugwig, *San Petroni in Bologna*, Leipzig 1904.

White John, *Art and Architecture in Italy: 1250-1400*, Baltimore 1966.

Willich, Hans, *Die Baukunst der Renaissance in Italien*, Berlin 1914.

Wundram, Manfred, 'Albizzo di Piero', in *Das Werk des Künstlers, Festschrift für Hubert Schrade*, Stuttgart 1960.

PHOTOGRAPHIC ACKNOWLEDGEMENTS

Alinar: 24 (above right), 63 (below), 124 (below), 128, 135 (below), 147 (above left), 151

Anderson: 120 (above), 137 (below left), 156

Brogi: 19 (below left), 20 (below right)

Jarson: 104

Klotz: 18 (above left and right), 19 (above left), 20 (above right), 28 (above right, below left), 29 (above right, below left), 38, 41, 42 (below right), 53, 55, 61 (above left, below left and right), 62 (above left and right), 63 (above right), 66, 67, 69 (above), 70 (below left, right and centre), 74 (below left), 75, 76, 84 (above left), 87, 88, 91, 97 (below left), 101 (above), 109, 110, 115, 116 (above), 120 (below), 124 (above), 127 (above left), 129, 132 (above), 136, 137 (above, below right), 138 (below), 141, 148, 149, 152, 153, 155

Klotz-Trachtenberg: 2, 7, 13, 14, 17, 19 (above right), 20 (above left), 27 (below), 29 (above left), 33, 37, 45, 54, 57, 58, 61 (above right), 62 (below), 63 (above right), 73 (below), 74 (above and below right), 84 (above right), 94, 97 (above, below right), 98, 101 (below), 102 (below left), 105, 107, 119, 123, 142

Monti: 42 (below left), 132 (below left), 138 (above)

Trachtenberg: 10, 23, 24 (below), 27 (above), 30, 34, 35, 84 (below), 146

Cover and colour plates: Scala Instituto Fotografico Editoriale S.p.A.

INDEX